BROTHER MENDEL'S
PERFECT HORSE

Also by Frank Westerman

ARARAT
ENGINEERS OF THE SOUL

BROTHER MENDEL'S
PERFECT HORSE

Man and Beast in an Age of Human Warfare

Frank Westerman

*Translated from the Dutch
by Sam Garrett*

HARVILL SECKER
LONDON

Published by Harvill Secker 2012

2 4 6 8 10 9 7 5 3 1

Copyright © Frank Westerman 2010
English translation copyright © Sam Garrett 2012
Maps © Hester Schaap

Illustration Eadweard Muybridge, *The Horse in Motion*, 1878

Frank Westerman has asserted his right under the Copyright,
Designs and Patents Act 1988 to be identified as the author of this work

First published with the title *Dier, bovendier* in 2010
by Uitgeverij Atlas, Amsterdam/Antwerp

First published in Great Britain in 2012 by
HARVILL SECKER
Random House
20 Vauxhall Bridge Road
London SW1V 2SA

www.randomhouse.co.uk

Addresses for companies within The Random House Group Limited can be found at:
www.randomhouse.co.uk/offices.htm

The Random House Group Limited Reg. No. 954009

A CIP catalogue record for this book is available from the British Library

ISBN 9781846550881

Typeset in Haarlemmer MT by Palimpsest Book Production Limited,
Falkirk, Stirlingshire

Printed and bound in Great Britain by Clays Ltd, St Ives plc

CONTENTS

Stud book   vii
Prologue   1

I

The 'Ts' in Lipizzaner   13
Blutauffrischung (New Blood for Old)   29
The Stork's Foot   47
K.u.k.-leute   61
The Black 'Mendelizes' to the Surface   80
The Obedience Test   95

II

The Return of the Tarpan   113
Heim ins Reich (Back to the Reich)   131
Plant 4711   143
Summoned to Military Servicing   165
The Breeding Station   176
Operation Cowboy   191

III

Bratstvo i Jedinstvo (Brotherhood and Unity)   217
Animal Farm   233
The Cold War Cavalry   256
The Human Zoo   265
Conversano Batosta   279

Acknowledgements   301

STUD BOOK

Conversano (Kingdom of Naples 1767)

(15 generations)

Kitty I (Vukovar 1938)

Conversano Savona x Bonavista
(Lipica 1911)   (Lipica 1913)

(1 generation)

Conversano Bonavista x Soja
(Piber 1925)   (Hostau 1945)

(4 generations)

Conversano Soja x Primula
(Wimsbach 1952)   (Piber 1961)

Conservano Primula x Nobila
(Piber 1967)   (Piber 1965)

Conversano Batosta
(Lipik 1987)

Conversano Nobila
(Deurze 1986)

PROLOGUE

For my sisters, my brother and I, the war proceeded peacefully. Not a summer's day went by without my going for a ride along the river. Father ran a depot for stallions in southern Poland. He was in charge of more than one hundred pedigree horses, the most noble horses in all the Reich. Each spring they would be stationed around various stud farms to cover the mares; by July they were back at our depot. Among them were slender English thoroughbreds, two Lipizzaners from the Spanish Riding School at Vienna, five Berbers confiscated in France, a handful of Arabs, both pure-blooded and cross-breeds, and also Noriker work-horses and obedient Huzuls, on which I had learned to ride at the age of five.

We lived at Schloss Ochab, a white mansion that served as the officers' quarters. Stallion depot Draschendorf was on the far bank of the Vistula, where the Polish saddlers lived, and the guards and stableboys – the youngest of whom slept in the hayloft above the stalls. Auschwitz was thirty-five kilometres upstream. We children didn't know what a Konzentrationslager *was. The word itself was too difficult, so we called it the* Konzertlager.

Just before Christmas we would select a fat pig for slaughter. 'Churchill, prepare to meet your maker,' my father said as he cut the animal's throat. I stood there hopping in excitement, even though I had no idea who Churchill was. The butcher made rolled meat and sausages out of it, which lasted us for months. On Christmas Eve my mother would sing hymns from the Evangelical songbook, accompanying herself on the piano. Father played the cello; he took lessons from a cellist he had brought in specially from Vienna, a woman of whom we were in great awe, because she was the only one who dared answer back to Father.

To his subordinates, but also to us, he was hard and strict. He never beat us with a belt, but he did box our ears. Every so often he would have the single stablemen line up and drop their trousers; the vet would then come along to check them for venereal disease.

In the summer of 1944, Father had a siren placed on the roof of Schloss Ochab and established sentry duty at night, so that we could sleep soundly. I began dreaming about der Iwan: that he was coming to get us, or the horses. We knew that the Russians were approaching rapidly, that they had already pushed back our soldiers far beyond the Dnieper. But at the Vistula, or so we were assured, they would be brought to a halt. Our house was on the safe side of the river, but the depot itself lay on the eastern bank. The horses were at all costs to be kept out of the hands of the Red Army.

Father began carrying out emergency evacuation drills. Without warning, he would trigger the siren, and everyone had to rush and saddle up half the horses and hitch the others to the carts and carriages from the coach house. Oats and hay, ropes, tackle, the tools belonging to the blacksmith and the vet – everything had to be loaded up and tied down, and within three hours there would be a column of men and horses waiting on the road. Once, during such a drill, when we had an important visitor at the depot, Father gave the order to march. He didn't send them across the bridge, but straight into the Vistula.

Everyone had to wade across the river and climb a hill on the other side.

'In case the enemy knocks out the bridges,' he explained to us that evening.

On 7 August 1944, the first swarm of Russian fighters appeared in the sky. I ran outside and stood beneath a beech tree, where I could watch them coming over. The air shuddered with the roar of their engines. There were so many that it began growing dark in the middle of the day. Among the hundreds of planes passing overhead, one opened its bay doors. A bomb slid out and hurtled to the ground behind our home, close to the private stables housing the coach horses and Hildach, Father's own horse. I braced myself for the explosion, but it didn't come. When we went to investigate, we found a 500-litre fuel tank. It had been filled with kerosene, but that had leaked and stood in puddles everywhere. 'A firebomb', Father said. 'Meant for us.'

I was nine years old. From that moment on, I knew the war would one day reach us.

My sister Beate, two years my elder, and I were taught to fire a pistol. 'Beate! Come now, act like the daughter of a soldier!' my father would say whenever she found something scary, or difficult. We didn't know that Father had been on at his superiors for weeks to be allowed to withdraw the stallions to behind the Oder. But no permission was given; retreat could be seen as a sign of weakness. No one was to know that the Reich was on the brink of collapse, so life went on as usual. During the first week of January 1945, everything was made ready for the new foaling season. On 16 January we celebrated Heidi's seventh birthday: she had invited a friend and everyone was cheerful. The next morning, one of my father's superiors phoned. 'Evacuate immediately!' was the order. The Russians had crossed the Vistula that night and were now regrouping before pushing on.

Mother packed the suitcases and summoned Beate, Heidi and me to say that we were allowed to take our school notebooks and one toy each. Sitting at the table, she prepared a huge pile of sandwiches. Heidi and I had to leave first, accompanied by a lance corporal. Our coachman was already waiting on the sleigh to ferry us to the station. It was still dark outside, the only light came from a slight glimmer on the snow. I had the feeling the landscape was waving us farewell. We had to wait on the platform for forty-five minutes, and along the way we had to change trains five times. Then we arrived at our refuge across the Oder, no longer in Poland, but in Czechoslovakia.

In the middle of the following night, our chauffeur arrived in the staff car with Mother and Beate and the two little ones. Father would come later, by horse and wagon. His soldiers and servants made the journey in five days, at twenty degrees below zero. Those on horseback were leading a stallion by the reins as well. At intervals, the riders had to walk for an hour in order not to freeze.

Our new place of safety was on the estate of a baroness, who had enough stables for all the animals. I felt more secure there, also because the Oder is deeper than the Vistula. But during the first week of February my mother fell ill; she had stabbing pains in her abdomen. Father took her in the staff car to the hospital at Olmütz, where she was admitted right away. He went to visit her every other day, and always took one of the children with him. Heidi, the first to go, told us that evening how Mother had been lying in the hospital bed, white as a sheet, her cheeks sunken. On 15 February it was my turn. When we arrived, Frau Hartwig, who had been taking care of Mother, was waiting for us at the gate. Father climbed out and talked to her, I could hear the tremor in his voice. I knew right away there was something wrong with Mama. It was terribly cold in the car, and I just sat there and waited. *Suddenly Father turned around. 'Friedel, Mutti ist tot!'* he said.

We entered the hospital, walked down high-ceilinged corridors, climbed the stairs. When I saw Mama's dress lying there, I couldn't bear it any more. Frau Hartwig and the nurses tried to comfort me, but nothing helped. Until Father put on his major's voice. Crying did not befit a soldier. We had been taught from an early age to hold back our tears.

Mother was cremated the next day at the cemetery in Olmütz, and we put her ashes in a copper urn. It was a shame we couldn't sing her favourite song, 'Befiehl du deine Wege', because the organist didn't have the music. When the service was over, Father took Beate and me aside and said that we, as the oldest children, must be exceedingly brave from now on. There were more difficult times to come, he said. We didn't dare to ask: 'What kind of difficult times?' But we both had the feeling that Father was sharing with us some important thing from the world of adults, and for that reason alone we felt very grown-up.

Immediately after my birthday, my tenth, Father left us. He had received orders to take as many horses as possible by rail in the direction of Dresden. There he would try to move them across the Elbe, and as soon as he succeeded he would come back and fetch us, along with the remaining fifteen stallions. Meanwhile, under the leadership of Sgt Wiszik, we were to form the rearguard of the Draschendorf depot. Father left on the Saturday before Easter. We never saw him again. Our farewell was extremely hurried, because railway carriages had suddenly been requisitioned.

Throughout April, we waited for him to come back. Every day we heard new rumours about the Russians. Far to the north of us, the vanguard of the Red Army was rolling towards Berlin, but the front behind that was spreading in our direction. And still no sign of Father. In late April, Sgt Wiszik took things into his own hands and planned our evacuation. In addition to two German corporals, our group also consisted of seven Polish stablemen. And then there were the fifteen horses, including Poseur, an English thoroughbred; Nero, a Holsteiner warmblood; Ibn Saud and Dakkar, two Arab half-breds, and the two Lipizzaner stallions from the imperial stables in Vienna: Conversano Olga and Conversano Gratiosa – two silvery-white gentlemen of sixteen and twenty-two respectively. To make things simpler we referred to them only by their maternal names, Olga and Gratiosa, which of course sounded funny for two stallions. Just before we fled they were re-shod by the village blacksmith.

Grandmother, who had been with us since Mother's cremation, sat with the youngest children in the tilt cart. She never went anywhere in those days without her carpet bag; it contained Mother's ashes. Father's chauffeur was to drive ahead with the car flying the banner of the Draschendorf depot, but at the last moment it refused to start and had to be towed. I sat on a flatbed wagon drawn by our Lipizzaners, next to a soldier named Sylvester. We did everything precisely as Father had told us to, but we had no mounted scouts in front of us or at the back. Standing there waiting to move, the entire caravan was about sixty metres long. We wanted to get going, but the local Wehrmacht commander had not yet given us permission. It was 30 April: we didn't know that Hitler had committed suicide that day. The commander didn't either, in fact.

It wasn't until 6 May that he let us go. We were planning to head west, along a route known as the Sudetenstrasse, which gave Prague a wide berth. Our destination was the big Lipizzaner stud at Hostau in the Bohemian Forest, close to the German border. But we got stuck almost right away: the road was too steep, it was raining, the wagons turned out to be overloaded. We may have covered twenty kilometres that first day, but no more. Luckily, we were able to spend the night in a flax mill, where we made our beds on piles of cloth. As soon as I closed my eyes, I saw red-faced Russians everywhere.

The next day, I had to ride one of the horses. Whenever one of the stablemen would go ahead, he would toss me the rope of the horse he was leading. We sold our only gelding for 600 Reichsmark to a family who had a cart but no horse. The roads were becoming clogged with refugees on foot and columns of prisoners of war who were being relocated. All things German were on the move. Everywhere we went we heard the lowing of cows waiting in vain to be milked. Whenever we passed an abandoned farm the Poles would hop off their horses and look for food, eggs for example, which they slurped down raw. After the midday break that day, which had lasted far too long, they began to mutiny. They demanded to be paid in advance, in zlotys, otherwise they had no intention of working themselves to death for 'the major's family'. Those were their very words. Grandmother climbed up on to the wagon and reprimanded them as Father would have. That helped somewhat, because they at least decided not to desert.

But during the night of 8–9 May, which we spent in the open, they got drunk. We were planning to strike camp at first light. I was going to drive the Lipizzaners, and I was ready to go. Suddenly someone screamed: 'Russians, everywhere!' There was no point in trying to leave. The faces of women, Mongol women, began appearing all around us. I had never seen female soldiers before, let alone Asiatic ones. They carried their rifles slung across their chests, and wore big cartridge canisters on their belts. Some were lying on their stomachs in the backs of wagons. I thought: German soldiers would sit up straight. Two of them came up to me, smiling – I could see their gold teeth flashing. The next moment they levelled their rifles at me. They waved the barrels to indicate that I must get down off the box. I was sure they were going to take me to Siberia. They weren't interested at all, however, in a blond-haired, ten-year-old boy. But they were interested in the two Lipizzaners. I had to hand over the reins, and that was that.

I

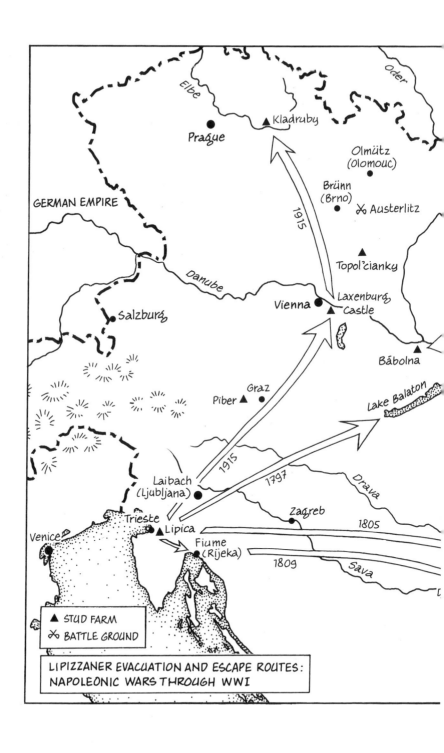

Oder

Elbe

▲ Kladruby

Prague

Olmütz
(Olomouc)

Brünn
(Brno)

⚔ Austerlitz

GERMAN EMPIRE

Topol'cianky ▲

Danube

Laxenburg
Castle

Vienna ● ▲

Salzburg ●

Bábolna ▲

Lake Balaton

Graz ●

Piber ▲

1915

1915

1797

Drava

Laibach
(Ljubljana) ●

Zagreb ●

1805

Trieste ●
▲ Lipica

Venice ●

Fiume
(Rijeka) ●

1809

Sava

▲ STUD FARM

⚔ BATTLE GROUND

LIPIZZANER EVACUATION AND ESCAPE ROUTES:
NAPOLEONIC WARS THROUGH WWI

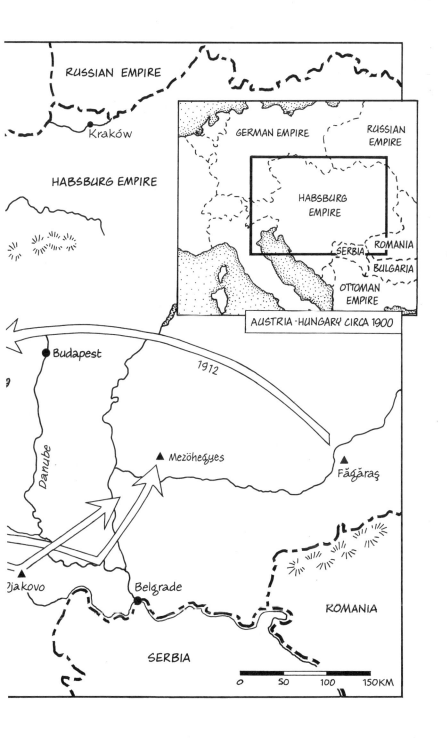

RUSSIAN EMPIRE

Kraków

HABSBURG EMPIRE

GERMAN EMPIRE

RUSSIAN EMPIRE

HABSBURG EMPIRE

ROMANIA

SERBIA

BULGARIA

OTTOMAN EMPIRE

AUSTRIA-HUNGARY CIRCA 1900

Budapest

1912

Danube

▲ Mezöhegyes

▲ Făgăraş

▲ ?jakovo

Belgrade

ROMANIA

SERBIA

0   50   100   150KM

THE 'TS' IN
LIPIZZANER

WHEN YOU GROW UP on the outskirts of town, there are two things you can do. You either go downtown – to the square in front of the cinema, where you smoke roll-ups and gaze up and down the main street that runs another thirty kilometres to another, bigger town.

Or you head out into the fields.

In my neighbourhood, the edge of town was marked quite concretely by the row of flats on Speenkruidstraat, three eleven-storey blocks standing shoulder to shoulder. At the end of the walkway on each floor, a fire escape wound down acrobatically to a ditch and a barbed-wire fence. It was there, at that exact spot, that the first field began. Crossing it you came to a rutted road that ran past sourish mounds of silage all the way to the Deurze Stream.

On warm summer days, we – those of us who had chosen the fields – would float downstream with the current in rubber boats. The spillway at Deurze was as far as we went. During my primary-school days, that was where the world ended. The stream there had a sloping bank that seemed made for sunbathing. But I had neither the patience nor the propensity for lolling about. One afternoon, while the others warmed themselves like lizards, I climbed the fence to scout out what lay beyond.

Walking past a stand of willows and an old bathtub that served as a trough, I came to another slope, steep as a railway embankment and with a row of poplars along its top. There was no way I could see over it, so I climbed up on my belly like a spy, using my knees and elbows. Craning my neck – like a lizard, in fact – I peered out on to a rectangle of white sand, worn with paths both circular and diagonal. Tight, symmetrical figures. The sand stretched all the way to a barn with its double doors closed. Just as I was about to rise to my feet, I heard whinnying.

A door slid open and, illuminated in the resulting darkness, was a white horse, standing hesitantly as though posing for a picture. The animal stepped from the frame with a graceless gait, led by a girl in riding boots with hair down to her buttocks. At twenty, thirty paces from my hiding place, they stopped. Face to face, even lip to lip they stood there, like two youngsters kissing.

Then another stable door opened and from that black square also a white horse appeared, not hesitantly but at a trot, snorting, its tail raised like a captured flag. A balding man with big sideburns was leaning back on the halter, yanking on it like an emergency brake, and together they spun a few times on their axis. Sand flew. I could smell the penetrating odour of horse.

The animal that was waiting began scraping one hoof rhythmically over the ground. 'Better put that hobble on her anyway,' I heard the man shout to the girl. She took a strap that hung from her belt like a lasso and slipped it with no little difficulty around one of the horse's hind legs; the other end she threaded between the forelegs and buckled it around the animal's neck. I understood that the two greys had not been brought out to trot around the exercise ring. Still, I was not prepared for what came next. The hobbled mare was: she swept her tail to one side and remained frozen in that position, like a statue.

The stallion, trotting proudly to and fro at the end of his slackened rope, shook his head then stopped abruptly. His black eyes remained fixed either on the tops of the poplars or on the high cumulus clouds above them, in any case far over my head. I pressed myself down further against the dyke in order not to be seen, but also in order not to see everything. Beneath its body, the stallion's telescopic member slid out segment by segment. I wanted to run away but I kept watching, transfixed. The horse's penis was black, with a flesh-coloured head, longer than I would have thought possible and sinuous and rubbery as an elephant's trunk. He pounced. The balding man seized the stallion's crooked organ and tugged at it to help him aim. Then the powerful male was transformed into a pantomime of helplessness, flailing with his front legs but unable to gain purchase on the mare's flanks. At every thrust his mane fell ridiculously over his eyes. I remember how he tilted his head to the left, then to the right, to set his yellow horsey teeth in the mare's withers. He bit her, she submitted – and all this took place as soundlessly and jerkily as in a silent movie.

∪

Freddy 'French Fry' claimed that people always felt like having sex, but that animals only did when they were rutting or in heat, and that that was the difference. He started talking about one of the girls who worked at the riding school and had hair like Kate Bush's, except she spoke German. Freddy said he would bet his Seiko that she could never hit the high notes in 'Wuthering Heights'.

Jelle and I, both thirteen, had no idea what he was talking about, but we agreed with him as a matter of principle. The three of us were walking along the stream, with Pjotr behind us. 'She went into a skid on the motorbike . . . *Bang* – right into a pylon. She was on the back, her boyfriend was driving. He was killed on impact.' Freddy wore a Palestinian shawl and was at least five years older than us.

Whenever a tractor or combine came rumbling down the brick lane we would pull Pjotr on to the verge and let him graze. The corn was so high you couldn't see the machines coming until the last moment, though the noise had already enveloped you like a cocoon of vibrating air. 'Good boy,' Freddy said. And then, to me: 'You could fire a cannon next to him and he'd just keep on grazing.'

Jelle, my neighbour who had started riding during the summer holiday, nodded earnestly, as though he suddenly knew all about horses.

That fearlessness didn't strike me as a healthy trait, though. 'But that means he's lost his instinct for danger,' I ventured.

Freddy came over and stood in front of me. He began explaining that that was precisely what was so great about the way animals had been tamed and bred since time began; a well-trained horse trusted people blindly. 'Trusts *you*.' The next moment, Freddy came up with something that he didn't seem able to get out of his head: it was time for me to try it, too.

I wasn't interested in horses. I had only come along with Jelle in order to hang out with Freddy, even though I knew little more about him than that he worked at the french-fry stand behind the Shell station on the industrial estate – and that, the one time I had been to his house, there had been a crumpled hundred-guilder note on the table. Like a scrap of paper lying there, waiting to be thrown away.

I patted Pjotr's neck, something I hadn't done or dared to do till then. 'But then we'd have to go all the way back and get a saddle,' I said.

That was nonsense. Without a saddle was no problem.

'But how am I supposed to get up there?'

Jelle folded his hands into a stirrup and tossed his head as if to say 'upsy-daisy'.

As I grabbed a tuft of mane with one hand and laid the other on the warm horse's back, I noticed that, from up close, all the hairs were either pitch black or white. From a distance Pjotr had looked vaguely grey and spotty, very different from how he looked now. When I said that, Freddy told us that Pjotr had been born black but would be completely white in a few years. 'He's a half-bred Lipizzaner. And Lipizzaner foals are born black. By the time they're eight or nine, though, they've turned white.'

It was the first time I'd heard the name Lipizzaner, a word that didn't make the sound of z's, but instead had a 'ts' that cracked like a ringmaster's whip.

I slid my knee over Pjotr's back and sat up straight, clenching him with my thighs to stop myself slipping off. As soon as I tensed my calves as well, the horse went into motion, still munching on grass and shaking its mane. I was wearing shorts, so I could feel every movement of his shoulder blades. They moved upward – forward, like the connecting rods of a locomotive. Powerful, regular. I sat and moved, without moving myself.

Why did this feel so tremendous? Freddy, Jelle, Pjotr and I walked past fields of potatoes and corn, but the only one who didn't have to walk was me. I was also the only one who could look out freely across the heads of corn. On horseback the world around you seemed different: the pebbles along the verge and the dry bed of the ditch let themselves be seen from another, more oblique angle. I had to duck to avoid branches I would otherwise not have noticed. When I looked back up, a vista opened that was broader than I'd seen before: I could survey the course of the Deurze Stream to where it passed the spillway and the new wooden bicycle bridge. My outlook had widened and deepened. I had been lifted on to shoulders, like a champion wrestler. No one was taller than two metres ten, but I knew myself to be a head taller than the tallest Montenegrin or the tallest Nubian. I felt elevated. You had footmen, and you had horsemen.

U

Almost every afternoon after school, Jelle and I could be found at De Tarpan. The paved yard of the riding school was our domain, we were allowed everywhere: in the tack room, on to the roof of the big barn to fasten down a rattling sheet of corrugated iron, amongst the audibly breathing horses in the stables and even into the owner's house. Although we didn't sleep there, it sometimes seemed as though for us, stableboys and girls, De Tarpan was home – just as it was for the horses.

I kept my parents at arm's length, they wouldn't have understood anyway. Although I never for a moment considered becoming a vegetarian, I stopped eating smoked horse meat. On the ceiling of my bedroom at home I drew a life-sized Arabian stallion in charcoal. Arabians have a concave muzzle, like the spout of an Oriental teapot. And they have one fewer pair of ribs than other horses: seventeen instead of eighteen.

Because I had no fear of horses, I was allowed to help break in the four-year-olds. When it was my turn to supervise the pony class on its outdoor rides, I would choose the steadily whitening Pjotr. Along with Jelle, I also trained the cross-breed gelding that belonged to the director of Goedewaagen's Royal Earthenware Factory, who had been slung from the saddle when he had caught his foot on an upright in the sliding door. Mr Goedewaagen had tried to scramble up from the sand, but remained on his hands and knees with his back sagging like a dog – and it was in that very same position that the ambulance personnel had carried him away.

In principle, all of the horses were at our disposal, except for the white stallion. He wasn't the biggest horse in the stable, but he did possess the most 'aristocracy'. He had an arched neck, a silvery-grey mane with an artistic curl to it and eyes that stood out by virtue of their size and blackness. Whenever a mare in heat walked past he would slam his flanks against the walls of his stall. His muzzle was covered in flecks devoid of pigment, he had an 'L' branded on the left side of his jaw and a 'P' on his right haunch, topped by an imperial crown. On the door of his stall was a nameplate: CONVERSANO PRIMULA.

Primula, or 'Prim' for short, belonged to Piet. In the five years I spent at De Tarpan, I never saw the owner of our riding school sitting astride his Lipizzaner. Piet trained Primula by walking behind him, like a coachman without the coach, his arms stretched out either side of the stallion's tail. At noontime, when there were no lessons to be given, he would take him out of the stall for this 'long-reining'. Others climbed on to their horses and spurred them on, but for Piet Bakker *this* was the exercise to beat all exercises. For it he needed no spurs, or jodhpurs or boots.

I once asked Piet what made Primula different from other horses.'

'His blood,' Piet answered.

'What is it about his blood then?'

'It's blue. Bluer than any other horse.'

I had been watching their exercises. Primula could canter so slowly, almost in slow motion, that Piet could keep up with him at a walk. That was how it was supposed to work: during the long-rein exercises, you weren't supposed to run. Your horse's power was primarily directed upwards, freeing him of the ground. This was easiest to see during the 'passage', when it looked as though Primula was bouncing on a trampoline and, for just the click of a shutter, hanging suspended in the air.

Harness racing was exhausting, hard riding. Horse races, according to Piet, were like the motorcycle TT rally in nearby Assen. But even the more sophisticated forms of riding weren't sophisticated enough for him. Jumping was track and field. Dressage: gymnastics. What we did at De Tarpan was the art of classical riding. Ballet.

After the midday session, Piet called me over to him on the white sand of the outdoor ring. While Primula chewed on a handful of concentrate, Piet told me that the Lipizzaner breed was the product of centuries of minute adjustments. Since 1580, at the Habsburgs' imperial stud farm on a ridge above Trieste, form had been given to a horse destined to bear kings and emperors. There the Austro-Hungarian equerries had created a pure and noble breed. Power and grace, loyalty and eagerness to learn – these traits had all, by means of selection and cross-breeding, been brought together in this one animal.

Piet ran his fingers down Primula's backbone, like a vet, and counted up the distinct vertebrae starting at the base of the tail. Between the thirteenth and the fourteenth he stopped and pressed against the cartilage. 'Amazing, isn't it?'

I probably shrugged.

This, Piet said, was one of the Lipizzaner's inbred traits: starting at the thirteenth vertebra, they possess a built-in flexibility. That makes them more supple than other horses when it comes to performing the levade, in which they rise up on their hind legs – like a controlled form of rearing. It was the pose in which the triumphant general would report to his sovereign, and in which he would later be immortalized on canvas.

Primula took a few steps to one side and began shaking his head. 'Has the inspection lasted long enough?' Piet looked at him the way a father looks at his son, and ran his hand down his neck.

'Do that,' he said to me.

I thought he wanted to show me that his stallion hadn't even worked up a lather, but he had.

'Well? Can you feel it?'

'What am I supposed to feel?'

'When you touch a Lipizzaner,' Piet said, 'you're touching history.'

U

It was for the pure-bred Conversano Primula, and only for him, that we built the grandstands.

The idea and the initiative came from Leny, Piet's wife, who had answered an ad in the local newspaper for a batch of church pews. She called Freddy over, because he could drive a tractor, and handed him a slip of paper with the address.

Jelle and I were allowed to go along, perched on our respective running boards. The flatbed trailer rattling behind, we drove into town, under the railway viaduct, past the Acmesa dairy and the head offices of the reclamation company where Jelle's father was the managing director.

I climbed off the tractor at the new traffic lights. Grongingerstraat 74, was that a left or a right at the end of the street? The lady I asked took the piece of paper and studied my face carefully. 'You're looking for the synagogue?'

'No, the church,' I said. 'We're here to pick up the pews.'

The address proved close by, just around the corner to the right. Number 74 was a narrow building with three high, stained-glass windows and an equal number of towers. The shoulders of the man who opened the door were covered in dandruff. He showed us in, crossing a floor of cracked tiles. A veil of dinginess had settled over the rows of pews, the baptismal font, the pulpit. The floor was dotted with little piles of dried pigeon droppings and here and there a shard of glass. This, he told us, was the old synagogue, which had been used after the war as a Dutch Reformed church. But the Reformed congregation had moved only recently to a smaller building, so this colossus could finally be torn down.

The word 'synagogue' stuck in my mind. Only twenty-five years later – at the spot where Freddy had turned the tractor around – would the city install a memorial stone with the inscription:

AROUND US HERE ONCE STOOD THE NEIGHBOUR-
HOOD WHERE 550 JEWS LIVED IN 1940. NO MORE
THAN 25 OF THESE CITIZENS OF ASSEN RETURNED
AFTER THE WAR.

When the memorial stone was unveiled, the Vanderveen department store published a book about the history of the Jews of Assen. It said that some of the furniture we had come for had been sent to Westerbork as early as 1940, to build a stage at the Nazi *Durchgangslager* (transit camp).

The pews that remained were four metres long. Leaden benches almost too heavy for three men to carry – Freddy at one end, Jelle and I at the other. The dust blew in our faces as soon as we went out the door. We slid the pews on to the trailer and lashed them down with longes. Three rows of four on the bottom, two rows on top.

Back at De Tarpan, Freddy drove straight to the visitors' area beside the outdoor exercise ring, where we unloaded the pews on to a platform made from old pallets.

When the grandstands were finished, and Piet came to inspect them, the pews had been arranged in four rows of five. He ran his hands over the armrests and felt under the seats as well, where we had already discovered a whole galaxy of chewing gum. Piet did not look happy. He told us to get some putty knives and scrape off the petrified lumps. He was even less pleased with the dismal condition of the wood itself. Using his bare hands, he broke off a chunk from one of the seats. Piet ground the wood to powder and hurried off to his lessons in the indoor ring.

Halfway there he paused, looked over his shoulder and shouted: 'Tear that rubbish apart. The rotten pieces can go in the wood-stove, the good ones we'll keep.'

Following Piet at a little distance, we went to fetch crowbars and claw hammers. Our grandstand was a write-off.

The easiest way to go about it, we discovered, was first to knock off the armrests, after which the middle sections simply fell to pieces. All you really had to do then was pry the back away from the seat. We vented our frustration at having done all that work for nothing on the pews themselves, and when Freddy suddenly remembered that his Seiko had a stopwatch, we made a game out of it. Taking turns in two-man teams, we would wait with sledgehammers poised for the third to shout 'Go!' Our faces red with exertion, we finally succeeded in tearing apart a synagogue pew in under six minutes.

∪

My last contact with Primula had been in a movie. In an almost deserted cinema in 1991, five of his sons and daughters paraded by on the screen. First Pjotr, then Lublice, Tarras, Latka and Sarpa – all half-breds who had already passed the age of selection and were therefore Lipizzaner white. Along with the pure-bred Lipizzaner mare Nobila, they were playing in a film based on Shakespeare's *The Tempest*.

The scene I was waiting for came about three-quarters of the way through. In all their whiteness, Primula's offspring came strolling down the long corridor of a palace. They appeared casually and without fanfare from doorways left and right – like members of an audience who accidentally wander on stage from the artists' entrance. As a group they formed the background to a love scene that took place amid an orgy of colours and shapes, to which the director – Peter Greenaway – seemed to hold the patent. Like a painter of light, he projected colourful, crowded *tableaux vivants*, one on top of the other, with as the single, fixed point actor John Gielgud, eighty-seven and still a force to be reckoned with, who played both Shakespeare and his creation Prospero.

At ease and seemingly without prompting, the horses pushed ahead until they were standing around Prospero's daughter and the chained Prince Ferdinand. Meanwhile, the two were declaring their love for each other – 'Admir'd Miranda, indeed the top of admiration' / 'I am a fool to weep at what I am glad of' – but the horses milled about imperturbably, sniffing at Miranda's dress, pawing at the carpet, until Nobila turned to face the camera and claim the entire screen for herself. Shakespeare/Prospero looked at the viewer and declaimed: 'We are such stuff as dreams are made on / and our little life is rounded with a sleep.'

There were, including myself, six people in the theatre. For a full ninety minutes we sat submersed in a fairy-tale world. We saw winged angels on swings, and greyhounds, the sleekest of all land animals. Shakespeare did not give one the impression that we flabby humans were the pinnacle of creation. He brought in a devil – 'a born devil, on whose nature nurture can never stick' – in order to underscore firmly the incorrigibility of the villainous streak in mankind. Against this background, the Lipizzaners radiated calm and innocence, as though they stood far above human machinations. They looked, it seemed to me, more sincere than their masters.

For the first time then, and for the first of many times since, I asked myself what it was that people tried to express through the animals with which they surround themselves. Or, in the case of the horse: what does the animal embody in the eyes of man? The horse, it occurred to me, is a repository of a host of human traits. Those characteristics have been foisted upon him – which is not to say that he is not imbued with them through and through. For starters, the horse was made a slave, obedient and tame. That took some 6,000 years, but the result was something to behold: unlike the zebra, the horse would eat from your hand. He would allow his hooves to be shod and his teeth to be flossed – as was the daily custom with the Arabs owned by King Hassan. In almost every culture, the horse was on a higher level to other grazers, he was their herder. And festooned with straps he used his muscle power to cleave the soil, thereby increasing the earth's yield; the surplus he dragged to town as though born to do nothing else. Many a civilization was elevated on four hooves, and when those civilizations collided, the speed and agility of their horses often served to determine the outcome.

A dog could be vicious (something seen as a typically animal characteristic), but a horse was brave and proud. In every age there lived men who loved their horse better than their wife. The dying wish of a Roman general? To see his horse one final time. And Emperor Caligula, a contemporary of Jesus of Nazareth, dressed his stallion Incitatus in purple and considered having him appointed consul. Since the most distant past, when the horse was first admitted to the circles of aristocracy, he has come to be treated less and less like an animal.

Conversano Primula was registered with a casting agency. For years he had played parts in advertisements for Verkade biscuits and chocolate bars. Sometimes he won bigger roles as well. I had once helped with the preparations for the Dutch feature film *Iris*. We spent two or three weeks teaching Primula to stand still in the dark as a car approached. In the evening we would tether him behind the sliding front door of the riding hall, Piet would come driving up with his headlights on and we would open the door and say 'whoa' and 'whoa fella'. His instincts as an animal of flight screamed at him to run away, but we finally brought him to the point where he would remain standing until the bumper almost touched him. Alert, but motionless.

After that we taught him to rear up whenever Monique van de Ven, who played the veterinarian Iris, tried to grab his halter.

The student trainee from De Tarpan was the only one of us allowed on the set. When it was over she told us that she had sat under a bush, in a wetsuit, to avoid growing numb in the downpour from the rain machine. Primula had done a magnificent job. In the film he displayed a will of his own – a pure white apparition under the hard, bluish spotlights, his indomitability serving as a warning for the calamity awaiting Iris.

U

The Lipizzaner was the horse to top all horses. More than any other breed, the Lipizzaner had come closest to the bastions of human power. He had performed at the coronation of shahs, parvenu sovereigns and Third World dictators – but also in Washington, at the inauguration of President Reagan in 1981. What is it about this animal that appeals to such men? Its power, held in check? Its obedience? Or perhaps it is the animal's white coat and the underlying notion of purity? The human species does not lend itself so readily to moulding and making; despite its knowledge and expertise, and despite the remarkable results humans have achieved with their own pets, it has as yet been unable to improve significantly upon itself. Man had designed the Haflinger, the Orlovdraver, the Clydesdale, the Friesian horse, the Connemara pony. More than four centuries of fine-tuning culminated in the present-day Lipizzaner, making it the oldest 'cultivated breed'. From generation to generation, the horses were selected for both outer and inner beauty – or at least for what passed as such at the Habsburg court of the moment. Each summer, a number of the best male four-year-olds were brought to Vienna. They had ascended to the pinnacle of the pyramid of civilization and became inhabitants of the palace, where they ate from red marble troughs. It then took ten to twelve years of training to school each individual stallion in all disciplines of the *Hohe Schule*. In the imperial manège, the fully qualified Lipizzaner would then perform his kinetic art to the strains of Handel, Chopin and Strauss. He danced.

As the credits rolled by, I waited long enough to see the special word of thanks to 'Piet Bakker and the De Tarpan riding school', and even after that I remained seated. The lights in the cinema came on, but I was caught up in my flow of thought. Man had created the horse after his ideal image of it, there was nothing religious about that. From the rugged *Equus ferus*, the wild quadruped of the steppes, he had moulded *Equus caballus*, an animal with sixty-four chromosomes: two fewer than his feral forefather. Neither God nor Darwin's slow evolution had had anything to do with it. The result was a new species which, with a little help in the form of stage directions, could perform Shakespeare.

BLUTAUFFRISCHUNG
(NEW BLOOD FOR OLD)

A T THE CENTRE OF the ring that was the world of Lipizzaners stood a Viennese hippologist named Hans Brabenetz. He knew their individual paces, their characters. He did not own a computer – the bloodlines of 5,000 horses were stored in his brain. Herr Brabenetz was the living, breathing filing system of the Documentation Centre for Old-Austrian Horse Breeds. With his wife, Suzi, he could be found in the Vienna phone directory, listed as 'certified horse-breeding professional'.

Pacing back and forth before the windows of my office, I practised three German sentences. Then I punched in the number and explained to 'Brabenetz!'(the 'r' dark and rolling) who I was and why I hoped to speak to him. I also told him that I would be coming to Vienna that weekend – to visit the Spanish Riding School.

'*Hofreitschule*,' he said. 'The *Royal* Spanish Riding School.'

'*Hofreitschule*,' I corrected myself.

'Herr Hartmann, before you go any further . . . Do you mind my asking your age?'

I dithered between repeating my correct name or stating my age. 'Forty-two,' I said at last.

'Ha ha, then I'm twice as old as you. I am eighty-four.'

After congratulating him on his seniority, I started talking about the Lipizzaners. What intrigued me most was the idea of their nobility – a human-bred animal that resided on the top rung of racial enhancement. If anyone could tell me about the background of this 'imperial horse', he could.

At his age, Herr Brabenetz said, the world around him no longer proceeded at such a clip. If I would go to the trouble of writing a letter, he would reply within two weeks. 'But before that, may I ask what it is you want from me?'

I started by describing Conversano Primula and his ancestors, who Piet had told me included famous stallions that had performed in Vienna. He listened for a minute, then asked: 'Have you ever been a soldier?'

I had to admit I hadn't.

'Then it's going to be difficult. If you have never served in the army, how can I explain these things to you?'

'I've been in wars,' I said. 'In the Balkans and the Caucasus.'

'*Ah, ich auch*,' I heard him say. 'Also in the Balkans, and almost in the Caucasus. We landed in the Crimea, 1942, but never got further than the Kertsh Peninsula . . .' He paused, then asked: '*Govorite po russki?*'

I replied in Russian.

Brabenetz growled. 'I *used* to speak it. You see, I spent two and a half years as a Soviet prisoner of war. We learned *Armee-Russisch* . . . But you know what, if you call me on Sunday, once you get to Vienna, I'll let you know whether I can receive you on Monday.'

U

Vienna, the mere sound of it, awakened in me the mood of Sunday afternoon visits to my great aunts, where boredom mingled in equal parts with cigar smoke. In heavy-framed honeymoon photographs on the sideboard – of Uncle So-and-so in a checkered sports jacket, and the corresponding aunt with her hair up in curls – the city displayed its gaudy side. And when the Vienna Boys' Choir sang their ethereal carols on TV at Christmas I watched slack-jawed, but that was because, according to my sister, they had been gelded at the age of ten or eleven.

As it turned out, my hotel, close to Vienna's Arenbergpark, stood in the shadow of two structures that looked like cooling towers, taller than cathedrals. Nothing could be less Viennese than this: windowless, drab, in a park full of skateboarders. The receptionist told me they were *Flaktürme*: air defence towers, each topped by four elevated crow's nests for anti-aircraft guns. *Flak*, from Fl(ieger) a(bwehr) k(anone), meaning 'anti-aircraft gun'. In 1943–4, six of these colossi had been built in the heart of Vienna, to raise the anti-aircraft guns above the city skyline. No one had ever got around to razing them.

I went into the park and laid my hand against the wall of one of the *Flaktürme*, you could still feel the seams where the concrete shuttering had been. And there was an entrance: a dark, vertiginous shaft leading to the cash desk of a modern art exhibition. Behind those walls it was as cold as a walk-in cooler. On the way to the top, by way of stairwells and service lifts, one kept passing statues and installations: a wilted rose garden, a miniature aircraft carrier stranded on a hill, a video spelling out the word P E A C E, over and over again. Outside, on the windy walkway, you looked over the Stefansdom and other city landmarks from a sixty-metre-high vantage. I saw the course of the Danube, tightly canalized and far from blue. That made me feel a bit more in place as well.

Vienna had a way of continually throwing me off balance. At Volkstheater station, where I left the underground, I found myself caught up in a demonstration. Waving the Austrian flag, the protestors crowded on to the escalators to street level. They unfurled banners reading NO TO THE EU DICTATORSHIP and chanted 'Austria stays free!'

Out on the pavement, I managed to give them the slip. Starting at the corner beside the station entrance was a baroque building so huge it would have taken ten minutes to circle on foot. These were the royal stables – not to be confused with the even more exclusive residence of the Lipizzaners – which, during the heyday of the Habsburg Empire, had housed more than 600 horses. In 2001 the complex had been converted into a 'museum quarter'. Paintings by Schiele, Klimt and Kokoschka had replaced the colourful collection of parade animals, which had once included thirty-two 'identical' Kladruber carriage horses, sixteen white and sixteen black (for funerals). In the courtyard stood dozens of purple plastic settees. Settling down into one, you couldn't help but wonder what had become of Vienna's iconic mustiness.

U

En route in the high-speed train through Germany, I had read Joseph Roth's *The Radetzky March* – to get a feeling for the old Austria that had given birth to the Lipizzaner. Writing between the wars, Roth had brought to life the twilight years of the Danube Monarchy. 'Vienna was, as they said later, the capital of peacetime.' That kind of tone. He wrote with fondness of Emperor Franz Josef I, whose patriarchal moustache and sideburns billowed and twined together. 'The emperor was an old man. The oldest emperor in the world. He saw the sun go down on his empire, but he said nothing. He knew, after all, that he would die before its downfall.'

Roth provided a painstaking description of the ineluctable fall of the once so sluggishly peaceful multi-ethnic state, which had extended from the Alps to beyond the Carpathians. This 600-year-old 'Holy Roman Empire' – wedged between the Prussian, Russian and Ottoman empires – had been run by twenty-four Habsburg rulers and was, by the dawn of the twentieth century, a worn and dilapidated house. The cohabitation of Poles, Czechs, Germans, Ruthenians, Hungarians, Slovenians, Croatians, Italians, Romanians, Slovaks and Jews had given rise to irreconcilable differences. The hairline cracks between the races *and* the classes had widened to become fractures. The writer, a Jew himself, let the reader feel the sweltering anti-Semitism, the burgeoning nationalism and the charged atmosphere at the gatherings of workers who had supposedly met only to perform gymnastics. At the same time he bore witness in unsuspecting Vienna to the splendour of the annual parade on the Day of Sacraments: 'an army of cherubs singing "God preserve us, God protect"', a Lipizzaner stallion drawing near 'with majestic coquettishness', followed by a strident voice: 'Hear ye, hear ye! The emperor approaches.'

And the emperor did approach: eight snow-white horses drew his carriage. And astride them, white-wigged in black livery embossed with gold, were his lackeys. They looked like gods, and were merely the servants of demigods.

After the war erupted in 1914, Joseph Roth fought on the Eastern Front to protect this world against the Russians. A hopeless cause. 'Time doesn't want us any more! These times want to bring forth only independent, national states! God is no longer believed in. The new religion is nationalism.' In November 1916 he was transferred back to Vienna, where he attended the funeral of Franz Josef as a guard of honour. A successor had already been crowned, but Joseph Roth felt orphaned – even though the greatest horrors were yet to come.

The same went for the 1,000 horses which together formed the Lipizzaner breed: with the demise of the Habsburgs, they found themselves in the hands of the new gods, the demagogues.

All the more surprising was to find that Vienna's faded glory was preserved by the very stallions of the Spanish Riding School. Amid the equestrian statues on Heldenplatz and in the little alleyways around the Hofburg, the Vienna of a century ago came alive. Beneath the arches it reeked of manure, there was the rattle of horseshoes and here one could actually still come to a nasty end beneath the wheels of a carriage. This tableau for tourists was the prelude to a choreographed performance by the Lipizzaners. The entrance fee varied from 26 euros for standing room to 142 euros for the plush of the imperial box. I chose one of the less-prohibitively priced seats, plus a tour of the stalls afterwards. The entrance to the manège (the 'Winter Riding School') was on the same side of the building as the former chambers of Empress Sissi, now converted into a museum where the preservation of the Habsburg dream was treated with equal earnestness.

My seat was halfway along the top balcony, but even from there the ceiling roses seemed high. I looked down on three candelabra, built up in layers like wedding cakes. The hall was a ballroom, the only one in the world that smelled of horse. A ringmaster with a wireless microphone walked out into the arena and told us a bit about the building's architecture and the tradition of the Spanish Riding School. The school had been started in 1580 with the arrival of nine Andalusian studs – hence the qualification 'Spanish' – to serve as the patriarchs of a new, imperial breed of horses:

well mannered and athletic of build, as befitted the House of Habsburg. 'Lipizzaners are human beings like us,' he went on, the soles of his shoes steadily tamping a single square metre of loose dirt. He repeated this claim in deadpan German, without elucidation and without irony. We would see white stallions who could dance a Viennese waltz, and the high points of the performance would be balletic moves such as the courbette and the capriole – 'airs above the ground'.

A march by Johann Strauss the Elder rolled from the loud-speakers. The horses entered, walking through the beams of sunlight that fell from a great height. First, the salute to the imaginary emperor; in unison, the riders doffed their bicorne style hats directly in front of the royal box containing the portrait of Emperor Charles VI, who had inaugurated this Winter Riding School in 1735. It was a Sunday morning, the hour of Mass. What followed was a forty-five-minute display of *magnificentia*, of beauty bred to impress.

Stallions that must easily have weighed 500 kilos switched so lightly from a left-handed to a right-handed canter that it looked like they were skipping. We were shown half-passes, pirouettes, transitions from marching on the spot (the piaffe) to an elevated trot (the passage), followed by the harmonious symmetry of formation riding by two sets of four horses at the same time (the quadrille). This was the High School of dressage – there was nothing higher.

Perhaps I was prejudiced by my experience with Piet Bakker and Conversano Primula, but the part I enjoyed most was the work on the long reins. The doors swung open to reveal only one horse: Favory Plutona. He wore no saddle. His gait resembled a graceful swaying of the hips. He revelled in it, and followed the fluid rhythm of the 'Pariser Einzugsmarsch' by Johann Heinrich Walch. Was it the grey directing the man who walked behind him, or the other way around?

Less subtlety but greater spectacle came with the school jumps – the absolute crowd-pleaser. In comparison with the postcards on which the stallions were shown floating head-high above the ground, the real thing was rather disappointing. The stamping that preceded the exercises had something nervous and grim to it – you could see this in the fixed gazes of both rider and horse. More interesting to me than their performance was the origin of these jumps. I'd first read about them in *Elsevier's Horse Guide*, a present for my fifteenth or sixteenth birthday, which said that the art of warfare (a gruesome thing, if you asked me) had brought forth the equestrian arts (a thing sublime), with as their highpoint the capriole: a vertical leap in which the horse first raises its front legs and then, at the highest point, kicks out with its hind legs. This explosion of force was designed to take out an adversary with a single kick. A deadly karate chop, in other words, to turn the Turk from the city gates. War had begot art: in stylized form, this jump was now seen as the supreme move in the High School of dressage.

Led by Tania, a Hungarian-born student working her way through college, I – along with a dozen other visitors – was admitted after the performance to the artists' foyer, the Stallburg. To reach this wing of the palace the horses needed to cross only one roofed alleyway.

'Stables of the emperor's equestrian guard since 1565', a plaque on the wall read. 'Heavily damaged by bombing in 1945. Restored in 1947–49.'

Favory Plutona was still lathered from the work he had done, and ran his muzzle back and forth in his marble trough a few times to say that he was hungry. From the arched ceiling above each stall protruded the bust of a horse's head in white plaster, but otherwise the interior was modern – with fire extinguishers behind glass and fluorescent lights in the corridors. In an outbuilding hung the heat lamps for an equine solarium.

Tania told us that the riders were also allowed to live in the Stallburg, but that only the *élèves*, the apprentices, exercised that privilege. 'Who is eligible to become a rider?' She tossed the question in the air like a majorette's baton, and caught it herself. 'You must be a man, no taller than one metre eighty, but with relatively long legs. Those, in fact, are the only requirements.'

We visited the saddlery, which smelled of leather and beeswax, and stopped finally at the stall of a black horse. There was not a single white or grey hair to be seen in his coat. Tania remarked that one out of every hundred Lipizzaner foals remained dark, either black or brown, which elicited a hiss of amazement here and there. There was, she said, a saying associated with the phenomenon: 'As long as dark Lipizzaners are born, the Spanish Riding School will live on.'

U

Back at my hotel room, I landed in the middle of an Animal Planet documentary about gorillas on a mountainside in Rwanda. 'What distinguishes man from animals', I heard the voiceover say, 'is that animals know no art and no religion.'

Is that so, I thought? 'And they don't commit genocide, either!' I was tempted to shout back at the screen.

But it was true: wild horses in France had never made paintings of the cave dwellers at Lascaux. Humans, on the other hand, had carved totems and crucifixes before which they danced or knelt. Sometimes the world of the human imagination was populated by horse-like creatures, such as the winged Pegasus who flew to the heavens and claimed a place among the constellations in order to inspire poets. Those poets in turn then summoned up new imaginary worlds in the form of poems or psalms, and it was precisely this capacity which made humans human. At least, that is, if you believed the scriptwriters at Animal Planet.

The question of the distinction between humans and animals continued to nag at me. My former biology teacher would have immediately altered this last sentence to read: 'between humans and *other* animals'. Again, there you had it. In a series of drawings made around 1500, Leonardo da Vinci had compared the facial expressions of humans, horses and lions – the expressions he portrayed were so interchangeable that one wondered which face belonged to which creature. Darwin had taken the notion of man as the God-appointed ruler of flora and fauna and knocked it on the head, but the peculiar thing was that man never stopped acting that way: as the tamer of nature which, once subdued, had to serve him in everything. The wild horses of the steppes had been captured with lassos, they had given birth to progeny that were converted into beasts of utility and then – with the exception of a few Mongolian Przevalskis – they were annihilated. Was that progress? Did the subjugation of a species always lead to improvement? 'The horse is the most noble victory ever achieved by man!' was the pronouncement made by Comte de Buffon, zoologist to the court of Louis XV. But if people were so good at moulding animal species to their wishes, why did attempts to improve the human race always end in murder and mayhem?

I turned off the TV and called Hans Brabenetz. He remembered me, and invited me to his home the next morning at nine-thirty. After hanging up I breathed a long sigh and opened a window; an afternoon without appointments lay before me. I decided to go to the Museum of Military History, to see the car in which Archduke Franz Ferdinand had been driven around Sarajevo in late June 1914.

As a journalist in the summer of 1994, wary of more contemporary bullets, I had visited the infamous street corner in front of Moritz Schiller's delicatessen. Now I wanted to see the holes in the black tourer itself. Nowhere else could one set eyes on such a precise junction which, once taken, had with a tectonic crash brought down a whole series of old, interlapping empires. 'It was Sunday, I was a student,' was how Joseph Roth remembered the moment. 'That afternoon a girl came by. They wore their hair in braids back then. She was carrying a big, yellow straw hat. The hat contained a telegram, a lightning bolt of paper. "You know," said the girl, "they've killed the crown prince! We're not staying here, are we?"'

The military museum had adopted a modern slogan: WARS BELONG IN MUSEUMS. Admission was free on the day of rest. In the first-floor gallery, two Russian blondes were standing beside a Turkish family as they watched a fencing demonstration. Once past the bust of Franz Josef, the exhibition halls grew more subdued, and more down at heel. The walls were hung with battlefield panoramas, the visitor could admire Austro-Hungarian uniforms in glass display cases. Victories won before the twentieth century were glorified unabashedly: there was an Ottoman army tent and cannon that had been seized from the Turks at Kalemegdan Fort in Belgrade in 1717.

As the paintings drew closer to the modern day, they became ever more gruesome. The one entitled *Die Baterie der Toten* (depicting a battle in 1866) showed more dying horses than soldiers. You could see it as an anti-war statement, as a predecessor of Picasso's *Guernica* (which also shows a dying horse), but that was not how it had been intended. The exhibition began increasingly to resemble a procession of dead horses, until one stepped across the threshold of 1900 and pride of place was assumed by the howitzers and gun turrets made in the factories of the Skoda family.

The curators, evidently, had been at a loss as to what to do with the two world wars. The second one was apparently still too fresh in their memories. It was only in 2001, after all, that a mayor of Vienna dared to say out loud that his country had mistakenly and for too long considered itself the first victim of Hitler's war. Since then there had been a boom in '1938' publications, all contritely broadcasting that very same message: the shelves of Vienna's bookshops were lined these days with titles like *Die Juden Wiens* (The Jews of Vienna), *Jüdische Frauen in Wien* (Jewish Women in Vienna) and *Der Anschluss: Ich hole euch heim* (The Annexation: I Have Brought You Home). The Museum of Military History, however, had not yet reached that point. Here they were still coming to terms with the First World War, only the opening phase of which was rendered with any conviction: a showroom-like display of an old car welcomed the visitor to the world of 1914. The open car was the length of a limousine, it had spoked wheels and running boards wide enough to accommodate the spare tyre easily. It was a four-cylinder Gräf & Stift. Number plate: A-iii 118.

I examined the oyster-shaped wound in the back door. The hole itself was no larger than a small coin, but the lacquer around it had been blown off the metal. Shortly before that happened, in Trieste, the archduke and his wife had allowed themselves to be paraded around in a landau drawn by Lipizzaners. In Sarajevo, however, a car had been chosen.

A plate on the motor cap read: LEISTUNG: 28/32 P(FERDE) -S(TÄRKE).

That the attack carried out by Gavrilo Princip and his fellow Black Hand commandos, Serb nationalists with claims of their own to Bosnia, had succeeded at all was an insane fluke: the bomb they had thrown earlier the same day had missed its target completely.

'Is this the real one, or did they make a replica?' a young boy in the costume of a knight asked his father.

'It's the real one.'

I had always found it astounding that, an hour and a half after that bomb was thrown, the motorcade through Sarajevo had resumed, and that Franz Ferdinand and Sophie's car had come to a halt only a few steps away from Princip. Who had fired twice, one bullet for Franz Ferdinand, one for Sophie.

'Maybe there's still blood in it?'

'No, man,' the father said. 'They cleaned that off a long time ago.'

But they hadn't looked carefully. Opposite the car lay the crown prince's uniform coat, a hole torn between the third and fourth buttons from the top. The blue material was stained a rusty brown.

∪

Hans Brabenetz was a little man. He had bristly hair and a white moustache, the eyes behind his large spectacles were moist and brown as a whelp's. When I arrived he was already standing in the doorway of his home, which stood directly beside the Maria Theresia barracks at the foot of Schönbrunn Park. The sweater he had on was like the ones you used to see at the army surplus shop: with epaulettes under which you could slip a folded beret.

I greeted him and asked how he was.

'That's not the kind of thing you ask a man of eighty-four,' he said.

His wife Susi was standing just behind him. She extinguished her husband's remark beneath a deluge of hospitality.

The hallway was a shrine – lined with oil paintings and pen-and-ink drawings of horses. Hans and Susi Brabenetz's living room, too, looked like an annexe to the military museum. I examined a collection of stirrups and a painting of Franz Josef in a coach drawn by two brown Kladrubers. There was also a triptych depicting the most famous cavalry regiments: the uhlans, the dragoons and the hussars. I recognized those names from the stories of Joseph Roth, in which they served as metonyms for 'honour' and 'elite'. Uhlans, dragoons and hussars looked down on the rest of the earth's bipeds, with the exception of the emperor and his entourage. 'All of them had endured miserable childhoods at the convent school, hard boyhoods at the military academy, cruel tours of duty on the border.' After the shots were fired in June 1914, they longed for war. A state of emergency was declared immediately, but to the officers' disappointment was lifted as the threat of armed conflict seemed to dwindle in the weeks after the assassination. Drily, Roth described their martial viewpoint ('Much nicer, of course, would be to have a war. But no war was coming for the time being. Orders are orders') and the resumption of the 'love manoeuvres' – collective visits to the brothels – born of boredom.

Frau Brabenetz began rattling cups and saucers and had us sit down on the greyish-green velour sofa. Her husband raised his voice: 'This Conversano Primula you were talking about. In what year was he born?'

1966 or 1967, I thought. But because I wasn't sure, I started by saying that he was the son of the famous Viennese stallion, Conversano Soja. Piet had always been adamant about that.

'Hmmm, *der Soja*,' Brabenetz said. 'But the mare's line is more important, and unless I am mistaken your Primula must have been born in 1967 and was descended from Kitty I.'

He stood up to look for something in a cabinet drawer. 'Kitty was an excellent broodmare,' he said, rifling through his papers. Before long he stopped his rummaging and cried out: 'Ah, here we have it! Now we're talking!' Herr Brabenetz turned on his heels to face me. Kitty, as it turned out, was a 'high-blooded' mare, a breeder's term that referred to the many Arabian pure-breds in her pedigree. She was the great-grandmother of Conversano Primula – he had inherited one-eighth of his genes from her. My host sank back down on the sofa and told me that Kitty had been born in 1938, in the stables of Countess Eltz at Vukovar. 'A super-mare.'

I said I was familiar with Vukovar, and with the castle of this Eltz family – or at least with the Vukovar that had been destroyed in 1992: I had stood atop the fresh rubble of Eltz Castle.

This brought us a little closer, for Hans Brabenetz had also been in Vukovar. 'But one war before yours.'

Susi said something that caused him to fall silent. Her husband seemed hesitant to talk about what he had done in Vukovar (wearing, I supposed, a German army uniform) during the Second World War. The conversation returned to horses. Countess Eltz's Lipizzaners, Brabenetz said, had included several famous studs, but they couldn't hold a candle to Kitty.

A good breeder, I would do well to realize, was primarily interested in the mare. The reason was fairly obvious: the Lipizzaner breed had precisely six stallion lines, the blood-lines with the paternal names Conversano, Favory, Pluto,

Neapolitano, Siglavy and Maestoso. It was those six founders of the dynasties within the breed who passed down their names from generation to generation. But there were only six of them! If you allowed for the Incitato and Tulipan lines as well, you had eight. But even then, the foundation of hereditary material was as narrow as a tightrope. In years when a breeding farm's genetic pool was on the verge of drying up, the foals fell in bunches. Sometimes hermaphrodites were born, or even animals with no gender whatsoever, stallions without balls, albinos. The degree of consanguinity could be no more than ten to twelve per cent – at higher percentages, degeneration would strike relentlessly. At one point, at the Italian stud farm Monterotondo, there were dozens of Lipizzaners walking around with thick tumours, like clusters of grapes, at the base of the tail. The problem of genetic depression was seen even in the best of families – perhaps *precisely* in the best of families. After all, wasn't the haemophilia of Crown Prince Alexei, son of the last Russian czar, a result of inbreeding among the Romanovs? The occasional mixing of herds, Brabenetz said, was pure necessity. Whether that happened in peacetime with the well-considered exchange of studs, or amid the turmoil of war – it resulted in the same, absolutely indispensable *Blutauffrischung*, the replenishment of blood.

I let the word '*Blutauffrischung*' linger on my tongue.

Brabenetz, I could see from the corner of my eye, was looking at me.

I asked what he meant exactly by the mixture of herds amid the turmoil of war, but he dodged the question. All he would say was that, with the fall of the central authority in Vienna, the Lipizzaner breed had been scattered across half a dozen countries. The rotation of stallions came to a standstill, and breeders in Hungary, Croatia, Romania,

Czechoslovakia and Austria had all gone about their business independently. Most were obsessed with the performance of the stallions. 'But a stallion that can perform a good capriole', Brabenetz said, wagging his finger for emphasis, 'will not necessarily deliver sons that can perform a reasonable capriole as well.' The important thing was the matriarchal line. 'A breeder must be able to look at the mare when she's only two or three years old and see the full-grown horse in her. She should look like a girl of twelve or thirteen, *platt und blöd*!' Susi was clearing away the cups and saucers, and her husband slapped his hands excitedly against his flanks and chest. 'No buttocks!' he shouted. 'No breasts!'

'Hans!'

A silence fell. Herr Brabenetz paused for a few seconds to allow the mood to settle. 'But now tell me,' he said cheer-fully, 'what is it you'd like to know, exactly?'

I handed over my cup and waited till Frau Brabenetz had left the room. Then I started describing my idea of looking at the horse – or, rather, human involvement with the horse – in order to better understand the peculiarities of our own species. How was I supposed to explain this? I said that I had come to view the horse, and particularly the Lipizzaner, as a human creation. I wanted to take what man had added to the horse over the centuries and soak it loose, peel it off and hold it up to the light. That could only serve to provide a clearer glimpse of the naked animal, *Homo sapiens*.

Brabenetz fiddled with the volume knob on his hearing aid. Suddenly he lifted a hand from his knee; he knew what I needed. 'Then you must come along with us,' he said.

An excursion was being planned to Lipica in the hills near Trieste, to the breeding station where the Lipizzaner had been given form – a sanctum that now lay within the borders of Slovenia. The trip would take place in one month's time.

He would act as the guide, his wife would be going too, and so would many 'Friends of the Royal Spanish Riding School'. I could profit from their collective expertise. He rattled off a whole series of names, but the titles that accompanied them were all I could retain – 'civil engineer', 'doctor' and a few times '*Hofrat*': councillor to a court that had been disbanded in 1918. Once I got to know this select company, a world would open up to me.

'And, of course, you can't write about Lipizzaners without having been to Lipica.'

THE STORK'S FOOT

PRIMULA WAS DEAD.
'He was twenty-eight, we still had the riding school,'
Leny says.

'We waited too long to do anything,' Piet adds. Primula, he told me, had foundered: the coffin bone in his forelegs had rotated and was pressing painfully against the hoof, and the membrane in between had become inflamed. 'In the end he could only stand on his hind legs.'

It is March 2007. We are having lunch in their houseboat on a canal beside the motorway to Groningen – behind a white windmill and a petrol station called The White Mill.

Leny dabs at a crumb with her forefinger and says that, in January 1995, Primula came down with another illness too. His winter coat began curling and looked woollier than normal, as though he were suddenly wearing a bedraggled astrakhan cape. Leny had recognized it as one of the symptoms of Cushing's Syndrome. 'I'd read about it, and said to Piet right away: "That's what he's got."'

They took Primula to the faculty of veterinary medicine in Utrecht, where blood samples were taken. The diagnosis arrived in the post two weeks later: Cushing's.

Piet and Leny called the vet that same evening. Their three

sons weren't at home, but none of them was particularly interested in horses and didn't have to be there to say goodbye.

They covered him with his own blanket. Leny had called the removal service, and the next day they came and picked up Primula with a crane and took him away in a lorry.

Leny is just the way I remembered her: stocky and resolute. As she gets up to fetch a dossier with Primula's papers, the houseboat rocks.

Piet is a different story. On a few occasions already, I had postponed plans to see him again. My recollection of him had still been that of a guru-like instructor whose scorn could make you shiver in the saddle. Piet had a shiny pate, a bald spot the size of a Bedouin's cap and a ring of curly hair at the back of his neck. You could easily have mistaken him for a concert pianist. Sometimes he would vanish for a week, only for it to turn out that he had been visiting Nicolae and Elena Ceauşescu's Lipizzaner stud farm in Romania – and he would come back with stories about the Securitate and bizarre encounters in Bucharest. Remembering his lessons, I could see him sitting, scrunched halfway down in an easy chair in one corner of the indoor ring. 'Auke! Give Auke a whack!' he would shout into the microphone. If Auke didn't immediately receive a flick of the crop, or received one that was too gentle (because the pony-girl on Auke's back wasn't strong enough), the voice would rise in a crescendo: 'I said: Auke! A whack!' The girl would worm her arm back and flap her riding crop a bit. 'That's petting him! What I said was: Whack! GIVE AUKE A WHACK! Do you hear me? Auke! Whack! Whack! Whack! Stop making me sound like a goddamned flyswatter!'

Sitting opposite from each other now, thirty years later, over a meal of black rye bread, cheese and ham, I notice that

Piet is balder, and that he's mellowed. The lines around his mouth aren't as deep. The hair at the back of his neck is thinner, with almost no curl to it any more.

I stir my coffee and ask how it all started: what had made them decide to bring a Lipizzaner to Holland?

'It was *his* dream,' Leny says from the next room. 'And I'd inherited some money.'

Piet planned to open his own riding school. It was in the winter of 1970, he was twenty-nine. 'I knew the Austrian state stud sometimes sold stallions that didn't go to Vienna,' Piet says, 'but I didn't have an address.' He called the Austrian consulate, but was rudely fobbed off. 'Lipizzaners are not for sale.' The official on duty obviously felt that horses belonging to the emperor, even though there was no longer an emperor, were not meant to fall into the hands of commoners. Piet had no intention of giving up. He was perfectly aware that in the old days there were no Lipizzaners to be found outside the imperial stables. The first Lipizzaner to come to the Netherlands had been a 'charger' belonging to the emperor's brother, Archduke Albrecht – who was captured in 1600 during the Battle of Nieuwpoort. Much later, in the early years of the twentieth century, Queen Wilhelmina of the Netherlands had owned four Lipizzaners originating from Hungary. But by the 1970s things had truly changed: the twin daughters of the managing director of carmaker DAF both had Lipizzaners, and the heir to a famous family of lexicographers had succeeded in purchasing a mare by the name of Nobila in Austria.

Piet wrote a letter addressed to the *Lipizzanergestüt, in der Nähe von Köflach* (Lipizzaner Stud Farm, close to Köflach), Austria – and actually received a reply. Dr Lehrner, the head of the stud farm, had three foals for sale that spring.

'So off we went,' Piet says. It was March, there was snow

everywhere. The train took them as far as Köflach, Leny tells me, but they had to hitchhike the rest of the way.

The building where Dr Lehrner received them was a former Benedictine monastery, the headquarters of the Piber State Stud – exclusive supplier of young stallions to the Royal Spanish Riding School. The director had slicked-back hair with a frivolous wave at the temples, impeccably Viennese. Seated at his desk, he turned his gaze on his visitors and asked whether they planned to buy a Lipizzaner in order to take part in contests. At the mere mention of the word 'contests', Piet grimaced, and they had passed the entry test. The director had a Land Rover pull up to the door and took his cloak from the rack. Chains on the tyres, they climbed through a series of hairpin bends to the high pasture at 1,600 metres, to the snowed-in 'sentry posts' with the stables for young stallions.

Three uniformed stablemen were standing at attention when they got out and tapped the visors of their caps.

The first animal led on to the frozen paddock was a stallion from the Maestoso line. 'But he had such a lazy gait, I didn't want him.' Piet leans his wrists on the edge of the table. He gulps. 'Only later did I realize . . . that sluggishness, that was strutting. It was gracefulness. Stupid of me not to have seen it right away.'

This makes me prick up my ears; I've never known Piet admit to being fallible.

The second foal was knock-kneed: he stood like a shy schoolgirl, his hooves turned inward. To correct this, the farrier had made for him special crescent-shaped shoes. Herr Lehrner cleared his throat, clasped his hands behind his back and called out: 'Present corrective shoeing!'

The senior stableman pivoted ninety degrees, clicked his heels and repeated 'Present corrective shoeing!', whereupon

the senior stableman's adjutant commanded his own subordinate to lift the animal's left front hoof.

Leny says that she had never seen such a blatant display
of militarism. Dr Lehrner paid absolutely no heed to the boy
who was still holding up that bent foreleg, not even when
the conversation had long turned to other things. Only
minutes later did he provide relief by shouting 'Front leg at
ease!' – an order once again passed down the entire chain of
command.

'That's right,' Piet says, 'we had run into a little bit of
Habsburg that had survived up there in the Alps.'

The third animal was three-year-old Conversano Primula.
He was a bit smaller than the first two, but his legs were
'drier', there was nothing soft and babyish about them, said
Piet.

The horse's big eyes appealed to Leny. 'They gave you
twenty-four hours to think about it; the next day you called
to say you wanted the little one.'

Piet clears the dishes. Leny opens the filing folder and
slides a sheet of paper to me across the table. STATE STUD
PIBER is printed across the top. PEDIGREE.

'The word comes from the French *pied de grue*,' Leny says.
'The stork's foot.' At some point, *pied de grue* was bastard-
ized to the more homely 'pedigree', but the idea behind the
original term remains quite lovely: the stork's footprint
resembles the branches of a family tree.

The chart showing Conversano Primula's lineage was
divided into preprinted, rectangular boxes, with space for
four generations: both parent animals, the four grandparents,
eight great-grandparents and sixteen great-great
grandparents. You could see at a glance how the Lipizzaner
nomenclature works; Conversano Primula's mother was a
mare by the name of Primula, while his sire was a stallion of

the Conversano dynasty: in this case, Conversano Soja, born in Austria in 1952.

I let my gaze wander over the names, dates, places of birth. Between the successive generations is a gap ranging from ten to no more than twenty-five years. Primula's grandfather, Conversano Bonavista, was born during the period between the wars, in 1925; his great-grandfather Conversano Savona entered the world in 1911 at the imperial stud farm in Lipica, close to Trieste, during the final years of the Danube Monarchy. Primula's stork's foot branched off from Italy to the Carpathians and from Czechoslovakia to the Balkans. His lineage hopped, skipped and jumped back through the twentieth century: as you followed the rungs of the various generations of paternal and maternal ancestors, you descended automatically into the crypts of Central European history.

I ask Piet and Leny whether I can make a copy of Primula's pedigree. They wave my question away and tell me to just keep it, they have a copy of their own somewhere.

More of Primula's papers appear on the table:

A veterinary certificate – with the results of blood tests for the contagious bacterial disease glanders and another malignant venereal disease (both negative).

An exit visa – showing the exact route from Austria to Holland by livestock carriage, via the border crossing at Kaldenkirchen.

An invoice – for the sum of 40,000 Austrian schillings.

A Dutch permit for importing a solidungulate (on condition that Primula remain in quarantine for one month).

A customs form from the Dutch border post at Venlo – with stamps dated 30 May 1970.

It was with this sheaf of documents that Primula had arrived in the Netherlands. He was received like an émigré, a prodigal son. The *Nieuwsblad van het Noorden* dedicated an article to the event: RIDING TEACHER IN ASSEN OWNER OF REAL LIPIZZANER STALLION. In the picture, Primula still looked like a plump adolescent, too heavy for the spongy soil beneath his hooves. His new owner – 'Mr P. C. Bakker (29)' – had announced his quite un-provincial ambition: 'With my stallion, I should be able to reach the level of the Spanish Riding School in Vienna.'

That was the Piet I knew: uncompromising, for himself and for others.

It was on 21 March 1971, he remembered straight away, that Primula had been saddled for the first time. 'My father filmed it, and you can see Primula standing there with a look that said: "Oh, come on!"'

I asked Leny whether she had ridden him too.

'A couple of times. But he always pulled so hard whenever you reined him in.' She looks at me from under her fringe. 'But that was impossible, you know, according to Piet. Oh no, Primula didn't do that!'

'No,' Piet says brusquely. 'Horses don't do that. Horses don't pull. It's the rider who pulls.'

His sudden firmness causes us both to fall silent. Piet and Leny remind me of a pair of motorcycle sidecar racers, with Leny as the passenger who sometimes leans into the curve in unison with her husband, and at other times hangs far out of the sidecar – but always with the goal of keeping the two of them in balance.

To break the silence I come up with another of Piet's equestrian maxims: 'And horses will never kick someone who lies perfectly still on the ground . . if you do get kicked, it means you moved!'

'Precisely!' Piet shouts – beaming now. At least *someone* hasn't forgotten his lessons in horsemanship.

'Especially when he was around mares in heat,' Leny continues. 'Then he almost yanked the reins out of your hands.'

Piet reels like a boxer who's taken a hard right hook. But then he recovers. 'Come on, let's go,' he says to me. 'I'm going to show you how to make a horse dance.'

U

Piet's jeep cuts a semicircle around the lake at Zuidlaren. It is drizzling, the road glistens. The rocking of the windscreen wipers shakes loose an avalanche of memories. In my mind's eye I see how Jelle and I were once told to report to Piet because we had left a hacksaw lying in the pony stall. He laid the evidence reproachfully on the ground in front of us, adopted a broad stance with his thin legs and took a verbal running start, beginning with the cave dwellers of Lascaux. Their respect for horses had been immortalized: apparently, hunters and gatherers fif-teen thou-sand years a-go had already understood something that had not yet sunk into our thick skulls. Piet pointed to the plaster bust of the tarpan horse on the front wall of the stables. The wild tarpan may have been wiped out, but his primal instincts had survived. 'Just like stupidity in humans!'

Piet's eyes seemed bigger than usual. He felt we were staring at him sheepishly, and he couldn't stand that, it made him furious. 'Now get the hell out of here, and I never want to see the two of you again!'

Jelle and I grabbed our bikes and cycled out of Deurze without a word. About ten minutes later we were cut off by a red Renault 4. The car listed to one side as it skidded to a stop. Piet hopped out and ordered us to get in. 'Lean your bikes against a tree.' Neither of us wanted to sit next to him, so we crawled into the back and huddled there like a pair of police suspects. Back at the riding school he had us walk ahead of him to the loft above the pony stall, where two cups of chocolate milk and two cellophane-wrapped almond-paste cakes were waiting for us.

Piet was a perfectionist who couldn't stand that the world around him was imperfect. Back then, young horses who proved unreceptive to his methodology of patience and repeated drilling were brought into line in fairly hard-handed fashion. I once arrived at De Tarpan just as he was pulling Robin, a chestnut bay of barely four years, by the halter to the middle of the ring. Piet was scolding him and shouting threats, he cracked his whip and bared his teeth. Robin shrank back, his eyes flashing. Every time the whip sounded I flinched and thought: make it stop! – but the disciplining continued. It didn't faze Piet. In the wild, he told us, things were much tougher still: in the wild, horses kicked each other black and blue in order to establish the pecking order. 'By the look of it, you lot failed to notice what intolerable behaviour Robin was developing,' he said. 'If you were paying attention, you'd have seen that he and I have now come to an agreement.' He had spoken to Robin in 'horse talk', in order to show him his place in the human–horse hierarchy. That was all.

The road cuts straight through the old peat pits, from one roundabout to the next. In the distance we occasionally see the sails and masts of boats on the lake. Glowingly, and with palpable nostalgia, Piet tells me about his first visit to the Spanish Riding School. 'I was around twenty at the time and my father gave me a round trip to Vienna.' He had taken a seat in the first gallery, beside a mustachioed Viennese man with a walking stick. From their perch they had looked down on the shoulder-in, shoulder-out: the standard warming-up exercises beneath the candelabra.

'At some point I said: "Really nice, isn't it?" But my neighbour didn't agree. He said: "Just wait, this is nothing yet."'

Then came the pirouettes, the flying gallop changes and the piaffe between the pillars. But the man kept repeating that this was 'nothing yet'. Until the doors at the far end of the ring opened again and Piet felt someone pinch his forearm.

'What I saw was a horse alone, without a saddle. I was viewing him head-on, so it looked like he was standing there on his own. He was snorting, regally, with a look that said "Now I'm going to show you people how it's done."'

The stallion that made its entrance was not carrying a rider. Behind him, though, was a man holding the reins. Walking almost free of constraints, the horse performed the same exercises and paces as the other stallions, but solely at the prompting of voice and rein. It was possible to teach a horse to distinguish up to thirty different sounds, and these 'vocal aids', in combination with the position of the rein and the pressure on the bit, were enough to help it run through the entire repertoire of classical equestrianism.

A thousand kilometres from Vienna, Piet had set out to do the same with his Lipizzaner stallion. And now, at the age of sixty-six, half a lifetime later, with De Tarpan closed, he owns only one horse: Conversano Nobila, son of Primula and Nobila, a mare long considered infertile. Bred and trained by his own hand to perform on the long reins. This grey, now twenty years old, is boarded at a farm just outside Zuidlaren.

Piet parks in the yard and calls to his stallion as he climbs out of the car. There is a whinnying in the distance, and as we approach Conversano Nobila sticks his head out over the lower half of his stall door.

'The spitting image of his father, don't you think? Look at those eyes!'

While Piet is currying him and picking the burrs from his tail one by one, I think about the extravagant opera *Rosa* (coincidentally – or perhaps not – by Peter Greenaway as well) about a man's love for his horse. That love goes so far that the main character's fiancée, consumed by envy, starts imitating a mare. To win his favour, in fact, she actually *becomes* a mare – in a bizarre metamorphosis from human to animal.

The 'human content' of a horse like Conversano Nobila intrigues me, but my initial reaction is one of surprise at his animal nature: as soon as he is led out of the stall he sniffs at the loose straw on the path between the stables, and once in the corral behind the farm he begins pawing at the sand as though in search of something he has lost.

'Mare's shit!' Piet simply watches and provides the subtitles: 'Which mares have been here while I was away?' Nobila is no longer responding to his master's voice. He lifts his head high, as high as he can, curls his upper lip so that I can see the pink of his gums – the better to track down what he smells. His tail is lifted too, and the horse droppings go tumbling to the ground. This is no mere act of defecation, but the planting of a scent, over that of his rivals. 'Good boy,' Piet says, 'and now let's get to work!'

I am again amazed by the ease with which Nobila – after one last shiver of excitement – shakes off his natural urges and gets down to work. Piet provides the almost imperceptible aids. Whenever he changes the position of the reins, his stallion performs the appropriate moves without delay. Nobila struts energetically, and at the command 'Come come!' he breaks into a trot – no further encouragement is needed.

I tell Piet that I have never seen him on a horse's back, and ask why it is he opted for the long reins.

'It's more equal this way,' Piet answers. 'There's no other interaction between man and animal that comes this close to the ideal of two equal partners.'

Unlike Primula in his day, Nobila wears a snaffle, a bit without a shank. Physically, therefore, Piet can only hold him in check with the soft noseband to which the reins are attached. Without an iron shank at the corners of the mouth, which rests on the stretch of exposed jawbone between the front and back teeth, the animal is harder to handle. But it also gives him a more autonomous air. Within classical dressage, which is in truth an unnatural activity, Piet strives for a maximum of naturalness. He has come to use the crop like a conductor's baton. 'I advise young riders to use a birch switch. A birch switch breaks as soon as you lose your self-control.'

I say – by way of understatement: 'You used to exercise your authority much more emphatically.'

'Could be,' he says in passing, as he puts Nobila through his lateral movements. 'But this is real authority!'

I remind Piet how angry he used to get at his horses, and at his pupils.

'Me? Angry?' Piet dismisses it with a laugh. The confrontation with the past is a hurdle at which he baulks. 'Leny says that too, sometimes, but I think that's a lie. The two of you must be mistaken.'

There is no pack of blue Gauloises in his breast pocket. It strikes me that he hasn't smoked this whole time, that he has apparently stopped smoking. Suddenly I have an inkling of what may have happened: the work with the long reins has changed him – in a loose paraphrase of the aristocracy's adage that riding ennobles the rider: give your son money and he will become arrogant and ill-mannered, but give him a horse and he will become a gentleman.

Piet insists, however, that he has always embraced a subtle style; subtlety, after all, was part and parcel of classical equestrianism and went all the way back to Xenophon, four centuries before Christ, who claimed that you 'cannot use a whip and spurs to teach a dancer to dance'.

In his textbook *On Horsemanship*, the Greek riding teacher had broken with the accepted wisdom of his day, which advocated force in the training of horses for war and for parades. Thanks in part to Xenophon, equestrianism in ancient Athens was far ahead of its time – as evidenced by the reliefs on the Parthenon showing horses in a 'collected gait': the back legs under the body, thereby providing not only propulsion, but also support. Xenophon's writings were rediscovered only during the Renaissance, but since then a command of the horsemanly exercises and figures has been elevated to an art, practised in its purest form at the Royal Spanish Riding School in Vienna.

And here, beside the lake at Zuidlaren, where Piet puts his white stallion through a complete choreography. A pirouette in gallop, for example: within seven strides, Nobila turns a full 180 degrees. Sometimes the legwork baffles the senses – you have no idea how the animal performs the movements it does.

Piet brings his horse back from a gallop to a trot, and from a trot to a walk. Then he has him stand still in the middle of the ring. Standing still, the weight distributed evenly over all four hooves, is a feat in itself. The effort makes Nobila foam at the corners of his mouth. 'All right now,' Piet says, and the Lipizzan stallion takes a few steps back, tucks its hindquarters beneath its body and shifts its weight back, further and further, until its front legs leave the ground and it raises itself in a levade. For a couple of seconds, Nobila towers above his master.

What I see touches me: I am looking at a quadruped doing its winning best to rise up and become a biped, like in a high-speed animation of evolution.

K.U.K.-LEUTE

WARS LEND GEOGRAPHY A helping hand by thrusting otherwise unknown territories into the limelight. The Bay of Pigs. Biafra. Vukovar.

'This is the main road to Laibach,' says the bus driver. 'From here it's about ninety minutes to our destination, Lipica.'

I had never heard of Laibach. My only vague association was with a right-wing hard-rock band that sang about intolerance. And nothing more. That was strange, because I thought I knew the Balkans like the back of my hand: I had lived and worked here as a correspondent in the early 1990s. The names Slavonia (a province in Croatia) and Slovenia (the country) were no longer cause for confusion. But Laibach?

Without slowing, our bus passed the Austro-Slovenian border. Rain clouds clung to the mountaintops left and right. Nothing about the surroundings reminded one of the political wildfires of June 1991, when Slovenia and Croatia unilaterally declared independence. For the Yugoslav leaders in Belgrade, that was a *casus belli* – and it was here, of all places, along the highway south of Graz, amid the alpine greenery and chalet-style farms, that the Balkan War combusted – with jet-fighter bombings and the incineration of customs sheds and exchange offices. On that stretch of burned earth now stood a blue sign with the EU stars.

'Laibach?' I asked the man sitting beside me.

'Ha!' he said. 'An Austrian in-joke. That's what Ljubljana was called a hundred years ago!'

My neighbour was dressed as a cowboy, but a very well-groomed one. His name was Peter. He was German – which made us the outsiders amid this company of Austrians. It was pure coincidence that I had sat down beside him: when I had climbed aboard our idling bus in a Vienna suburb, half an hour before departure, it was the only seat left. All the 'Friends of the Spanish Riding School' had already settled in; Hans and Susi Brabenetz were in the front row.

'Do you have any idea who your travelling companions are?' Peter had asked as soon as we met. Leaning over to me, he said in a low voice: '*Das sind alle k.u.k.-Leute.* These are all k.u.k. people. Does that mean anything to you?'

I had heard of 'k.u.k.' before; it was the abbreviation and, by the same token, the shibboleth for *kaiserlich und königlich*, imperial and royal, an echo from the days of the Double Monarchy, when everything was better.

I told him that I had met Mr and Mrs Brabenetz already, and wondered whether the others were cut from the same cloth.

The German wiped a grin from his lips with thumb and forefinger. He nodded, then asked whether I could put his hat in the baggage rack above our heads. The black leather Stetson he handed me was quite unlike the other headgear in the rack: ladies' hats with brooches and embroidered flowers. My gaze travelled over the knots at the back of their owners' heads and the distended earlobes with jewels dangling from them. The ladies smiled when they saw me; if their husbands moved at all, it was only their moustaches.

The men's dress code consisted generally of a collarless hunting vest of grey cloth with billiard-green piping and leather buttons. When we stopped for a break at a petrol station close to Laibach, it looked as though the entire cast of a Sissi film had poured out across the car park.

Back in the bus, Hans Brabenetz took the microphone. He began with a joke: he hoped we were seated comfortably, because Lipica, purveyor of horses to the royal household, lay 'eight days' from Vienna. We were left to work it out for ourselves: a day's journey on horseback amounted to between thirty and forty miles; the distance to the Stallburg 300. 'You may be thinking: couldn't they have found a more convenient place, closer to Vienna? The answer is no. The coastal range along the Adriatic was the best choice.' The equerries of the House of Habsburg had purchased the Lipica estate in 1580 from the bishop of Trieste. At the time, it was a Renaissance-style villa with a walled courtyard, stables and a chapel – far from any village or settlement. It had been the bishop's wont to spend the summers there in solitude. Lipica, it was important for us to know, lay just outside the mild climatic zone of the Adriatic Sea, in the Karst Mountains. It was there, four hundred metres above sea level, that the Spanish-bought breeding stallions, the best in the world, were stabled in order to produce offspring with the lively mares from Trieste and its environs – and later, from 1584, with the mares of standing expressly imported from Andalusia as well. The first foals born at Lipica had the widest possible range of colours and markings. But the equerries were masters of their trade, and quickly began emphasizing certain traits. On 7 December 1658, Emperor Leopold I signed a list of twenty-three directives with which the breeders of his personal horses were to comply. According to Brabenetz, though, the true success of the breeding programme lay in Lipica's location. 'In summer the climate is pleasant enough, but in autumn a storm wind rises that often continues unabated till spring.' I saw the leader of our excursion gesture with his free hand, to illustrate how the Lipizzaner's physique, as it were, had been carved out by the relentless mountain wind. A rigorous climate, lean and hardy vegetation – everything had served to improve the build and character of the Habsburgs' horses. Brabenetz predicted that we would be surprised by the aridity of the region, which owed its ruggedness to underground limestone formations; calcium dissolves in water, giving rise to funnel-shaped wells that empty into caves and subterranean rivers. At the same time, the landscape was dotted with crags of bare granite and other erosion-resistant stone. The soil was hard and rocky, which had produced a horse with compact hooves that did not split or break, even on the paving stones of the Hofburg, the imperial residence.

After Brabenetz's explanation, the atmosphere in the bus became freer, louder too. No mention had been made of the war. Not the most recent one, nor the one that had led in 1914–18 to the loss of Slovenia, thereby cruelly cutting off Lipica from the Spanish Riding School. The excitement that hummed through the bus was caused by a 20-euro-cent coin: the newest minting, of Slovenian design. Someone had accepted it as change at the petrol station, and now the passengers were crying shame at how Slovenia had dared to depict two Lipizzaners on the reverse.

When the coin reached me, I asked one of the Friends whether Austria had never done the same with its currency. 'A long time ago, yes, when we still had our own money,' he said.

Here and there wallets were being drawn to check whether there were perhaps more of these subversive coins in circulation. Someone fuelled the fires of discontent by claiming that

Slovenia was attempting to copyright the name 'Lipizzaner' as exclusively Slovenian. Amid the rising consternation I noticed that my fellow passengers were carrying snapshots of horses – behind the little plastic windows in their wallets which other people usually reserve for photos of their loved ones. The horses were not all Lipizzaners. My neighbour handed me a business card showing a Shagya Arabian in full gallop, a black one. You could buy his sperm, by the strawful. 'He's got fantastic credentials,' the German said.

I told him that I didn't own any mares, but showed him Conversano Primula's pedigree to reciprocate. I had found pictures of Primula's father, grandfather and great-grandfather in books about the Spanish Riding School, and I told him that I planned to follow the wanderings of these Lipizzaners across the length and breadth of Europe. What had happened to them during the world wars? In whose honour had they performed – and to what end? Concerning Conversano Savona, the great-grandfather, I had discovered that he was 'an excellent *levadeur*' – a performer of the levade and the product of one of the final foaling years at imperial Lipica. Next to his date of birth, the pedigree stated: *1911, k.u.k. Karster Hofgestüt Lippiza* (Imperial and Royal Karster Stud at Lippiza). Savona had stood one metre fifty-seven at the shoulder. At the age of sexual maturity, his description read: A sturdy, somewhat tall and narrow stallion with sufficient character and large, expressive eyes. As a stud, he had passed these traits (known as 'fundamentals') unfailingly to his progeny, making him a hallmark stallion.

'Yeah,' my neighbour said, 'you can have a great stallion, but if he doesn't pass down his traits his sperm is worthless.'

∪

I first noticed the neatly cropped lawn, solid green and slightly rolling. The lands of the Lipica estate stretched out across a valley floor intersected by straight lanes lined with lime trees and well-kept white fences on both sides. A neat English estate, that's what it looked like, only more arid. Not exactly inhospitable. The boulders left behind in the Ice Age had been removed from one of the fields: a two-hole golf course had been laid out on it. A pair of men in a golf cart trundled along silently across the lawn as the bus drove on to Hotel Maestoso and the adjacent Grand Casino Lipica. Our hotel had been built during the Tito era, as you could tell from the box-like architecture and lettering that would now be called 'retro'. We had found our way into the centre of Lipica without seeing a single horse. Waiting in the lobby for us was a glass of wine and a word of welcome from a young man in an Italian suit and pointy shoes: Zoran, the commercial director.

Zoran wore his hair in a ponytail, with matching goatee; he knew enough Austrian–German to greet us with *Grüss Gott*, but possessed no special antenna for other Austrian sensibilities. We stood around in a semicircle. Hans Brabenetz, who was much shorter than Zoran, walked up to face him and jabbed his walking stick into the carpet.

The commercial director went on talking about facilities and capacities. He said that Lipica was doing well, 'especially now that we have the euro'.

My companions murmured and shuffled their feet.

Zoran fixed his eyes on a point far behind us and spoke of the metamorphosis Lipica had undergone in the late 1970s to prepare for its 400-year anniversary celebration in 1980. Two hotels were built, a sauna, a swimming pool, tennis courts, an indoor riding hall. President Tito was the patron of the jubilee, but shortly before the summer-long festivities,

Comrade Tito had died; past endless rows of mourners, his body was transported in a blue train from Ljubljana via Zagreb to Belgrade.

The commercial director was about to add something about the history of Lipica under Tito, but made the mistake of beginning the sentence with: 'In his day . . .', which allowed Brabenetz to interrupt. 'His day, young man, that is *my* day. And I speak on behalf of many of us when I say: it is *our* day.'

Zoran appeared to lose track of what he was planning to say, and made a leap to the present. 'These days most of our guests are couples. She comes to see horses, he comes to play golf.'

'And what is your breeding objective?' Brabenetz asked.

'What do you mean exactly?'

'What kind of horse do you have in mind during breeding – what does it look like, what are its characteristics?'

'Hans!' I heard Frau Brabenetz whisper. She stepped forward and expressed her thanks for the warm welcome.

The commercial director raised his glass and, as 'honoured guests from Vienna', awarded us the privilege of entering the grounds of the stud farm without a guide. We could come and go as we pleased.

∪

The background material for our trip included a historical overview of Lipica, in which I read that the stud ('the alma mater of the Lipizzan') had been hastily evacuated three times around the year 1800 alone. And always for the same reason: Napoleon's approach.

The first exodus had been in March 1797 ('amid severe weather conditions'), in response to tidings that the young French commander – twenty-seven at the time – had crossed the Alps with an army of 30,000 men. The court equerry at Vienna ordered the immediate evacuation of all livestock from Lipica. In four columns of seventy-five animals each, with the stallions kept apart, the group travelled inland on foot in the freezing rain – from the mountain ridge above the Adriatic coast to Lake Balaton. It was springtime: foaling season. A foal was born every day, each birth delaying progress by an hour – the time needed for the young animal to stand on its own long legs after being licked clean.

One year later, after the signing of the Treaty of Campo Formio, the animals were able to return. The stables and outbuildings had been pillaged, but the hay was already being brought in from the fields and the only well Lipica possessed turned out not to have been poisoned. Eleven miles away as the crow flies, Napoleon was making his triumphal entry into Trieste. As a peace offering he was given a Lipizzaner stallion, hastily sought out and not too large.

In 1805, less than a decade later, Napoleon – Emperor Napoleon by now – went to war against the Habsburgs again, and this time forced his way into the heart of Vienna. Lipica was evacuated and the rounded-up genetic material withdrawn to Hungary once more.

The period from 1809 until the Battle of Waterloo in 1815 marked a third Hungarian exile. This was the six-year interregnum during which Napoleon ruled over the Adriatic provinces, including Lipica. Only after he had exited the European stage and the political borders were redrawn during the Congress of Vienna did the horses come shuffling home.

I turned the page and saw maps showing these equine odysseys. Against the backdrop of shifting Central European borders, the escape routes were marked in different colours, including the dates and duration of the exile. I couldn't take my eyes off them. These were not the trails of pillaging left by Genghis Khan and his hordes, or the routes of the various Crusades. These were the escape routes plied by herds of domesticated and expertly bred single-hoofed animals, led by stableboys, as they crossed *pusztas* and mountain ranges. Altogether they had forded the Danube four times – sometimes swimming with only their ears, eyes and dilated nostrils above the surface. Straining their necks, they had clambered up on to riverbanks, had shaken themselves dry like dogs – and were then driven on, to keep them at all costs from falling into the hands of the enemy.

U

The horses' domain began on the far side of a little arbour with canary-yellow pillars, belonging to the casino. When I went out to visit the stud farm directly after checking in, the visitors from the last tour were just being herded out. The atmosphere felt charged, in a summery way: perhaps because there was lightning in the air, or maybe it was the smell of fresh-cut hay. As a special envoy from Vienna I was indeed allowed to enter the original Lipica: a cluster of old buildings huddled together on a hill. Cutting away from the visitors' route, I ended up at a feed silo, a dunghill and, a little further up the slope, an unpainted barracks of the kind one sees everywhere in the countryside of the former Eastern Bloc. A group of shabby-looking men were sitting on a low wall outside, scratching their stomachs. I asked where I could find the *velbanca*, the elite stable for the breeding stallions, which dated from 1703. With the neck of his beer bottle, one pointed at a building behind me, a few metres down the slope but with one side wall visible from where we were. That wall was punctuated by a sort of ventilation shaft in the shape of a wheel. I walked over and peered down, almost from roof level, and saw the white backs of ten stallions – separated by ornamental barriers of hardwood and cast iron. Together they produced the peaceful sound of animals chewing. If there were a Mecca for Lipizzaners, this was its Kaaba.

A hundred metres further, behind a little church with a cobalt-blue dome, lay the foursquare loafing barn for the mares – white dams with their black and brown foals. They were standing up to their ankles in straw and barely bothered to look up. The foals, their chests still jutting out like seahorses, chased each other and collided wildly. A blackboard on the wall showed which mares had already foaled. The youngest animal was two days old.

Conversano Savona, too, had frolicked around this barn. At the time of his birth in 1911, Lipica still belonged to the emperor. For a full three and a half-centuries, it occurred to me, these rubble-lined paths had remained closed to the general public. Then came the war. The emperor, the czar and the sultan were driven from their palaces; the Lipizzaners from Lipica.

The historical overview we'd been given described the demise of the Habsburg royal stud in terms cold and businesslike. The prelude had been the relocation of the stud farm at Făgăraş, founded in 1874 at the foot of the Carpathians in Transylvania. As unrest spread deep into the Balkans, that herd of Lipizzaners had been moved – ostensibly because of an infectious eye disease – to a farm at Bàbolna, more than 500 kilometres away, between Budapest and Vienna. Then the First World War threatened the survival of the entire breed. At 8 p.m. on 18 May 1915, five days before Italy declared war on the enfeebled Austro-Hungarian Empire, a messenger from the emperor arrived in Lipica with evacuation orders. Within twenty-four hours, the first transport of seven livestock carriages left from the station at the nearby village of

Sežana. In record time, the population of some 200 animals was withdrawn to the far side of the Alps. At Lipica, the Italian invaders found an empty *velbanca*, deserted pastures and an empty loafing barn. The emperor evacuated only his horses, however, from the border area. Not the farmers. In the mountains above Trieste bitter fighting ensued, villages were burned to the ground. Of the local population, only the stablemen of Lipica, boys from Sežana, escaped unscathed: they had joined the equine exodus, sharing the animals' carriages and sleeping in the same straw.

By rail, the Lipizzaners were transferred to Franz Josef's summer estate just south of Vienna. The youngest animals travelled on, to the Kladruby stud farm on the Elba, east of Prague. Animals foaled in 1912 or earlier (including Conversano Savona) were housed at the fairy-tale Laxenburg Castle on the Danube: it would have been hard to find a safer haven inside Europe during the First World War. But despite their peaceful place of exile, the uprooted herd proved restless. Where it was normal for four out of every five mares to produce a healthy colt or filly each year, after their flight from Lipica that was down to one out of every ten. To make matters worse, thirty-one mares in foal died for no apparent reason during the first half of 1916: the Lipizzaner population shrank to beneath the critical limit of 1,000 horses.

U

When he saw me at lunch the next day in Hotel Maestoso, Hans Brabenetz waved me over to his table. He wanted me to sit on his left, the side of his good ear. And so, what did I think of the excursion so far?

I told him I had been particularly impressed by the *velbanca*.

What he meant, though, was the breeding material, the quality of it. We had just come back from a tour with the veterinary director. If he wanted an expert opinion, Brabenetz realized, he would have to turn to the other guests.

'Friends, I believe we can safely state that our young Slovenian colleagues are well on their way, but that Lipica cannot hold a candle to our own Piber stud.' That statement called for a toast. Next, Brabenetz began introducing me to the group around the table. I made the acquaintance of Frau Bachinger (the mother of a rider at the Royal Spanish Riding School) and Herr 'Hofrat' Kugler (director of the unfortunately bankrupt and now defunct Lipizzaner Museum in Vienna). Sitting beside me was a lady who once, as a special concession and in tribute to Empress Maria Theresia, had been allowed to perform the drills in the Winter Riding School. There was also 'Professor' Zimmerman, but what he was a professor of remained unclear to me. And then you had the biologist from the University of Vienna, who had such a heavy Carinthian accent that Brabenetz put him in his place by referring to him as 'another of our foreigners'.

I nodded in greeting to everyone and announced my aspiration of gaining access to the archives of the Royal Spanish Riding School. My hopes were, in fact, fixed on the *Hofrat*, who seemed to be thoroughly familiar with those archives. And indeed, it was Herr Kugler who spoke up. Most of the documents, he said, were kept in boxes that had no labels or any other form of filing system. What he was saying, in so many words, was that for an outsider like me, the archives would be utterly impenetrable.

'And what do you hope to find that has not already been described in the official chronicles?'

I was actually hoping for more clarity about the 'German'

years. But saying that, I had noticed, could put me on thin ice, as it had during my first visit to Brabenetz. 'All the movements back and forth,' I therefore said. 'The official tours, but also the forced evacuations.'

Hofrat Kugler said that, 'for obvious reasons', the archives contained lacunae during the wartime period. What's more: the state had commissioned him to collect and publish the most important documents. It was highly unlikely that anyone else would be allowed simply to browse through the remnants.

The others also adopted pained expressions.

And if I wanted to try regardless?

In that case I would have to appeal in writing to the most gracious Frau Gürtler.

'She is the proprietress of Hotel Sacher,' someone said.

'Directly opposite the National Opera,' someone else added. 'The most expensive hotel in all Vienna.'

I would do well to realize that the lady in question had, for years, been the organizer of the exclusive 'Opera Ball' for the crème de la crème of Viennese society, and recently had been appointed director of both the Royal Spanish Riding School and the federal stud at Piber.

'By way of a sideline,' someone noted.

Intentionally or not, my travelling companions were giving the impression that Frau Gürtler was, if not the most powerful, then certainly the most unapproachable woman in Austria.

When the waiters came to bring our coffee, Zoran appeared in the dining room. He was carrying a clipboard, and asked who was interested in descending into the local limestone caverns, the biggest in Europe. The rest of us could drive up into the mountains to see the colts. No one plumped for the stalactites and stalagmites – the chief topic in the bus a little later was how badly, almost insultingly so, the Slovenians had misjudged their guests.

Half an hour later, we climbed out and found ourselves on a windy ridge. There wasn't a horse in sight. For as far as one could see, the crests here were draped with pasture-land. We had parked close to a barn where the young stallions returned to be fed in the evening. Putting on a pair of tinted glasses, Hans Brabenetz assumed his pose of general indignation. The two stableboys in green and white overalls who were walking around the corral had no idea how to deal with this crowd. They threw pitying glances at the ladies' shoes and outfits. Still, everyone was there to see the colts.

'Mightn't it be possible for you to drive them over in this direction?' Brabenetz asked. The stableboys looked at each other and exchanged a few words in Slovenian. The eldest of the two shrugged. The younger boy went scuttling away to fill a zinc bucket with a few kilos of feed concentrate, then climbed on to a bright red tractor and went chuffing off towards the horizon.

While we waited, a man in a cableknit fisherman's sweater approached and spoke to me. I'd never noticed him before. He had seen me taking notes, though, and wanted to say something. 'It's ridiculous.' Taking me by the elbow, he led me away, beyond earshot of the rest. 'I'm sure you've noticed by now: these people say "*Schnäuzel*" when they mean "snip". But in Austria we just say "*Schnippe*", you know. It *is Schnippe*.'

My German, I told him, wasn't good enough to pick up such nuances.

'But it's not a nuance!' The man turned to face me and pushed his glasses further up the bridge of his nose. 'I don't want you to get the wrong impression of us. This group is not representative. Before I retired I was a publisher of schoolbooks, and I can assure you: Austrian schoolchildren learn to speak German. That is our national language.' He stopped as a lady came by, walking her little lapdog.

'Most of the men here are retired officers. They're loaded with ribbons. It's Empress Maria Theresia this, Empress Maria Theresia that. The good old days. Don't get me wrong: I'm not a communist. But Austria has to look to the future.'

For the last ten years or so, the publisher said, children's textbooks no longer oozed nostalgia. But myths died hard. To see that, all I had to do was look around – these people still hadn't come to terms with the loss of the empire. And for almost a century, the idea that Austria had fought for a just cause during the First World War had proven ineradicable. He pointed to the north, where we could see the snowless peaks of the Julian Alps: that was where the front had been, up the valley of the Isonzo, a mountain stream along which the Italians had sought access to the heart of Austria. Did I know that, during twelve battles over a three-year period, at least 300,000 people had been killed there?

I had no idea. My knowledge of the First World War was blatantly deficient. I was about to tell him that Dutch schools didn't teach you much about that period – but it was not an excuse I felt comfortable making.

His grandparents, he told me, had given everything to the emperor, including their wedding rings. 'They donated them to the war effort. They were given cheap iron rings in return.' Germany and Austria had learnt nothing from the First World War. Especially not the professional soldiers with their blood-and-iron mentality.

I asked what he meant by that.

'The tendency to jump to attention for anything that exudes authority.' The man believed that after a few glasses of schnapps they were still capable of bursting out into '*Gut und Blut für unsern Kaiser | Gut und Blut für s Vaterland*' (Property and blood for our emperor | Property and blood for the fatherland).

'But isn't that simply folklore that will die out of its own accord?' I was thinking of the veterans at memorial services, the wreath-laying crowds that dwindled with each passing year.

He shook his head: new nostalgists were cropping up all the time. In fact, the monarchy's popularity had risen so much that distant heirs to the Habsburg throne were now daring to claim the old family castles. 'But *they're* the ones who started the war, and *they're* the ones who lost it. Not the common people. Not my grandparents!'

But then, I wanted to know, how in the world had he ended up with the Friends of the Spanish Riding School?

'You mean: with this club of monarchists?'

I nodded, perhaps a little more emphatically than I'd intended.

'I love horses,' he said. 'I suppose that's all one can say about it.'

∪

Waiting for the young stallions to appear, I tried to imagine the chaos and desperation that must have followed in the wake of the First World War. It wasn't easy. The historical overview we had been issued dealt only with the legal settlement of the Lipizzaner affair – as a curious footnote to history itself. In 1918, as soon as Austria–Hungary and Germany had suffered defeat all around the tattered edges of their empires, the Lipizzaner breed had become an outlawed, endangered species. Across the floodplains of the Elba and the Danube they had outlived the dominion of their creators and patron-protectors, the Habsburg-Lothringens.

The treaties signed in Paris (Versailles, Saint-Germain and Trianon) had reduced the contours of the deflated empire to the present-day pork chop of Alpine Austria. South Tyrol, the Istrian Peninsula and a chunk of Slovenia, including Lipica, were awarded to Italy. The Lipizzaners were dispersed across six new Central European states – as in a diaspora.

Germany, which had had its wings clipped at least as decisively at Versailles, was forced to pay a reparation in kind of 125,000 horses for the victors' farms.

Austria was obliged to surrender a portion of its Lipizzaners and a separate treaty was drawn up to arrange for the redistribution of the herds. The breed had been the personal property of the emperor, but he had lost everything – his crown, his titles, his holdings. While Europe lay in ruins and countless disabled veterans were dragging themselves back to what was left of their homes, an international commission turned its attention to the horses' medical files and pedigrees. It was hard for me to believe my eyes. After a complicated game of give and take (this mare in return for that rare stallion), the population gathered at Laxenburg was split into two herds – both with the greatest possible variation in bloodlines. As victor, Italy was awarded just over half the Lipizzaners evacuated from Lipica: 109 animals. Enough for Benito Mussolini to establish his own military stud farm in now-Italian Lipica.

Austria was allowed to keep ninety-seven. Conversano Savona was among them: as a blue-blooded grey in a republic that had formally abolished its nobility.

∪

The red tractor had almost disappeared when someone shouted: 'Here they come!' At first, I couldn't see anything. The hilly landscape was a greyish-green with grey spots: the sky above it a light blue. Somewhere on the horizon, amid this palette, a dark serpent was twining along: seventy young stallions, coming down the slope at a gallop. I saw a swell of horses' bodies moving forward in waves and heaves. Sometimes the ribbon disappeared into a fold in the landscape and was lost from sight for thirty seconds or more. One never knew where the stallions would reappear, but when they did they were suddenly much closer. Soon you could make out the individual animals and feel the earth tremble. I stepped to one side, from where we had gathered in the corral, directly in front of the open barn doors.

The others remained where they were. I divided my attention between the onrushing herd with their flattened ears and the joyous faces of Frau Brabenetz and Frau Bachinger, who stood watching arm in arm. The horses shot through the funnel-shaped fences of the corral without slowing. In the final straight they accelerated to a sprint. But where was the finish line? Never before had I witnessed so many horses racing towards me simultaneously. Their hooves flung sand and pebbles from the ground. The noise they made was not a ruffle, not a stamping, but a wall of sound. The ladies from Vienna apparently had no intention of moving aside. I had flattened myself against the white wooden fence. Just as I was about to scramble over it, I heard a wild whinnying. Looking up, I saw the animals come screeching to a halt, as though on command, amid a cloud of dust – at an arm's length from Frau Bachinger and Frau Brabenetz. Their handbags still slung over one shoulder, the ladies promptly began patting the greys like blue-ribbon winners.

The corral had been transformed into a chaos of humans and animals, but what did it matter? Stallions that nibbled at shawls and hairdos were barely reprimanded. Hans Brabenetz stood in the midst of it all, his chin held high. 'Bravo!' a lady in a hat shouted to the horses – like an opera lover cheering her favourite tenor.

THE BLACK 'MENDELIZES'
TO THE SURFACE

THE CONVERSANO BLOODLINE RAN back more than two centuries to the stallion Conversano himself (who bore no maternal name), an animal of outstanding quality born in 1767 in the Kingdom of Naples. When Conversano reached the age of seven, Count Kaunitz saw to it personally that he was taken to Lipica to provide fresh blood. He was black.

A black patriarch for a white breed appeals to the popular imagination every bit as much as the white mares that bear black foals. The breeders, however, were fairly oblivious to all this; they worked on the basis of intuition and experience. The stallions they sent to Vienna at first comprised all colours and markings, from spotted and flecked to sorrels and isabelles. This was only natural; the Lipizzaner was of mixed blood – a new breed formed of the best equine material, culled from Denmark all the way to Egypt. But after a time the greys became dominant, with even the blackest of foals starting to grey within a year. '*Kaiserschimmel*' – imperial greys – they were called, and they were enormously popular at the royal court. Their nickname, though, owed nothing to the breeders, who were quite amazed to see non-greys becoming increasingly scarce. The majority of the descendants of browns or blacks crossed with greys turned out to be greys themselves. Entire herds ended up white. New Lipizzaner studs were set up far from Lipica in the eighteenth century, in the Balkans, the Carpathians and other territories belonging to the Habsburg crown. It was at these farms in particular that the breeders did their utmost to preserve the entire range of colours. In order not to compromise too much on quality, however, they regularly made use of greys as well, and still the number of coloured horses continued to dwindle.

But just when it was assumed that the coloured Lipizzaner had become a thing of the past, a foal that remained black or brown would pop up here or there. Treasured for its rarity, the black Lipizzaner took on a sort of supernatural status – as sought after as the black tulip among bulb-growers.

One of the participants in our Slovenian excursion – an entrepreneurial type with a permanent growth of designer stubble and a Blackberry that summoned him sultrily with the words 'Master, you've got mail' – had his sights set on buying a black Lipizzaner. There was one in the stables at Lipica, and a real beauty at that.

'How old is this animal?' he had asked, without even glancing at the veterinary director.

'Seven,' our guide said. 'He's completed his basic training now and is about to start a career in our own riding school.'

We had already attended a show at the Slovenian *rajtšul* (riding school) in Lipica – a performance by professional riders who had been schooled in Vienna.

'How much would he cost?'

The veterinary director laughed politely – the horse was not for sale.

The Austrian raised a hand in the air. 'Wait,' that hand said. He held his mobile to his ear and began pacing the corridor, immersed in consultation with his base camp ('love at first sight', we heard him say). Meanwhile, one of us fed the coveted horse a handful of hay and scratched him on the head. His call finished, the businessman now took the director aside. From their body language it was clear that the one was making an offer that embarrassed the other. The Slovenian rocked back on his heels, defensive and at the same time resolute. The black Lipizzaner was the pride of Slovenia.

∪

Of all horse breeds, the Lipizzaner is the most exhaustively documented. A list of scientific publications as long as your arm provides details on maternal descent, blood types, inbreeding, digestion, pigmentation, benign tumours and pure-bloodedness. For a Lipizzaner to be recognized and registered as such, Austria applies a set of obligatory physical standards: a shoulder height of between 152 and 158 centimetres, a trunk no longer than 165, the nasal profile not too concave. Inadvertently, the forms on which these stipulations (thirty-seven in all) are checked off resemble the Nazis' 'Aryan tables' (which cited as the most important feature the distance between the forehead and the back of the head). Stringent criteria applied to determining the Lipizzaner's pure-bloodedness. Foreign taints to the pedigree were tolerated, as long as the 'five-generation rule' applied: a Lipizzaner could be denoted as pure-blooded if both parents descended from at least five generations of pure Lipizzaners. Coincidentally or not, all candidates for the SS had to present a Greater Aryan certificate, a family tree dating back to 1 January 1800 'as proof of Aryan descent for five generations'.

Selection and exclusion – that's how breeds have always been enhanced.

It was amazing to consider how long heredity had remained

misunderstood, and at the same time how badly the science of genetics, which made its appearance in 1900, had been abused during the century which followed.

None other than Charles Darwin had gone in careful search of the mystery behind traits which disappear only to reappear sporadically generations later – but was unable to unravel it. How bizarre that his evolutionary theory encompassed life on earth in its entirety, yet he had no clue about the mechanism of heredity. That the variant best suited to survive in nature ultimately replaced its weaker competitor Darwin had unearthed in 1859. But how did such variations arise in the first place? The widely accepted 'giraffe hypothesis', advanced by the Frenchman Jean-Baptiste Lamarck, supposed that the giraffe's long neck was a result of having to crane for increasingly higher-hanging leaves. An adaptation acquired over the course of a lifetime, Lamarck said, was passed on to the individual's descendants; Darwin dismissed that claim as 'veritable rubbish'. Long-necked giraffes had a better chance of survival than short-necked ones, which was a completely different matter. But even that observation provided no answer to the question of what it was that reproduction actually reproduced.

Darwin pursued just such an answer in his voluminous *The Variation of Animals and Plants under Domestication*. With his half-cousin Francis Galton, he also conducted tests on animals, performing primitive blood transfusions between dissimilar breeds of rabbits. The rabbits died. Galton, a mathematical genius, drew a distinction between all things congenital ('nature') and the things which an organism learned during its lifetime ('nurture'). Propensity *and* environment provided a plant or animal with its ultimate form. The only question was, however, to what *extent* did the two factors play a role? And could one really view them as being distinct? Could the hardness of the Lipizzaner's hoof, for example, be credited to the stony ground of the Karst mountains – to environmental factors, in other words – or had it (by now) become a genetic trait?

In 1883, Galton coined the term 'eugenics' to describe attempts to improve the human race, comparable to those made by the animal breeder. The breeder excluded weak and defective individuals from reproduction by selling them to the butcher or having them castrated (negative eugenics), and took steps to promote the reproduction of the best (positive eugenics). The possibilities seemed limitless: species had evolved, and during that process human beings had climbed to the highest heights; logic indicated that 'an even greater destiny' lay in wait. All that remained unclear was the mechanism of heredity itself. Darwin consulted the breeders of horses and pigeons time and again. What did they focus on? When did they see the differences arise, and how? Alongside their practice of artificial selection, he posited 'natural selection' as the mechanism that caused one species to survive and another to bite the dust. The subtitle to *On the Origin of Species*, accordingly, read 'Or the Preservation of Favoured Races in the Struggle for Life'. But, as Darwin admitted readily: 'The laws which determine heredity remain largely unknown' – a quote I came across in a biography of the monk Gregor Mendel (1822–84).

Mendel *did* read Darwin (there are lines and scribbles in the margins of his German-language edition of *On the Origin*), but Darwin had never heard of Mendel, or of the visionary insights he had achieved in the seclusion of a monastery garden. 'The priest who held the key to evolution' – that was how they referred to him after his death. Had anyone asked this cigar-smoking monk about the mystery of the black Lipizzaners, he would probably have started his reply by refuting the idea that terms such as 'blood' and 'blending' had anything to do with heredity. At that point the imperial horse breeders would have laughed in his face – the improvement of livestock, after all, was all about 'blood', 'bloodlines' and 'blood relationships'. They saw themselves as blenders of blood and, when it came down to it, as among the best in the world at doing just that. But Mendel, through the application of statistical analysis, had arrived at a radically different understanding.

Generally speaking, the facts of his life as summarized drily in his biography told a tragic story. He had made a discovery that ranked with those of Copernicus, Newton and Darwin, but during his lifetime had been unable to convince another living soul of its importance. Was Mendel born too early? Did he fully realize the significance of his discovery? Or was the failure to appreciate him a consequence of the chronic drowsiness suffered by all Habsburg backwater towns in the second half of the nineteenth century?

Gregor Johann Mendel was the only son of a tenant farmer from the Austrian province of Moravia, north of Vienna. His father had to work three days a week as forester for his landowner (*Robota*, this feudal arrangement was called), but was crippled by a falling tree. Had his son not received such excellent marks at school, he would surely have followed in his father's footsteps.

Using all the family's available funds, the boy was able to continue school up to and including the university entrance exams. 'Then, he found himself forced', Mendel wrote of himself later in the third person, 'to find a way out of the situation of bitter anxiety concerning his daily bread. In the year 1843 he applied for and was granted admission to the Augustinian monastery at Brünn.'

Johann changed his name to Gregorius, took a vow of

chastity and was ordained into the priesthood – a few months before the revolutionary year 1848, during which Europe's monarchies were shaken to their foundations. Confronted with rebellious liberals, socialists and neglected minorities, Vienna agreed to the establishment of a national assembly. The first session was held in the riding school at the Hofburg: in the interests of democracy, the Lipizzaners remained in their stalls. The system of *Robota* was abolished, but otherwise the occasion was dedicated largely to bickering. It was only by means of a desperate give-and-take that the Habsburg dynasty finally survived the uprisings of 1848. Thereafter the rebellious provinces were brought back into line with an iron fist, and the national assembly was disbanded within the year. The final gain, however, amounted to a settling of accounts with the most rigid conservatism of the church and the nobility.

In Brünn, Brother Mendel used to his advantage the ground which science had recently won from faith. He performed his priestly duties as an assistant teacher in natural history, and also found time to begin experimenting with pea plants. He was not the kind cut out for administering spiritual assistance to the dying: the mere sight of ill people made him feel ill himself.

On 8 February and 8 March 1865, Mendel delivered two addresses to Brünn's Natural History Association concerning his longer-term experiments with *Pisum sativum*, the pea. Step by step, he explained how he had first selected seven strains of pea for his tests, strains which differed in the colour of their pods (green or yellow) or the length of their stems (shorter than thirty centimetres or longer than seventy). He had used a brush to cross-pollinate them, transferring pollen from the one flower to the stamen of the other. Then he had counted how many green or yellow-podded, how many short- or long-stemmed plants there were among their descendants. The revolutionary feature of his approach was the application of statistics to nature – which bore surprising fruit. Having carefully examined 12,835 plants, he announced that the passing down of selected traits occurred in accordance with fixed numerical relationships. Even more important than this perceived pattern was the observation that those traits did not degenerate, that no yellowish-green or medium-long pea plants turned up. From this, Mendel concluded that hereditary characteristics were transferred by bearers (which he called '*Elemente*') that did not blend during reproduction, but were passed on unchanged. One needed to draw a distinction between the capacity to develop a certain trait and the trait itself. The trait itself was not necessarily expressed, and could remain dormant for generations before showing up much further down the line.

Such as the black coat of the original Conversano.

His audiences did their utmost to follow his arguments, but none appreciated the magnitude of his discovery. Nevertheless, the secretary of the Natural History Association moved that the text be included in their periodical. There were no objections. *Versuche über Pflanzen-Hybriden* (Experiments on Plant Hybridization) appeared in the association's journal in 1866 – a publication which opened the door, upon its rediscovery in 1900 (the moss on Mendel's headstone was by then sixteen years thick), to new types of racial improvement, and to correspondent Utopias that would ultimately leave no one unaffected.

ᴜ

Mendel had spent nine years crossing varieties of garden peas in his 35 m × 7 m plot in the monastery; in the fifth form of secondary school we had reproduced his experiments in nine weeks, but using fruit flies. Our biology teacher, a bearded man with a tendency to gesticulate wildly, liked to provoke us. In the intellectual sense too, and in the best Socratic tradition. About genetic manipulation and the accompanying social pitfalls. About Darwin and whether we were actually descended from chimpanzees. ('No, stupid!')

Our biology teacher told us that Darwin had for years delayed publishing his theory of evolution, being nervous about the reactions of his fellow Victorians. And it was not until twelve years later – in 1871 – that he dared write: 'Man is descended from a hairy quadruped, furnished with a tail and pointed ears.' *Homo sapiens* was a primate who shared with the other primates an ape-like ancestor, though this did not prevent Darwin awarding special status to man. On the contrary, he was intrigued by the human tendency to protect the weak and even to keep them alive by artificial means – in seemingly total contradiction of the principle of natural selection. Altruism, Darwin went on to reason, served to promote the degeneration of the species. Hastily, almost as though shocked by his own words, he then added that such reflections were not a plea for leaving weaker individuals to their own fate or denying them the right to reproduce.

We split up into two-man teams for our experiments with *Drosophila melanogaster* (fruit flies), which proved anything but boring. Among those tiny flies were individuals with white eyes rather than red, or blunt wings instead of tapered. Our mission in breeding new generations was to keep an eye on precisely these physical traits. Stopper bottle, magnifying glass and test tube within reach, we got down to business. We dipped cotton balls in ether to anaesthetize the insects, allowing us to examine them more closely.

During the theory lesson at the start of the sessions, we

had learned that the carriers of heredity came in pairs, one half from the mother and the other from the father. They were in the nucleus of every cell in our body, on string-like chromosomes to which pairs of genes were also attached, too tiny to be seen with the naked eye. Those were the bearers of certain traits, like blunt wings, or tapered ones. At the moment of reproduction, these pairs of genes stripped away into two halves, 'alleles', each of which then ended up in a random germ cell or ovum. When a male sex cell fused during fertilization with a female one, those halves once again became entangled. In every new pair of genes, therefore, one half (allele) came from the mother, the other from the father.

You had to keep your wits about you or you could easily lose your way in the fruit-fly experiments. In practice, the allele responsible for tapered wings won out over the one for blunt wings, and was therefore called 'dominant' – we were to indicate it with a capital letter (A, for example), to distinguish it from the 'recessive' or subordinate allele for blunt wings (a). A fruit-fly larva would only develop into a blunt-winged individual if it had inherited a lower-case a from both parents and therefore possessed the gene pair 'aa'. The other possibilities (AA or Aa) always produced flies with tapered wings, due to the dominant A.

If you crossed a blunt-winged fruit fly (aa) with a tapered-winged one with two dominant alleles for tapered (an AA type), then all of the descendants would have pointy wings, because they had all inherited an A and an a and were therefore Aa themselves.

$$AA \text{ (= tapered)} \times aa \text{ (= blunt)}$$
$$\vee$$
$$Aa \text{ (= tapered)}$$

Yet if you went on to cross the members of this first generation (Aa) with each other (Aa × Aa), it turned out that this could also produce blunt-winged (aa) flies.

$$Aa\ (= tapered) \times Aa\ (= tapered)$$
$$\vee$$
$$AA\ (= tapered) + Aa\ (= tapered) + aA\ (= tapered) +$$
$$aa\ (= blunt)$$

Statistically, therefore, one out of every four descendants in this second generation was a blunt-winged fly.

As a student, you couldn't help but respect Mendel, who had deduced all this without knowing about chromosomes, genes and alleles. And what went for peas and fruit flies also went for people and horses. The grey factor – that is to say, the allele that produced the greying of the Lipizzaner's coat – was dominant over the one that produced a colour. That was the whole story.

U

'My time will come,' Gregor Mendel once predicted to a fellow monk. His garden-peas study was sent out to more than one hundred scientific libraries throughout Europe. He himself distributed an additional forty copies to specialists and other interested parties, and established correspondence with the greatest German-language botanist of his day, Professor Carl Nägeli of Munich. After the careful initial exchanges, the greeting 'Honourable Sir' faded into 'Honoured Friend'. Mendel told the professor that the results of his research were at odds 'with the current state of science', and sent him packages of seeds with which he could reproduce his experiments.

Nägeli did nothing with them.

At the instigation of his friend in Munich, however, Mendel sowed a field with hawkweed. 'I consider myself privileged to have found a colleague as skilled and successful as you,' the professor praised him.

In June 1870, Mendel complained that his eyesight was declining. He no longer had the sharp vision needed to pollinate the hawkweed manually. And after being appointed abbot in 1868, he also had little time available for his research. For his social contributions – not his scientific ones – he was awarded the Franz Josef Order.

In 1867 the Habsburg Empire had been transformed into the celebrated Dual Monarchy, ruling over Austria and Hungary. On the hills of Buda, astride a Lipizzaner from the Maestoso line, the emperor of Austria had been crowned king of the Magyars.

As abbot, Mendel followed his own insights, and the relationship with his bishop cooled. His monks at Brünn were allowed to disseminate Darwin's theory of evolution rather than the story of Creation. The abbey itself had never been considered particularly devout; the bishop had threatened before to close it, saying that 'every ray of spirituality' there seemed to have been extinguished. Mendel began smoking Virginia cigars. The walls of the monastery entrance he had painted over with worldly scenes of beekeepers and breeders, and – why not? – with a kneeling St Isidor, patron saint of agriculture. And when one day he received a visit from a French seed merchant who wanted to hear about his experiments with peas, he could no longer summon the energy to rail against his fate as a neglected scientist. 'That is a long story,' he told the man. 'Too long to go into.'

Gregor Johann Mendel died of a kidney infection on 6 January 1884, at the age of sixty-one. The celibate father of genetic science left behind no offspring of his own.

The epilogue to Mendel's life story – under the heading 'Belated recognition' – covers a few dozen pages.

1900 – the year in which he was rediscovered – was also the year, therefore, that gave birth to the field of genetics. Working independently of each other, three scholars – Hugo de Vries in Amsterdam (in March), Carl Correns in Tübingen (April) and Erich von Tschermak in Vienna (June) – published the rules of genetics as set down by Mendel. All three lauded his genius. This revolutionary discovery called for a new way of thinking about the breeding of plants and animals; it called for equations, and the calculation of probabilities. Mendel, posthumously, had presented the breeder with a tangible set of tools.

In England, the zoologist William Bateson – a disciple from the very start – immediately recognized the enormous repercussions for 'Man's power over Nature'. Bateson announced that he could imagine no other breakthrough that would have such a profound effect on mankind.

From St Petersburg to Los Angeles, scientists went in search of Mendel's published experiments with peas – and, lo and behold, *Versuche über Pflanzen-Hybriden* turned out to be right there on the university library shelf. Unread, the pages still uncut.

As with the history of warfare, what happened next with Mendel's legacy is best expressed in dates:

1901 – William Bateson has *Versuche* translated into English.

1904 – Bateson makes a pilgrimage to Brünn, but notes less enthusiasm about Mendel there than he had hoped.

1906 – The Augustine monks dedicate one corner of the abbey's entrance to the memory of their former abbot.

1908 – Thomas Hunt Morgan, the first Nobel Prize laureate in the field of genetics, sets up a 'fruit-fly lab' at Columbia University in New York.

1909 – The Darwin memorial year (hundredth birthday/ fiftieth anniversary of *On the Origin of Species*) brings evolutionary theory and the laws of genetics closer, thanks to improved understanding of the phenomenon of 'mutations', or abrupt changes in genetic material.

1910 – The international association 'Friends of Science' raises a statue to Mendel at Brünn.

∪

In 2007, the breeding of Lipizzaners was organized according to the Mendelian model. At the agricultural university in Vienna, located on Gregor Mendelstrasse, half the zoology department was working on little else besides Lipizzaner genetics. If a foal somewhere did not turn grey, you might hear the specialists say: 'The black "mendelizes" to the surface.'

The University of Ljubljana kept up its end as well: Slovenian zoologists from the biotechnology faculty bombarded the stud-farm managers in Lipica each year with prescribed breeding schemes.

'Our breeding objective?' The veterinary director didn't have to think about it long. 'Bigger horses,' he said. 'With more pronounced withers. That aside, we're simply out to preserve the classic traits.'

In the breeding strategy devised in Ljubljana, each stallion and each mare were given a number, behind which lurked a whole gamut of genetic factors. Computer programs had been designed to calculate the ideal pairing partners. Just before the breeding season started, the results were faxed to the stud farm.

'But they are not always the best recommendations,' the veterinary director admitted. 'And if my intuition says I should do something else, then I do something else.'

Was he saying that he placed no faith in a scientific approach?

That wasn't it.

But then what was it?

That was hard to say. 'Look, these are not chickens.' The Lipizzaner breeder rubbed his hands together. 'They're more like us. You can empathize with them, almost like equals.'

THE OBEDIENCE TEST

M Y ORDER WAS WAITING for me on the shelf of an open
cabinet: a film tin the size of a café serving tray, the
description written in felt pen on the label:

Title: *Die Spanische Hofreitschule zu Wien*
Director: Wilhelm Prager
Producer: Universum-Film AG (UFA), Berlin
Length: 414 metres
Film censor: all ages, free of blasphemy
Classification: artistic value, edifying for the populace
Premiere: 14.12.1939, Gloria Palast, Berlin

I sat down at the special console for 35 mm films, before a
bank of buttons and a screen. But it was lunchtime; I would
have to wait until the on-duty archivist came to thread the
reel for me and the time allotted me had begun.

Arranging the viewing, the train to Berlin's *Hauptbahnhof*,
the taxi ride to Fehrbellinerplatz with its imposing Nazi
building fronts – all of it had gone so *pünktlich* that I had
arrived *überpünktlich* before the concrete facade of the
German film archives. I was too early, but the doorman nevertheless led me down the tiled corridor to the viewing room.

He was, as it turned out, informed of both my arrival and my extraction. 'So you're the Dutchman who's come for the white horses.'

That indeed was what I had come for. Or, more precisely: for the most controversial documentary ever made about the Spanish Riding School. By the Germans, in 1939, one year after the *Anschluss* with Austria. With a bit of luck, I'd even get to see Conversano Bonavista, who at the time had been a fourteen-year-old school stallion – the most renowned of all Primula's forefathers, his name among the few chiselled into the marble pantheon of the Stallburg: CONVERSANO BONAVISTA 1925–1953. I would recognize him by his chunky build, his strikingly short neck and the unpigmented spots around his eyes and mouth.

There had been little warning of the stir that Bonavista, like his father Savona, would create during the interbellum. The Spanish Riding School, badly in need of a lick of paint, had been stripped of its 'Royal' designation in 1918, and during the 1920s was allowed to continue with a handful of stallions on condition that the doors of the Winter Riding School be opened to the public. The masses showed little interest: Vienna had other things on its mind besides dancing horses. Reading the chronicles of Joseph Roth, one encounters a city in upheaval. Within the boundaries of the new republic, the former metropolis of the Danube Empire was a top-heavy place: one-quarter of all Austrians lived within the limits of Vienna. Swarms of beggars wandered past the stately porticos. 'The hospital has a ward for the reconstruction of the man destroyed by the forces of war,' Roth wrote. 'The cosmetic surgery ward. It is here that those who have been shot to pieces in the war are helped to regain God's image.' Photographs of armless or legless veterans were displayed in shop windows to promote the 'anti-war museums' opening here and there. On the street and in parliament, the merits of closing the Spanish Riding School had been discussed more than once. What, after all, was the point of maintaining such an aristocratic institution? Voices were raised regularly, saying that the Winter Riding School would be better converted into a public swimming pool, or a cinema. It was only by responding promptly to the needs of the day, such as benefit performances for tuberculosis patients, that the Riding School's management was able to keep the Lipizzaners from the knacker's yard. But the glitter was gone. At the entrance, postcards were sold showing white horses performing the levade or a capriole, with revenues going to the Broom Fund, for the purchase of brooms and pitchforks for the Stallburg.

$$\cup$$

The windows of the film archive were blacked out with brown curtains. Sansevieria and shoots of lemon geraniums graced the windowsills. I began leafing through folder K310888, which went with the film I had ordered. It contained newspaper clippings about the director, Wilhelm Prager. Stuck to the inside cover was an instruction leaflet, explaining to the uninitiated how they should watch 'films from the National Socialist period'. How very German. I was warned that the film I was about to see was made during the era of orchestrated Nazi propaganda, which had paved the way for the Holocaust. This was followed by a quote from Goebbels who, in 1933, had demanded that German films from then on have 'popular contours', and stated that art had a right to exist only when it was 'rooted in National Socialist reality'. The rest was *entartete*, degenerate, and would be eradicated in all its vulnerability.

A filmography of Wilhelm Prager was also included: he had directed more than fifty films, eleven of them about horses. This latter fact, the author of an obituary noted, reflected his predilection for sports and agriculture, and the bridge which the horse formed between the two. Born in 1876, Prager had lived to the age of seventy-nine. He had, at least later in life, a mouth like a humourless stripe. His directing breakthrough came in 1925 with an edifying ode to the human body: *Wege zu Kraft und Schönheit, ein Film über moderne Körperkultur* (Routes to Strength and Beauty, a Film about Modern Physical Culture).

'Proto-fascistic' the instruction leaflet ruled. The film was a paean to the beauty of athletically built men and women who kept their bodies in shape with dance, gymnastics and the occasional steam bath. *Mens sana in corpora sano*, a healthy mind in a healthy body. Even Benito Mussolini appeared before the camera, to demonstrate his limberness.

In retrospect, *Wege zu Kraft und Schönheit* could be seen as a source of inspiration for later Nazi propaganda. Leni Riefenstahl had made her screen debut in Prager's film: she is one of the enchantingly dressed slave girls in a Roman bath, applying balsam to a naked woman. A film historian had once demonstrated how much the composition and lighting in a number of stills from Riefenstahl's *Olympia* – her two-part film dealing with the 1936 Olympics in Berlin – resembled certain scenes from *Wege zu Kraft und Schönheit*. The resemblances were striking, but so were the differences; in the final account, Riefenstahl was no longer interested in the individual, but in the collective. Her crowd scenes from *Triumph des Willens*, about the colossal NSDAP rallies, were seen as the absolute pinnacle of cinematographic propaganda. When she did pick out an individual from the crowd, it was only as a serviceable cell in the supra-organism of which he was a part: the Aryan race. Leaving out his humanity, she portrayed the human as a herd animal.

The critics viewed Wilhelm Prager as less political, less inclined to propaganda. He seemed sincerely interested in movement and rhythm, and in 1928 was the first film-maker to be commissioned by an Olympic Committee to record the summer games, in Amsterdam. Prager's leap from athletes to highly trained horses was not all that drastic; the real discrepancy was found in the timeline at the bottom of his filmography: in 1928, no books were yet being burned in Germany and Austria; by 1939, however, the anti-Semitic race laws were already in force ('for the protection of Germanic blood and Germanic honour') and the German peoples were being readied for the Polish campaign.

With one twist of the knob I could make the film play, slow it down, freeze a frame and run it backwards. The volume could be adjusted with a slide control. Otherwise, there was nothing for me to do. The archivist moved behind the projector table and closed the curtains. 'If there's anything you need, I'll be across the hall, in room 323.'

As soon as I set the reels in motion, a bird's-eye view of Vienna appeared. There was a crackling sound, like fire in a hearth, then suddenly it was drowned out by a blare of trumpets. The Winter Riding School appeared on the screen with its forty-six Corinthian columns, a brass band playing in the uppermost gallery. The musicians themselves weren't visible, only their instruments. Swastika banners hung from the railings.

The rather harsh and excitable tone was established, but the following scene was actually quite relaxed. The camera rolled backwards through the corridors of the Stallburg where the trained stallions waited, curried and inquisitive, for the start of a special performance. Then, from a side corridor, came the riders, one by one, led by Erste Oberbereiter (chief equestrian) Zrust, and behind him his eternal shadow Lindenbauer, who I recognized from photos in which he was putting Conversano Bonavista through the *passage*. These were Austrians, *k.u.k.-Leute*, from head to toe. They wore gleaming spurs and black leather boots that covered their knees, not because boots happened to be back in fashion, but out of a sense of tradition. At 3 minutes 20 came a meeting with two, also jackbooted, *Wehrmacht* officers and a lady in a uniform dress.

'*Heil Hitler!*' Zrust raised his arm, his visitors returned the salute in perfect unison. Both delegations were standing in a courtyard, the Germans in the shade of a tree, the Austrians in the hot sun – as though at roll-call.

Had Zrust and his deputies felt ill at ease, or were they actually impressed by their new leader in Berlin? The fact was that the Germans had marched into Austria in March 1938 to loud cheering and, what's more, they had given back to the Riding School its 'Royal' designation.

The Germans had also immediately appointed a new Riding School commander: Alois Podhajsky, an Austrian in the service of the *Wehrmacht* since the *Anschluss*, who had begun his military career during the First World War as a dragoon in the 4th Emperor Ferdinand Regiment. Podhajsky later wrote his memoirs, and in them the reader can see how much the *Wehrmacht*, the NSDAP, the SA, the SS and even the State Ministry for Food Supplies and Agriculture craved control over the white horses. A multilateral tug of war began. Podhajsky described the 'countless delegations' who frequented the Stallburg. They poked and patted everything in sight and stared around in amazement. The SA Brownshirts, the security police, were the rowdiest of the lot, but one *Wehrmacht* general finally took the matter all the way to the top. From Berlin, a decision was handed down that the Piber stud would be placed under the aegis of the Ministry of Agriculture, and the Royal Spanish Riding School directly under the army high command.

The directive included a proviso intended to placate Heinrich Himmler's SS:

> The Army High Command is prepared to offer members of the mounted SS the opportunity to improve their equestrian skills at the Royal Spanish Riding School.

At 4 minutes 50, Zrust began introducing the stars of the show, one by one.

'Favory Africa!' he shouted – upon which Favory Africa came trotting into the arena and stopped in front of the German inspectors. The horses were announced by name, not their riders. I sat up straight and, damned if it wasn't true, the fourth stallion was a bullseye: 'Conversano Savona!' So it wasn't Bonavista, but old Savona himself. I stopped the film, ran it back thirty seconds and let him reappear – frame by frame this time – from the shadows of the archway. The first glimpse was the white of his muzzle, then the sunlight on his mane. As if for a military inspection, Savona turned ninety degrees, so you could admire the line of his back. Standing still was something he normally refused to do: his stableboy could barely keep him from nibbling at the ornamental shrubbery.

'Conversano Savona is able to perform the perfect levade,' I heard Zrust say.

Director Wilhelm Prager had cast eight prize stallions for a performance in what was, by far, the world's most beautiful riding school. To the rhythm of martial music, his montage cut between panoramic shots and details of a lifted leg or a gleaming eye. To depict the history of dressage as well, Prager showed the ancient tapestries from the series *Le Manège Royal.* These portrayed the 'airs above the ground', as taught at the French court as early as the sixteenth century. The tradition of the Spanish School elaborated upon the methods of riding master Antoine de Pluvinel, who in turn had refined the Greek horsemanship of Xenophon.

Conversano Savona showed what he did best: the levade 'between the pillars'. Among the other greys, his docked tail made him easy to pick out and his supple movements were a joy to see. The dial, with which I could view him in slow motion, gave me an instrument with which to dissect each movement into a series of consecutive positions. I could freeze the flow of time at intervals of tenths of a second, reminding me of the famous photographic sequences made by Eadweard Muybridge in the nineteenth century. In those photographs, taken in 1878, the viewer can also see, quite clearly and for the first time ever, the locomotive sequence of the horse.

The eccentric Muybridge, a photographer in San Francisco, had been hired by the governor of California to settle an old dispute: did a trotting horse lift all four feet from the ground simultaneously, or didn't it? For painters throughout the ages, the gallop had been a source of major vexation: their standard solution had been to portray a horse with legs extended front and back, as with a jumping jack – as a result, countless horses have galloped through the history of art in cartoon-like poses. The trot, however, was even more mysterious, because of the irregular moments of suspension. The new invention of photography could help provide the answer, but in order to make his pictures Muybridge first had to improve contemporary shutter mechanisms. When he finally succeeded in photographing a horse moving at speed, he was able to demonstrate the existence of a suspended moment during the trot. Muybridge immediately went on to design a machine, the zoopraxiscope, with which he could project a series of photographs in rapid sequence and so conjure the illusion of motion.

Yet Wilhelm Prager, it occurred to me, had gone further than Muybridge, and not only because the state of technology allowed. Consciously or unconsciously he had portrayed the horse, in this case the improved and highly trained Lipizzaner, as an *Übertier,* a super-animal.

The annexation of the Royal Spanish Riding School by the German high command on 18 June 1939 was celebrated as a minor *Anschluss* within the greater one. Originally, Zrust, Lindenbauer and their colleagues were to have delivered the Hitler salute during the performance, but the new director, Alois Podhajsky, prided himself on having banned 'that disgusting gesture' immediately upon his appointment in 1939.

Podhajsky's life was inextricably entwined with that of the Viennese Lipizzaners. Halfway through the film he appears on camera, on horseback. He wears a military cap and sits bolt upright in the saddle. But not on a Lipizzaner. The narrator says: 'With this horse, a German thoroughbred, he won a medal at the Olympic Games in Berlin.' Bronze – as I remembered having read in his memoirs.

From the minor and major events Podhajsky had described emerged the portrait of a man shaped by the age in which he lived.

He had learnt the levade astride Conversano Savona.

His father had served the emperor as an officer in the Austro-Hungarian army.

Born in 1898, Alois had moved as a child from one garrison town to another: from Mostar (Herzegovina) to Travnik

(Bosnia) to Esseg (Croatia) to Lemberg (present-day L'viv, in the Ukraine) to Chernivtsi (across the Carpathians, now in the Ukraine as well).

At the outbreak of the First World War, his dream came true: at the tender age of eighteen, he was allowed to join the cavalry.

That proved a disappointment. ('Only seldom did the opportunity arise to gallop at the enemy with sabres drawn.')

In October 1917 he was wounded in the neck. ('I too have paid my blood sacrifice to the dying Colossus, the holy alliance of the peoples of Central Europe.')

His recovery was slow, he was unable to speak for a long time and felt dejected. ('Almost all the playing fields of my youth were suddenly located in foreign countries.')

Podhajsky's spirits rose again only in 1927, when he was made cavalry inspector for the Austrian republic.

In 1933 and 1934 he experienced two glorious years as an apprentice rider at the Spanish Riding School. ('Because they themselves were paragons of self-discipline, my instructors, through their Lipizzaners, taught me the mentality indispensable to achieving the highest degree of dressage.')

His participation in the Berlin Games, on the other hand, was a source of lifelong frustration. He, an Austrian, had been the best. But both gold and silver were reserved for the German equestrians; the jury was that corrupt.

He needed only two sentences to dismiss the *Anschluss*: 'In 1938 my life was unexpectedly shaken by the course of world history ... Austria was devoured by the German Empire, and its officers by the *Wehrmacht*.'

In the summer of 1939, Major Podhajsky and his white horses made a triumphal tour of Germany. With the announcement of the mobilization, as prelude to the invasion of Poland on 1 September, he almost lost his best stableboys.

But he succeeded in convincing the high command in Berlin to release several sergeants from front-line duty in order to care for his Lipizzaners. ('A more positive expression of appreciation for European culture could not be imagined!')

∪

I had been warned repeatedly that, if I hoped to understand the fortunes and misfortunes of the Lipizzaners under the Third Reich, there was one fact I had to keep in mind: Adolf Hitler was an Austrian. He was from Braunau am Inn, a border town, but Austrian through and through. Braunau was also the first place he visited in March 1938, during his victorious progress in the wake of the *Anschluss*. Everywhere he went he was received with equally delirious enthusiasm, and Vienna – where he had twice been refused admission to the Academy of Arts – was the grand finale. From a balcony at the Hofburg he addressed a crowd of hundreds of thousands.

'This country is German,' he declaimed. And: 'I announce to history the entry of my native country into the German Empire.' From where he stood he looked out over Heldenplatz below, with its famous equestrian statues towering above the crowd.

The Opera, Burgtheater and Spanish Riding School, more or less the holy trinity of Austrian culture, were transformed at one fell swoop into prize German property. After his speech, the Führer could have walked down the palace corridors to the Winter Riding School and the Stallburg. But Hitler was not a horse person. He wore boots but no spurs. Insiders even claimed that he was afraid of horses. On his birthday in April 1933, the German equestrian periodical *St Georg* honoured him with a full front-page portrait under the heading: 'The man who helped Germany back into the saddle.' But in that same year he refused to accept the jumper Wotan, three-time winner of the Coppa d'Oro Mussolini, as a gift. In a telegram he said he was 'deeply moved' by the offer, but his mind was made up:

I am, after all, already a co-owner of this horse, and so it makes no difference to whom it belongs, it remains a delightful and cherished possession of the German nation.

Hitler was a vegetarian. He liked dogs. At the front, in the mud of First World War Belgium, he had adopted Fuchsl, a white terrier. Later, during his own world war, he owned a German shepherd, the bitch Blondi. Lipizzaners, though, were considered 'Austrian' in the extreme. He was enamoured of *Körperkultur*, and the skills the stallions displayed – balancing finely between dance and gymnastics – came awfully close to that. What's more, the animals were white, and considered racially pure.

U

Towards the end of the film, Oberbereiter Zrust led the German delegation into the royal loge – a square room with a fireplace and decorative candelabras on the walls.

'Lady and gentlemen, may I invite you to be seated.'

In the centre of the room was a low table bearing a vase of flowers, with four chairs around it. The only woman in the group removed her gloves, arranged her dark-blonde hair. The swastika insignia pins on her lapels flashed. When their host was seated as well, the camera cut to a long shot from above. What you saw was an audience of four, with the best seats in the house: a niche just behind the low boarding of the Viennese Winter Riding School.

Then came the horses, three of them in a row, at a canter. 'The obedience test!' Zrust announced.

But instead of going into the arena, the horses were steered into the confinement of the loge itself. Cantering easily, they turned in a carousel around the table, without touching anyone or anything. The circle they described was so tight that there would not have been enough room for four horses. After their dance they left the loge on the far side.

The Germans began applauding. But Zrust called for silence: this was only the first half of the test. Once again the three greys made their entrance, this time at a right-hand canter. Conversano Savona, with his trimmed tail, was in the middle. Rhythmically, at four, five strides to each revolution, the stallions now circled the table clockwise. I pressed 'pause' to get a closer look at Conversano Savona. He was twenty-eight when this film was made, and still fiery and virile. He had performed until his seventh year to the glory of the emperor, until his twenty-seventh for the republic, and now in his old age he was displaying his obedience, almost play-fully and innocently, to the 1,000-year Reich.

Pressing 'play', I let him disappear into the wings.

II

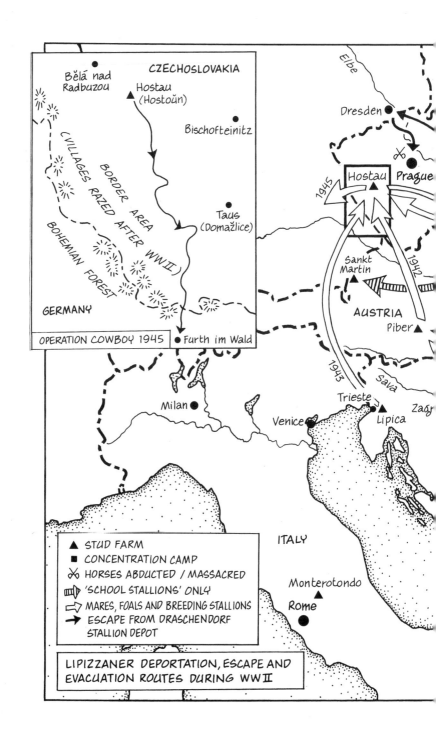

CZECHOSLOVAKIA

Bělá nad Radbuzou

Hostau (Hostoûn)

Bischofteinitz

Taus (Domažlice)

Elbe

Dresden

Hostau Prague

CBORDER AREA
(VILLAGES RAZED AFTER WWII)
BOHEMIAN FOREST

GERMANY

Sankt Martin

AUSTRIA
Piber

OPERATION COWBOY 1945 • Furth im Wald

1945

1942

1943

Sava

Milan

Trieste

Venice Lipica Zagr

ITALY

▲ STUD FARM
■ CONCENTRATION CAMP
✄ HORSES ABDUCTED / MASSACRED
⬛ 'SCHOOL STALLIONS' ONLY
⬜ MARES, FOALS AND BREEDING STALLIONS
→ ESCAPE FROM DRASCHENDORF STALLION DEPOT

Monterotondo

Rome

LIPIZZANER DEPORTATION, ESCAPE AND
EVACUATION ROUTES DURING WWII

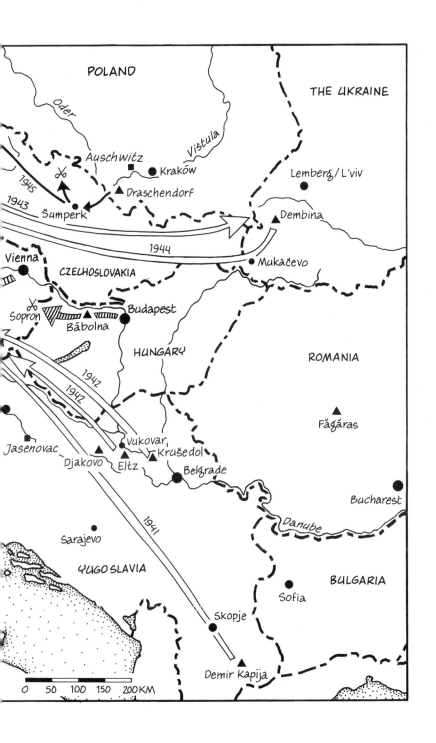

THE RETURN OF
THE TARPAN

HITLER'S RACIAL POLICIES WERE preceded by experiments with horses and cows. Starting in the 1920s, two zoo directors, the brothers Heinz and Lutz Heck, had attempted to prove that the proto-horse and the proto-ox could be 're-bred'. They endeavoured to draw purity from the mixed genetic pool of domesticated livestock.

The Brothers Heck had been raised at the Berlin Zoo, where their father was the director. Lutz succeeded him in 1931; Heinz, two years his junior, was placed in charge of Hellabrunn Zoo in Munich. Both brothers shifted their zoos' emphasis from exotic to indigenous species, including bears, lynxes and otters – with the new wolf den in Berlin as the main attraction. Out of patriotism, and curiosity, they set about 'reconstructing' live aurochs (last seen in 1623) and tarpans (of which the last wild mare had fallen into a ravine in the Ukraine during a drive in 1880). Lutz assembled herds of feral Corsican cattle, Spanish fighting bulls and other rough-and-ready ungulates, selecting them for aggressiveness, colour, size and the shape of their horns. The proto-ox may have been extinct, but parts of its genetic material, they reasoned, must live on in our modern-day cattle. By means of guided reproduction, the genes of the original prototype would fall into place like the pieces of a puzzle – then you had revived a dead species.

Heinz pursued the same ideal in Munich, using Polish Konick ponies, direct descendants of the last tarpans in captivity. On 22 May 1933, with the second-generation offspring, he struck the jackpot: 'A fabulous foal appeared!' Heinz wrote later. 'He was almost completely grey, with a black mane, a black tail and a broad black stripe down his spine. He displayed all the traits known to have been possessed by the former Teuton horse – we had our first proto-horse! An animal had been born that no one had ever dared hope to behold.'

It was Lutz who established the link between the revival of the tarpan, and later that of the aurochs, and myths of the grandeur of the German people: through the veins of these resurrected creatures flowed 'the pure blood of the ancient inhabitants of the German forests', the wild oxen and horses of the epic *Nibelungenlied*. Lutz was particularly skilled at highlighting the social significance of the 'breeding-back' experiments. From the products of cross-breeding, from mongrels in fact, one could retrieve the pure line. This meant that, by means of selective breeding, the ongoing degeneration of the German folk could be reversed. Within several generations one could filter out the more diffuse elements from a race and, at the same time, tap into common Aryan genes. Lutz Heck joined the SS and became friends with Hermann Göring, for whom he organized hunting parties on the Schorfheide heath north of Berlin, where the recreated tarpans had been reintroduced.

∪

The story of the Brothers Heck was familiar, because I happened to know some modern-day 'back-breeders'. They had been among the vanguard of ecology students at the Agricultural University at Wageningen, where I studied in the 1980s. Most had an engineering degree in zootechnics, a discipline which traditionally focused on improving the quality of the udders or the milk yields of dairy cows, but the back-breeders were not interested in those applications. On the contrary, they applied their knowledge to reversing domestication. Their goal was to return horses and cows, 'large grazers' in their jargon, to their wild state.

Had you asked them 'What is your breeding objective?', they would have had a ready answer: to achieve horses and cattle which, in appearance and character, resemble their extinct predecessors. In practical terms this meant that they – like Lutz and Heinz fifty years earlier – preferred a foal that bit and kicked to one that came up and licked your hand inquisitively.

I had met one of them: Carolien – a strapping woman who thought nothing of plunging her arm up to the shoulder into a cow's pelvic canal. Back then, Carolien had introduced me to a few of her kindred spirits, none of whom wore make-up and all of whom, male or female, dressed in drab greys and greens. The back-breeders would eat meat, but only if it came from the weaker members of their own herds.

'We'd be pleased to sell it,' Carolien told me, 'but the average consumer would find it too tough.'

You could get rid of that toughness by letting the cuts of meat age to the point where the cells begin decomposing. 'If you do that it's nice and tender but, well, then it's past its shelf life too.'

During a period in which the faith in a society that can be created to perfection was steadily waning, the back-breeders embraced the notion of a 'creatable' nature. And, in the late 1980s, the times suddenly turned in their favour: a failed land-reclamation project bestowed upon the overcrowded Netherlands a nature preserve of un-Dutch proportions, the Oostvaarders Lakes. This swampy area was inhabited by the flora and fauna characteristic of a temperate river delta. A richly variegated ecosystem developed, despite the lack of two essential links in the food chain: large grazers and their natural enemy, the wolf. The idea of reintroducing wolves proved unpopular, but no one much minded long-haired cattle or mousy-grey horses. To the back-breeders fell the task of filtering the proto-traits out of the modern domesticated herds, and allowing them to re-express themselves as lookalikes of extinct horse and cattle species – and, into the bargain, of creating the consummate ecosystem.

Carolien and her colleagues followed in the footsteps of the Brothers Heck not only in spirit, but also to the letter: they made use of Heck cattle, the descendants of the animals that had been presented as proto-oxen and portrayed on many a Nazi poster. The offspring of Heinz's tarpans also formed the raw material for the Dutch nature-builders. As far as they were concerned, though, these animals in no way reeked of Nazism – or at least no more than a Volkswagen did. The back-breeders considered themselves progressive. For them, the future lay in rolling back man's subjugation of nature.

But just when they had started introducing the descendants of the Nazi-totem animals to a man-made wild, the back-breeders ran into competition from a new breed of stirpiculturist. Their main contender was every bit as unconventional as the heirs to the Heck brothers, but cut from very different cloth: he was a transgeneticist who arrived on the scene on 16 December 1990, in the person of Herman de

Boer, professor of biotechnology at the University of Leiden. On that day, Professor de Boer celebrated an auspicious birth by treating his staff to the traditional Dutch wheat ruskets sprinkled with aniseed comfits – blue comfits in this case, for the calf born only hours earlier in his laboratory was a bull. The animal was named Herman, after his creator. To the naked eye, one could not see that that the calf bore in its cells a built-in section of human DNA.

The professor and his staff wore special T-shirts for the occasion, printed with the slogan: 1990 – THE YEAR OF THE GENETICALLY ENGINEERED COW.

At every breakthrough, large and small, in the run-up to their triumph, he and his lab-coated colleagues had flung their arms around each other's shoulders and joined in the DNA yell: *Deeee – Ennnn – Aaaaaa!*, seven times in a row, until they were hoarse.

In theory, Herman's daughters-to-come would produce mother's milk. Or in any event, milk containing lactoferrin, a component of mother's milk.

'In biotechnology, Mother Nature has found a new lover,' said Herman the Professor. The champagne corks popped, there was cheering and clapping, but from beyond the fences of the Pharming company came the sounds of shrill protest. The Animal Protection League plastered Holland's bus stops with posters showing mothers with udders. Did the professor believe he could play God, or the Devil? Had he forgotten who Mengele was? At night, shadowy figures in balaclavas destroyed a number of field stations for genetically engineered corn and potatoes. Responsibility for the attacks was claimed by a group calling itself The Raging Potatoes.

'Terrorists', the newspapers ruled. 'The tail-end of the Red Army Faction in the Netherlands.'

Yet these were no run-of-the-mill vandals; the pamphlets

they distributed read like scientific publications, albeit without the footnotes and bibliography. Given the damage caused, the Dutch intelligence service decided to keep an eye on this new band of musketeers – and made a failed attempt to infiltrate it using students from the Agricultural University at Wageningen.

During editorial meetings at the magazine I worked for in the early 1990s, we too wondered aloud who was behind this violence. What kind of people could both commit vandalism *and* have university training in genetics? Because I had studied at Wageningen and was therefore considered familiar with the breeding ground of The Raging Potatoes, I was sent to find out.

U

At a staunchly vegetarian squat in Wageningen I met the members of the contact group Biotechnology and Society, some of whom were working on their dissertations. I was vaguely familiar with them, these anarcho boys and girls with their mildly frivolous trappings. In the buttonholes of their black coats they wore clown's bells. They all had a bedraggled look, like the dogs who belonged to their household. 'Human beings once evolved from prey to predator,' one said. 'To celebrate that fact, they perform ritual slaughter.'

'Ritual murder,' someone else corrected him.

'Bullfights,' said a third.

The agreement was no names. We were seated in the shared kitchen of an old house along the dyke, amid crates of vegetables from the collective market garden. One of the squatters, a doctoral student with an array of rings in his ear, had told me beforehand: 'We are to The Raging Potatoes what Sinn Fein is to the IRA.'

Forty thousand years ago, he said, evolution had got out of hand. What palaeontologists called the great leap forward in fact amounted to the consolidation of man's hegemony over the animals. *Homo sapiens* had escaped from the peloton of the species and succeeded in subjugating all other creatures to his will. Darwin was quoted: 'Animals whom we have made our slaves, we do not like to consider our equals.'

I should look at it this way: wild animals had been waylaid on their evolutionary paths. They were caged, tamed and bred in the service of man. But that domestication had not been limited to horses, wolves or goats; African slaves were also thrown in chains and sold on the markets of the world.

A girl sitting on an old couch with her dog added to that list the repression of women. Power always came down to control over genetic material.

I had to stop and think about that one.

'By means of sexual morality,' the girl with the dog said.

Suddenly, everyone had stopped talking.

'That's why people respond so hysterically to homosexuality, because it means Mummy and Daddy's genes aren't being passed down the way they're supposed to.'

I said: 'And so now you people are out to reverse the course of history, or rather of evolution?'

'No,' the doctoral student said. 'We're trying to keep certain excesses from repeating themselves in the name of genetics.'

'The Holocaust,' I said.

'Sure, or what about apartheid?'

U

During my tour of the animal-testing laboratories of what was called the BioTechnion, I saw cages containing genetically modified rodents that looked like normal mice, except that they were three times the size of their non-manipulated counterparts.

'High-risk waste' read the sign on a tray covered in mouse droppings.

'What's high-risk about mouse droppings?' I asked the manager.

'They're carcinogenic,' he said. When I didn't respond straight away, he said: 'They cause cancer.'

The head of Molecular Biology at the ITAL (Institute for Applied Atomic Energy in Agriculture) opened the door of a secure laboratory. A lab assistant wearing a surgical mask and Plexiglas safety glasses was dunking ultra-thin slices of carnation stem in a Petri dish. With her tweezers she immersed the green confetti in a soup of special bacteria that served to carry foreign genetic traits into the plant cells, for the purpose of creating carnations that lasted longer in a vase.

'What I do is unfamiliar, and therefore scary, and therefore dangerous,' she said with a sardonic laugh.

I was led along to an enclosed cubicle marked 'quarantine' – it was separated from the rest of the lab by an airlock with a pair of heavy steel doors. The technologists working with germs on the far side of the portholes were covered from head to toe in white suits.

'After each experiment, all life in the cubicle is gassed,' the head of Molecular Biology said.

I had heard that The Raging Potatoes, whose attempts to eradicate dangerous technologies had even reached as far as this laboratory, had forerunners in Germany. Close to Cologne, a female commando unit had scaled the fence around an experimental plot at the Max Planck Institute, where thousands of petunias with a built-in corn gene were in full bloom. They foiled the experiment by planting a few everyday house plants of their own here and there. Less playful was the act committed by The Seething Viruses in Darmstadt, who burnt down the local genetic institute on New Year's Day 1989 – according to their pamphlet, to head off the pioneers of 'human breeding'.

U

Before long I had collected an armful of arguments for and against genetic engineering. But how to weigh them against each other?

There was no denying the past: Mendel's insights, half understood, had produced the blackest pages in history. Gene technologists like Herman de Boer defended their work by the parable of the breadknife: one and the same tool could be used to slice bread or to cut someone's head off. They applied their technology, they claimed, strictly to noble purposes. But that did not alter the fact that their tools were still sticky with old blood. There was no way simply to erase the past and start with a clean slate. And it was precisely that message that was given during the public lecture I attended later.

The title of the talk was: 'Nature vs Nurture: Genetics in the first half of the twentieth century'. The venue was the wood-panelled dining room of Hotel de Wereld in Wageningen.

There were about forty people in attendance, including a few punkish types who had apparently not been told that the white rat as a fashion accessory had become passé, at least beyond Wageningen. Seated on one of the broad windowsills, a shaven-headed boy was letting his rat run through his cupped hands like a treadmill.

The floor beneath our feet was hallowed ground: it was here, on 5 May 1945, that the German surrender in the Netherlands had been signed. A framed photograph showed a German and a Canadian general sitting opposite each other uneasily. Above the door was a sign reading CAPITULATION HALL – these days, wedding parties were held here as well. It was still light outside. Through the windows you could see the 'No More War' monument at the corner of Liberation Street.

The speaker, as it turned out, was a denim-clad philosopher of science. On a screen behind the rostrum appeared a prediction from 1922: 'In the near future, mankind will be able to synthesize life forms that are unthinkable in the natural world', which turned out to be a quote from the man known as 'Lenin's biologist'. This Nikolai Vavilov was a first-generation Mendelian who considered it his mission in life to ensure successful harvests. Under the czar he had been sent on expedition to Persia and Afghanistan, in search of frost-resistant strains of wheat and rye. His family of Petersburg merchants was 'proletarianized' by the Bolsheviks in 1917, but that did nothing to curb Nikolai's enthusiasm. In the process of assembling what was to become the biggest seed bank in the world, he travelled to the cradles of the cultivated crops: corn in Mexico, the potato in Peru, wheat in Palestine. All the seeds and tubers he could lay his hands on he had shipped to Leningrad. In an interview in Paris, he said: 'What I am interested in is a worldwide agrarian philosophy. Or rather: a Marxist agrarian philosophy. Allow me to cite Marx: "Scientists used to study the world in order to understand it; we study it in order to change it."'

The listeners chuckled. Vavilov's words and deeds had fallen on fertile soil.

Across the Soviet Union, Vavilov had set up dozens of strategically located seed banks, based on the idea that a plant breeder should have at his disposal the broadest possible palette 'in order to provide guidance for evolution'.

By 1924, Vavilov's collection included 64,000 species and varieties. Geneticists elsewhere were either full of admiration, or mocked him. The mockers set no store by Mendel, but rather in Lamarck's hundred-year-old thesis: a trait acquired by an organism during its lifetime can be passed along to its progeny. Bringing back frost-resistant rye from Afghanistan was, in their view, needlessly complicated; rye plants that survive a period of extreme cold become frost-resistant by themselves. In other words, you can 'harden' organisms or otherwise force them to adapt to their surroundings, and those adaptations remain inheritable.

We heard that a certain Paul Kammerer, a Viennese expert on reptiles and amphibians, had resurrected Lamarckism shortly after the First World War. In addition to his work as a zoologist, Dr Kammerer was an accomplished musician, a Freemason, an atheist and a pacifist. He could make salamanders change colour by changing the colour of the substrate in their terrariums. This was what had long been referred to as a chameleonic trait, and was not seen as world-shaking news. But it was through his experiments with amphibians that Kammerer created an international furore. In his Vienna laboratory he had forced the midwife toad, a species that normally mates on dry land, to reproduce in water. He was interested in observing how these creatures would cope in a wet and slippery environment. The midwife toad does not possess 'nuptial pads': swellings on the palms of its forefeet that other amphibians use to keep from sliding off each other's backs. After some difficulty, these terrestrial frogs were able to mount for mating, and then the miracle happened: suddenly the fourth generation possessed nuptial pads. Terrestrial midwife toads had been born with a trait belonging to aquatic toads, and not by cross-breeding but by adaptation.

On tour in the United States in 1924, Dr Kammerer was

hailed by the *New York Times* as 'the new Darwin'. The pads on the feet of his terrestrial toads proved the correctness of Lamarck's thesis. Heredity was not engraved in the plasma of the germ cell, but was something that could be moulded by environmental pressure. Inborn traits were unimportant; what mattered were the acquired ones. Nurture had triumphed over nature, and with that were negated all claims to superiority by the Aryan or the nobleman.

The speaker also showed us a quote from the idealist Paul Kammerer: 'These amazing results open an entirely new road for the improvement of our race, for the purification and strengthening of all mankind. And that in a lovelier and more dignified fashion than has until now been propagated by fanatical racists.' Kammerer spoke out against the *Hakenkreuzler*, the skinheads of the Viennese student body who were taking to the streets in aggressive gangs each Saturday in the 1920s, bearing swastika banners. He railed against the rabid anti-Semitism that had manifested itself early on in Austria in the form of 'Don't Buy from Jews' campaigns and the promises from politicians and priests of a 'Jew-free Vienna'. In Moscow, the Soviet Minister of Culture recognized in him the profile of the socialist hero, and ordered a film, *Salamandra*, made about this foreign genius who had proven that one's origins did not define one's future. The surroundings in which you grew up, that was the thing. Given a classless, egalitarian society, a new and uniform brand of human would automatically arise.

Lamarckian heredity was such a crucial – indeed, indispensable – link in the creation of *Homo sovieticus* that Kammerer was offered a lecturer's chair at the University of Moscow. And he would indeed have left for the Soviet Union had the journal *Nature* not published the results of its peer review in August 1926, a report which showed that Kammerer's terrestrial frogs had acquired their nuptial pads by means of a subcutaneous injection of Indian ink.

The speaker paused for a sip of water. 'A few weeks later,' he went on, 'Kammerer sent his comrades in Moscow a letter.' He was innocent, he insisted, but because he had no way to prove it, he could only offer his apologies for the commotion created. Kammerer closed his letter with the words: 'Tomorrow I hope to gather sufficient courage to put an end to my ruined life.' The next morning he shot himself through the head.

We walked outside in silence. The street lights had come on, but strangely enough the here and now had gone out of Hotel de Wereld; my thoughts were floating somewhere between Vienna and Moscow.

Though Kammerer was banished to the sidelines of history as a fraud, his death in no way ended the struggle between the Mendelians and the Lamarckians. The Soviet Union was not about to give up. In August 1927, less than a year after Kammerer's demise, *Pravda* parachuted in a new standard-bearer of Lamarckism: the obscure Trofim Lysenko, a man without a university education. On a kolkhoz, a collective farm, somewhere in the Soviet Republic of Azerbaijan, he was said to have turned winter wheat into spring wheat by 'treating' the seed, and not by cross-pollination.

Lysenko's star was on the rise. This proletarian man of practice was said to moisten the seeds and then freeze them, whereupon they were suddenly transformed into varieties that produced abundant harvests. The promise of Lysenko's method grew and grew, particularly during the famine of 1932 and 1933; a famine that was the result of Stalin's programme of agricultural collectivization, and led to millions of deaths and widespread cannibalism in the Ukraine alone. In the wake of that catastrophe, heads had to roll; the age of the great purges dawned in the Soviet Union. And as the leading man at the Lenin Academy for Agricultural Sciences, Nikolai Vavilov was next in line for the Gulag. The case stated against him was that he, with his bourgeois background and overseas contacts, had committed 'agricultural sabotage': his fixation on the setting up of seed banks had caused him to lose sight of the people's needs.

A Mendelian viewpoint was suddenly being referred to as 'a class-hostile position on the biology front'. At conferences, Lysenko was allotted more and more time for his speeches.

At one such meeting in 1936, Vavilov asked him: 'So you possess the ability to alter species at the level of their hereditary traits?'

'Yes, comrade.'

Lysenko declared Mendel's 'pea laws' null and void. Mendel was a monk, and a German one at that, who had produced a false, statically conservative doctrine which the Bolsheviks rejected, opting instead for dynamism and progress.

Vavilov, 'Lenin's biologist', was dethroned in 1938 by 'Stalin's biologist'. Two years later he was hustled into a black car and taken to a Gulag prison on the Volga, where he died as a martyr for genetics.

That was the East.

ᴗ

But what about the West?

The first, immediately striking thing there was: in Europe and America, the drive to breed better humans was embraced in equal measure by the left and the right, by progressives and conservatives. The vast majority of geneticists wanted to apply breeding techniques to society. In 1920, the chairman of the American eugenics movement foresaw the supreme revolution for mankind 'when human mating is raised to the same high level as that in horse breeding'. He dreamed of a day when a woman would demand the 'biological-genealogical history' of a marriage candidate, 'just as an animal breeder will not accept a stallion without a pedigree'. Society, the first biographer of Gregor Mendel wrote in 1924, must demand a great sacrifice from paupers and invalids: that they 'forego parental bliss'. Rebutting political leaders whose empathy led them to defend the weakest, many geneticists brought to bear the principle of the 'survival of the fittest'. Although 'fit' or adapted was not the same as strong, Darwin's theory was often distorted into an equation for 'might makes right'. Those who wished to preserve the defective and the deformed were defying the laws of nature. Add to that the futuristic view of Nietzsche's *Übermensch*, who would look back on today's humans in 'painful shame', and you had the principal ingredients of Social Darwinism.

In the interests of making a start somewhere, the Dutchman Herman Bernelot Moens proposed the one-off crossing of a Negro male with a female chimpanzee. He predicted the birth of a half-human, half-ape, a primal creature that could shed light on both man's origins and his destiny. In a tract published in 1905, he put it thus: 'Man must elevate himself to such a degree that religious belief seems childish to him. Only then can a higher type of human , the *Übermensch*, arise, who looks down upon contemporary humanity as we do upon the ape-man.' Horses and donkeys produced mules, so what reason was there to suppose that the experiment would not work? The taboo on bestiality could be circumvented by employing artificial insemination, 'thereby avoiding any further ethical objections'. Moens assembled a list of impressive recommendations, and even a promise of funding from Queen Wilhelmina of the Netherlands, but saw his project founder with the arrival of the First World War.

In both Scandinavia and America, eugenics got off to a successful start. The way was led by California, where the castration and, from 1900 on, sterilization of criminals became common practice. To lend a helping hand to natural selection, tens of thousands of indigent women were rendered infertile against their will. At the same time, racial segregation and strict taboos served to prevent the abomination of white women bearing the child of a black man. More and more countries took action to keep their undesirable subjects from reproducing. After the application of Mendelian insights helped to improve vastly their grain harvests, the Swedes became particularly enthusiastic. In 1921 they were the first country to open an Institute for Racial Biology. After measuring and photographing tens of thousands of Swedes, the subjects were divided into desirable and less desirable genotypes. The next step was the sterilization of the inferior, on a voluntary basis at first.

Finland and Norway joined in, and in the early 1930s Denmark decided to banish promiscuous or 'erotically imbecilic' girls to the uninhabited island of Sprogø, where the ferryman saw to it that no male human set foot. '*The right to live* must be distinguished from the right to *give new life*', a Dutch defence of eugenics put it in 1926. 'The dissemination of the defective seed always undermines society' – and the improvement of living standards could do nothing to change that. Hadn't Plato in his *Republic*, after all, depicted the ideal society as a stud farm, where all physical or mental shortcomings were excluded from reproduction?

It was on to this bandwagon that Germany hopped in 1933.

In the free state of Danzig, Gregor Mendel's portrait was printed on a 10 pfennig postage stamp. HEALTHY CHILDREN, read the text at the top left. GLOWING FUTURE was printed in the opposite, right-hand corner. The National Socialists described their doctrine pithily as 'biology applied to politics'. Every facet of their principles had a link to natural processes: the urge for *Lebensraum* could be explained by the concept of the 'biotope', of a species' perfect ecological surroundings; the Führer principle could be observed among alpha males in a wolf pack; the natural phenomenon of territorialism justified the war of aggression. Pacifism was unnatural. With Hitler in the chancellery, the Organic Age had displaced the Technological Age. The NSDAP's Racial Policy Bureau focused on categorizing people as able-bodied, inferior or, for the remainder, as 'non-starters'. The German people, Hitler's ideologists claimed, needed a 'race doctor' to rid them of noxious, foreign taints. A traditional doctor healed the individual organism, but that after all was only mortal. The *Erbanlage* (gene), on the other hand, lived on – it was much more important to keep *that* healthy. *Aufartung durch Ausmerzung*, racial improvement through annihilation, became the core of this project for human back-breeding.

The number of hours dedicated to biology lessons in German schools rose by fifty per cent, at the expense of foreign languages. The objective: to 'biologize' popular thinking.

At a second-hand bookshop I bought a pair of German textbooks from the Nazi era: *Inheritance, Race, People* for the primary schools, and *Family Science and Racial Biology* for the secondary schools. Under National Socialism, pupils were instilled with a love for the Teutonic forests, where Ur-Germans brought down wisents with dagger and spear. Early on, girls were instructed in mothering, and everyone took part in experiments with fruit flies: the Ministry of Education was ordered to see to sufficient quantities of glass jars, chloroform and fruit flies, to ensure the continuity of lessons in Mendelian genetics.

And German children learned to recite this verse by heart:

> Keep your blood pure!
> It is not yours alone
> It comes from far, it flows much further
> Thousands of forefathers give it substance
> The entire future flows into it

At the back of their textbooks were blank pages on which each pupil had to draw his own family tree – as a pedigree. Room was left to fill in the colour of the eyes, skin and hair of each ancestor.

'No boy or girl', Hitler wrote in *Mein Kampf*, 'should be allowed to leave school without first acquiring a total understanding of the absolute necessity of having blood that is pure.'

HEIM INS REICH
(BACK TO THE REICH)

P OST FROM VIENNA. PROTRUDING from the letterbox was
an envelope from Hans Brabenetz – his name and address
were printed in block capitals on the back.

As I opened it with a house key, I marvelled at the
phenomenon of the letter – a curious medium, something
you associated with the past, or at least with a tradition. In
Brabenetz's letter ('as promised') I found a copy of a centuries-
old family tree. In Lipica I had shown him Primula's pedigree,
which went back as far as Conversano Savona; now he had sent
me the pedigree of Savona himself, with as his most distant
ancestor the mare Perletta, born in Lipica in 1838.

On the final evening of our excursion, we sat and talked
in the lobby of Hotel Maestoso. Raising his index finger, Hans
Brabenetz once again recited his motto:

He who breeds the horse and dreams Olympia's palm
 to win
Shall choose a mother to his aims akin.

'Virgil,' he said. 'The *Georgics*.'
All it took was one question to get him going: 'So how
does one go about becoming a hippologist?'

Brabenetz clenched his walking stick between his knees and rested his hands on the handle. 'Do you know the Hungarian writer Molnar? Molnar would have said: "Well, how does one go about becoming a prostitute? The first time you do it out of curiosity, then out of love, and after that for the money."'

Our guide had the bravura typical of old men who have nothing left to lose. We were drinking beer. Opposite us, a Bosnian Muslim sat flipping through a coffee-table book. He looked like a cleric, dressed in plus fours and a high-collared smock. On his head was a dark-red fez.

The true hippologist, Brabenetz confessed, will always admit that the thoroughbred Arab possesses a more noble countenance than the Lipizzaner. 'In fact, the Lipizzaner's proportions are rather skewed. His forelegs are too short, his head is too massive, he has no withers, and his back, well, it's not really right at all.'

Brabenetz had not been brought up with this professional expertise. He came from a family of artisans, tailors to be precise. They owned no horses. Hans grew up in Vienna's 13th District, around Schloss Schönbrunn – the area where he and Susi still lived. 'As a boy I knew every horse in the neighbourhood by name, and after school each day I would go by and say hello to them.'

He was born in April 1923 and attended secondary school in the late 1930s. I was curious to hear whether he had been taught from the Nazis' biology books – with their emphasis on genetics and the physiognomy of Jews, Gypsies and criminals.

'Not at all,' he said. 'Austria was too Catholic for that. Maybe there were textbooks like that after the *Anschluss*, but I never saw them.'

Had he ever experimented with fruit flies?

I was met with a blank stare. He had wanted to join the cavalry. During the 1939 mobilization he hadn't yet been of age, but one year later, when he reached seventeen, he had signed up as quickly as possible. 'While I was still in the recruitment office, I had my first setback. "We don't work with mounted units any more," was the first thing they told me after I had joined up.'

Fortunately, artillery horses were still used to pull the cannons. During his officer training, Brabenetz learned to ride and drive horses. 'Even a sergeant felt like a demigod in those days,' he said. 'In the barracks, the non-coms all had a room of their own.'

In June 1941 – with an eye to further advancement – he had volunteered again, this time for the invasion of the Soviet Union, Operation Barbarossa.

> *An Neckars Weiden, am Rheine,*
> *Sie alle meinen, es wäre*
> *Sonst nirgend besser zu wohnen.*
> *Ich aber will dem Kaukasos zu!*

> On Neckar's willowy banks,
> and on the Rhine, it's said,
> there is no better place to live.
> Yet I want to go to the Caucasus!

That was based on Hölderlin, the poet. That was what they used to recite.

Brabenetz grinned and, before I could react, offered his excuse: 'You see, I was young and naïve.'

The Jewish boys from his class, he told me of his own accord, simply disappeared one day. 'And believe me, at the time I never stopped for a moment to wonder why.'

In the summer of 1941, Brabenetz's regiment landed at the Crimea. They chased the Russians out before them like rabbits, across the dusty plain behind the Yalta coastal range. Driving a team of horses loaded with radio equipment, he had followed the advancing front. Then autumn came, and he and his unit were left to spend the winter on the Kertsh Peninsula. 'The counteroffensive came at Christmas. We didn't fight, we just walked. Across the snowy steppes. Those who fell froze to death. I saw it happen to a friend of mine. All I could do for him was take the chain with his identity tag on it, so that we could report him killed and not missing. But I didn't dare to take off my gloves. I just walked on.'

He showed me the palms of his hands, full of rough and calloused scar tissue from the frostbite he had suffered in the final days of 1941. In the lazaret, Hans Brabenetz had to be spoon-fed like a big, eighteen-year-old baby, because both his hands were bandaged. Once he recovered he was sent home for three weeks' sick leave.

Back in Vienna, in March 1942, he had visited the morning training session with the Lipizzaner stallions. He sat in the first gallery of the Winter Riding School, the sole visitor. In the arena below, German officers were being given riding lessons by a man with the stern eyebrows of a flamenco dancer: Colonel Podhajsky, the German-appointed commander. Brabenetz liked the fact that the instructor used the Austro-Hungarian and not the Prussian equestrian terms. That was special; even the monkeys in the Vienna Zoo had by then been dubbed 'German monkeys' and the elephants 'German elephants'. 'In fact, for seven whole years we Austrians *were* Germans.' It had filled him with pride to see that the Royal Spanish Riding School had held its own as a bastion of Austrian identity.

Meanwhile, Podhajsky had spotted the visitor. He gestured to him to come down.

'I hurried down the steps and saluted. "What are you doing here?" he asked. And before I could say anything: "Why aren't you working? Why don't you make yourself useful and grab a broom?" I tried to reply, but he was too fast for me. "Name?" "Unit?" Only when he asked what business I had being in Vienna, did I have the chance to tell him that I was on sick leave. "Well then, don't you have a girlfriend?" "Yes, Herr Oberst, but she works until five o'clock."'

Posthumously, Podhajsky became a popular hero of whom no one spoke ill. In equestrian circles far beyond Austria he was known as 'the good Nazi' – on the basis of one achievement: he had piloted his noble Lipizzaner stallions safely through the Second World War.

'*Ein schwieriger Mensch,* a difficult fellow,' Brabenetz ruled, 'just like Herbert von Karajan.'

I searched his face for a glimmer of sarcasm, but saw total earnest. Podhajsky, he went on, held the rank of colonel because that went with his function, but everyone could see that he had never been to the front: he wore no medals on his chest. 'On the last day of the war he took off his *Wehrmacht* uniform and quickly put on an armband with the Austrian red-white-red on it.' He snorted as he said this.

Podhajsky himself never viewed this defection as an act of disloyalty. In his autobiography he recounted how his wife Verena had taken his uniform away in a laundry basket and disposed of it, a few hours before the Americans rolled in. That was why he was never taken prisoner, while Brabenetz, a good deal lower in rank, was arrested on the spot and had to perform forced labour in Byelorussia for two and a half years.

I was reminded of our first phone conversation. 'Have you

ever been a soldier?' Brabenetz had found that very important. For him, a military background was a prerequisite for understanding anything about the world of horses. I hadn't understood the connection at the time, but now it began to dawn. It had to do with the typical martial mentality of the professional soldier, who thought in straight lines, angularly at the very most, but never flexibly or 'by contingency'. That was the way he was trained, or perhaps even broken in. The military man *pur sang* had distanced himself from a whole range of human traits – spontaneity, creativity, independence, compassion. His soldierly upbringing in the barracks, or nurture, had made him more and more like the domesticated animal. All soldiers respond reflexively to vocal aids ('At ease!') called 'orders'. The soldier can stand motionless at attention or lift his knees rhythmically while marching on the spot, one-two, one-two, as in the piaffe. The well-trained soldier has, as a matter of course, mastered the goose-step. Military guards and other elite units were also trained in marching with the legs extended, often with torso and head turned ninety degrees to face the leader, as in the equestrian shoulder-in.

Hans Brabenetz's discerning eye and breeder's instincts were not the product of any formal education. During his officer's training, the *Blut und Boden* (blood and soil) curriculum did not feature detailed biological tuition, but was limited to slogans directed against Jews and Bolsheviks. In 1942 he was transferred to Croatia. Along the Danube, close to the city of Vukovar, he trained recruits to hunt partisans. Besides the locals who fought for Hitler's cause, there were also the dyed-in-the-wool fascists of the Ustaša, the Croatian anti-communist guerrilla army, but they went their own way. And one also had the Domobran, the standing army of the Croatian vassal state. It was Brabenetz's task to teach Domobran conscripts to be ruthless in their fight against Tito.

I asked whether he had known then about Jasenovac, about the murders of partisans, Serbs and Jews that had taken place in that camp – without ovens, but on an industrial scale nonetheless. This 'Auschwitz of the Balkans', after all, had been located close to his barracks, and many Croatians had vented their hatred quite openly – with one archbishop to the fore, who proclaimed 'It is no longer the tongue that speaks, but the blood!'

Brabenetz shook his head: the name 'Jasenovac' he had heard only after the war, and that the Ustaše had taken advantage of the war to rid themselves of the Serbs – that had been news to him as well.

'The Ustaše were your allies,' I said.

'Well, I saw them a few times, but I never had any dealings with them.' As a regular *Wehrmacht* officer, there were many things of which he had not been aware. 'Often, everything seemed to be under control,' was how he put it. 'You could walk into a yard with no problem, to talk to a farmer, but afterwards you weren't sure whether you'd been talking to a farmer or to a partisan.'

Most of the 'farmers' he had dealt with, he went on, were tenants on the estate of the Eltz family; Frau Antoinette Gräfin von und zu Eltz had dedicated herself to the breeding of Arabs, Noniuses and Lipizzaners.

Hans Brabenetz rubbed the elbow patches on his jumper and told me about an army veterinarian by the name of Frielinghaus, who had also been sent to Vukovar. Dr Frielinghaus had been granted a very special mandate by the Berlin high command: his mission was to buy up racially pure Lipizzaners for Hitler's racially pure Reich.

Apparently, in the thick of the war, the German top brass had actively pursued Lipizzaners that were dispersed around the Balkans. At least ten questions sprang to mind, but Brabenetz was not about to be interrupted. Countess Eltz, he said, had been reimbursed royally, and she had handed over a total of about two dozen horses. At the time, Frielinghaus had told him about meeting the countess. She was sitting at her desk when he came in, dwarfed by a study 'the size of a granary'. She had offered to help transport the horses, but that wasn't necessary: the horses selected for Hitler had excellent hooves.

'And your Kitty was one of them.'

So there was that as well. But first I asked about that active acquisition policy – what was the idea behind it?

'To safeguard valuable breeding material.'

'But only Lipizzaners?'

Brabenetz raised his head and looked at me through his tinted spectacles: with the exception of a few Arabs, yes, only Lipizzaners.

The Führer, I realized, had implemented an ambitious programme aimed at bringing back, *heim ins Reich*, as many Lipizzaners as possible, having collected them from all over the Balkans: from a monastery in Serbia, the Eltz family castle in Vukovar, and even from the Macedonian stud, where the king of Yugoslavia used to have his Lipizzaners bred. With the exception of those belonging to the countess, the animals were simply confiscated. The herd belonging to the exiled King Petar II was transferred to the Piber stud by way of Skopje and Belgrade. Although the exact motive behind it all was not immediately clear to me, a certain pattern could be discerned in the confiscation, transport and uniting of the

Lipizzaners. Piber, as it turned out, was not the final destination: in October 1942 the stables there were cleared as well, as were those at Lipica a bit later on. As soon as Mussolini fell in 1943, German troops took over the cradle of the Lipizzaners, and the animals once again went on transport – just as they had in 1797, 1805, 1809 and 1915.

All these Lipizzaner populations were guided across the Alps by Adolf Hitler's hand and brought together like long-lost sons in the village of Hostau, in the Sudetenland.

'As an Austrian,' Brabenetz added immediately, 'I reject the term "Sudetenland". That is a purely National Socialist concept. I prefer to speak of "German Bohemia".'

Most of the evacuations were carried out under the pretext of 'the partisan threat' – a claim that was not entirely confected: one of the Lipizzaner stud farms in Croatia had been emptied by Tito's forces, the suspicion being that they were keeping the animals hidden in the densely forested hills nearby, or that they were using them for reconnaissance patrols.

Only the Lipizzaners from the 'safe' Axis countries of Hungary and Romania stayed put – there wouldn't have been enough room for them at Hostau anyway.

'You know,' Brabenetz said, leaning towards me 'you're lucky I'm still alive. Once I'm gone, there's no one else who could tell you these stories first-hand.'

Suddenly his wife was standing beside us: Susi Brabenetz had come to ask her husband to go with them for a walk.

'*Spazieren?*' His voice reverted immediately to a deaf man's volume. 'But I'm in the middle of a conversation!'

Hans Brabenetz looked over his shoulder towards where a little group of excursionists had gathered on the lobby's slippery tiles. This time, though, he stuck to his guns. Frau Brabenetz shook her head gently, turned around and led the group outside like a traffic warden.

Hitler's haven for the Lipizzaners, her husband continued, was tucked away in the Bohemian Forest, in the modern-day Czech Republic, close to the German border. That area had once belonged to the Danube Monarchy, and was later a part of Czechoslovakia. It was inhabited by a great many ethnic Germans or *Volksdeutschen*, who, wishing to become *Reichsdeutschen*, had begun in the 1930s to demand with increasing vehemence that their sternly led neighbour annex the region. In October 1938, when the well-oiled German military machine rolled in, they were met in every town and village by a solid hedge of arms raised in salute. This annexation of the Sudetenland, a few months after the *Anschluss* of Austria and barely one year before the invasion of Poland, was Hitler's last 'non-aggressive' conquest, with the blessings – 'peace in our time' – of Great Britain, France and Italy in the form of the Treaty of Munich. The Czechs were thrown out of their houses and driven away in long, slow processions. Only when the Sudetenland was finally more German than Germany itself did the Lipizzaners arrive.

The stud farm where they were housed had once been used for cavalry mounts. With the arrival of the new herds, Hostau, consisting of 600 hectares of meadowland around a stately mansion, was transformed into a model breeding station. A German newspaper predicted that this little village of potters and ropemakers would, from now on, be famous not for its ceramics, but for its noble Lipizzaners. Here the world's most famous white horses had found their 'beautiful green pastures'.

It became the largest Lipizzaner stud farm in history, and its commander, Major Hubert Rudofsky, had been a close acquaintance of Hans Brabenetz.

'I saw him as my foster father,' Brabenetz said. He described Rudofsky as a true horseman who, as a matter of principle, had never learned to drive a car, and whose vanity led him to change his uniform sometimes as often as three times a day – 'just like Hermann Göring'. Among other ways, their friendship had expressed itself in the fact that Brabenetz had inherited most of Rudofsky's valuable collection of equestrian drawings and paintings, which hung on the walls of his home in Vienna.

Between 1943 and 1945, Major Rudofsky had overseen more than 300 Lipizzaner breeding mares and a large number of stallions, a herd augmented each spring by the birth of around one hundred foals. By May 1945 there were – counting these foals – some 400 Lipizzaners at Hostau, approximately two-thirds of the breed's reproductive capacity. I thought about Colonel Podhajsky in Vienna, who had been in charge of only forty stallions – and about how it was he alone, Alois Podhajsky, who had been placed on a pedestal as 'the man who saved the Lipizzaners from the turmoil of the Second World War'.

That was unfair. The mares were more important.

We fell silent. The Bosnian man opposite us got up; I wondered whether he had been listening.

Brabenetz leaned back and remarked that it was all Hollywood's fault. The fault, in fact, of producer Walt Disney: he had made a movie that was based ostensibly on Podhajsky's memoirs. 'But it was purely a fantasy.'

When I asked about the title, Brabenetz dismissed the question. The truth, he felt, would be of greater use to me. 'And the truth of the matter is that Podhajsky was revered after the war, while Rudofsky was locked away in a Czech prisoner-of-war camp.'

I asked whether Rudofsky had children, and whether they might still be alive.

'He never married.' After his release, Rudofsky was

banished to Germany. There he had waited passively until 1973, when Podhajsky died and he cautiously emerged from the shadows. Brabenetz had stood up for him by urging the authorities in Vienna to correct the skewed historical record and officially recognize Rudofsky's role in the Lipizzaners' survival.

'And?'

'He received that recognition in 1985, in the form of a certificate of appreciation and a gala performance in his honour. But once Hollywood has established a certain view of things, there's nothing you can really do.' Rudofsky died the following year, in 1986. Hans Brabenetz had spoken at his funeral. On behalf of the Friends of the Royal Spanish Riding School he had laid a wreath on the man's grave – and that was it.

I asked about Hostau: was there anything left to see?

'Nothing. The Germans were chased out again in 1945. Not a person remained, and not a horse either.'

I suddenly felt the urge to visit the place where Hitler had rounded up virtually the entire Lipizzaner population. Without a doubt, the very sand would still bear the imprint of a fanatical belief in racial superiority.

Brabenetz could read my mind. 'Don't bother,' he said. 'The only thing there is a warehouse for potatoes. Nothing more.'

PLANT 4711

IN AUGUST 2002, THE Vltava overran its banks and wreaked
havoc in the city. Torrential summer rains over the course
of a week caused the river to rise to seven metres above its
normal level. Prague's underground rail tunnels were flooded,
as was the low-lying zoo, where an elephant drowned and a
seal escaped from its saltwater basin – the animal was fished
out of the Elbe later, more dead than alive, close to Dresden.

> Hi, it's me with news about the Military Archives. The
> building has been in a terrible state since the 2002 flood.
> But miraculously enough, the documents dealing with
> the military stud at Hostau were not damaged. Three
> cardboard boxes full, they tell me.

That was Martina's first report on the Lipizzaners' Bohemian
past, as found in the Czech archives. I had asked her to do
some digging around concerning the stud farm ('*hřebčín*',
she taught me, with an 'r' that rolled around the tip of your
tongue) at Hostau (Hostouň in Czech). Her own tongue was
adorned with a metal rivet, topped by a little black ball.
Martina was a 'fashionista' with dark, choppy hair who had
studied Dutch and Japanese at Olomouc. Her manga years

were behind her now, indeed she'd had her fill of Japan and the Japanese entirely and was preparing to write her doctoral thesis on colonial Dutch literature from a feminist perspective – a 'gender perspective', as she corrected me. I had met her at a literature festival in a Prague theatre, where a blue arrow was painted high up along one wall: THIS WAS THE WATERLINE DURING THE 2002 FLOOD.

Because my mobile couldn't receive photos, Martina emailed me a few pictures of the Military Archives. What popped up on my monitor was a weather-beaten building, undeniably in Habsburg style, with a partly wrecked front wall. Ostensibly decorative gratings hung crookedly in front of the windows, the window frames and panes themselves having been washed away. Tarpaulins had been stretched above the entrance gate to keep visitors from being hit by falling rubble.

Martina provided me with a detailed progress report, first by text message and after that, in more expanded form, by email. When she arrived at the old parade grounds, she had first checked in at a cargo container that served as the porter's lodge. Hanging from an old-fashioned hat rack were a policeman's baton and a walkie-talkie.

'Oops,' she texted, 'you're not allowed to take pictures here.'

I learned that the archives were only half-staffed and half-stocked. All the documents on the ground floor had dissolved in the brown waters of the Vltava in 2002; only the storeroom on the upper floor had remained dry.

At the top of a staircase Martina had found a reading room with fluorescent lighting and an austere station-hall clock. She used her mobile to take a few snapshots: I saw Formica tables and broad windowsills with yellowish-green house plants.

The Hostau boxes were duly waiting for her at the lending counter. Shortly before the flood, she told me, the filing cabinets from A to K had moved to the first floor in preparation for a planned refurbishment.

Martina: 'So what do you think of that!?'

'Beginner's luck,' I texted back – accompanied by one of those winking emoticons, to make sure the irony wasn't lost on her.

She was fond of dogs, not of horses. But her professional pride didn't allow for the cutting of corners, and she plunged enthusiastically into the Lipizzaners' past. An archivist had given her a list of the boxes' contents, and she was expected to mark those items that were of interest. That selection was then presented to an invisible censor in an adjoining room, who would give or withhold his *nihil obstat* for viewing.

The very first request came back by return post.

'*Spáleno*,' was the reply. Burned.

The documented history of the biggest Lipizzaner stud farm of all time had apparently been decimated not only by water, but also by fire.

What did emerge were orders from the Red Army dating from the summer of 1945, which also applied to the military stud. There were tables showing the punishments meted out to those looting the hastily deserted homes of Germans in and around Hostau; 'Measures to prevent the spread of venereal diseases and alcoholism'; and the weekly rations:

Soldiers	Prisoners of war
25 g butter	–
40 g lard	–
125 g margarine	10 g margarine
750 g meat	–
500 g bread (daily)	250 g bread (daily)

And the horses?

Not a word about the horses. Only a request from the veterinary staff for supplies to carry out blood tests for equine typhoid, and the announcement of a public auction of horses 'discharged from military service'.

For archive material marked *Tajne* (Secret), Martina had to wait an hour, sometimes longer. The censor first had to assess and then release them, bearing his initials and a stamp reading DECLASSIFIED. Once again, however, they contained nothing about the Lipizzaners. There was a speech by a Czechoslovakian brigadier general from 1948 ('This year, our country moved ahead along the only possible path, the path that leads to socialism. This is what the people have decided! This is what mankind has decided!') and orders to make 'fond' placards for the fifty-second birthday of the first people's president. As of 1949, Hostau had ceased to exist as a military stud farm and the paper trail came to a dead end.

Martina was irate, even more disappointed than me. 'We live in an information vacuum,' she wrote. 'At school, in history lessons, my teachers always dawdled endlessly over the First World War, so they wouldn't have to talk about the second one. Let alone the communist period; even now, almost no one here knows how to deal with that.'

She had already closed her laptop when a man in uniform appeared at her table. 'Are you the one interested in the horses of Hostau?' It was the censor. Someone else had been at the archives a while back, asking about the same subject, he said. He hadn't been able to help him either.

Thank God for Martina's persistence.

The other person, it turned out, was a German who was mapping the evacuation routes of warhorses. As a child, he had been on one of those transports: his entire family, along with a herd of breeding stallions, had tried to get from Poland to Hostau ahead of the advancing Red Army. The boy's mother had died en route, and then he lost his father. 'He had an old Red Cross telegram with him,' the censor told Martina. 'It said his father had died in Prague in 1945, in Pankrác prison.'

She had copied the German's name and address from his calling card.

'As a son, of course, there were all kinds of questions he had,' the censor said. 'But he got here too late. The prison records were lost in the Vltava flood.'

U

Waiting for me at the juice bar in Munich's *Hauptbahnhof* was the man who had fled for Hostau, horses and all. He was reading the *Frankfurter Allgemeine*; it wasn't a newspaper he had bought on impulse, he'd read it daily for the last fifty years.

'Ehrenfried Brandts,' he said, as soon as he'd folded his favourite paper. 'But by all means, call me Friedel.'

He had short hair, the kind of grey that had obviously once been blond. His build was tall and thin, even fragile, but he looked younger than seventy-two. My description of him as a 'cartographer of equestrian evacuations' evoked a smile, but he felt compelled to admit immediately that he had no first-hand knowledge of the Hostau stud. 'I was on my way there in May of '45, with fifteen stallions. We were looking for refuge, but we didn't make it.'

Friedel Brandts chose his words carefully. On the phone he had suggested that we meet in Munich, because he went there regularly. Now he invited me to lunch at the Intercity Hotel – a rusty cube riveted to the side of the droning station hall. We took a table in a five-star interior and ordered salmon carpaccio with a horseradish mousse.

'So I really know very little about the Lipizzaners in the Second World War. Except that two of them were stolen from under me.'

His thoughts were obviously elsewhere. Brandts clenched a toothpick between his teeth as though trying to bite back something. His father, he continued, did know Hostau: as the commander of a military depot for stallions in occupied Poland he had been a direct colleague of Major Hubert Rudofsky, who ruled the roost at Hostau. They held the same rank, were part of the same chain of command and even exchanged a stallion now and then – but that was all.

To understand the maelstrom into which Hitler's horses had been drawn, he said, I would first have to develop an understanding of the Nazi stud-farm system as a whole. That's what he had been doing. His slender hands opened the clasp of his bag and pulled out a book entitled *Pferden zwischen den Fronten* (Horses Between the Fronts). He had written it himself. He slid it to me across the table, a gleam in his eye. 'Came out just last month.'

It was a mixture of travelogue and reconstruction, a self-narrative and a historical account. At the back was a map of the European continent, between the meridians of Berlin and Minsk, with a tangle of dotted lines showing the escape routes of costly stallions and mares.

'And you can't really understand the horses' story without knowing something about Hitler's *Generalplan Ost*,' he said helpfully.

I had read a bit about that. The term itself sounded as neutral and low-key as '*Endlösung*', the Nazi euphemism for their 'Final Solution'. It stood for the blueprint for a new society of the pure-blooded in the recently annexed Eastern areas which, to that end, had first to be purged of Slavs, Jews and Gypsies. A popular replantation of some five million Germans (who were to be *ausgesiedelt*, like seedlings) would ensure the Germanization of countries such as Poland, Byelorussia and the Ukraine – which, with their fertile arable soils, would then become the granary of the 1,000-year empire.

Within this *Generalplan Ost*, horses played a twin role: they dragged the cannonry and they ploughed the rich soil behind the lines. Six weeks after the invasion of Poland, a start had been made by rebuilding the former stud farms that had been badly damaged by blitzkrieg bombings. The job was given to fifty-nine-year-old Gustav Rau, Hitler's chief equerry.

'*Ein Machtmensch*,' Brandts said. A man in love with power. Had he known him?

'Did I know him? Whenever he arrived to inspect our stables, he always came into our house with a lit cigar. No one else would have dared do that, but Rau was impervious to everything.' His father's boss liked to say that he had an open line to the Führer, a claim which – true or not – had made a lasting impression on him. Friedel Brandts recalled how they always hid three-quarters of the contents of his father's humidor, just to be on the safe side, because Hitler's equerry had a tendency to help himself immoderately.

He could talk for hours about Gustav Rau. Rau's wife Hertha had made an equally deep and unpleasant impression on young Friedel. Sometimes he had to bring her fresh vegetables with his horse and wagon, a drive that took hours – and even when he carried the crates to her shed, she never offered him a glass of lemonade, not even on blazing hot days. But his research and reflections on Rau's virtually unparalleled diligence and professional expertise had caused his memories to become less clouded by rancour. The title 'chief equerry' (*Oberlandstallmeister*, sometimes shortened to *Oberland*) was one Rau had acquired in 1933, the year he was made the most powerful horseman in Germany. During the war he was given complete freedom to shape 'the horse of the future' – by employing his talent as a breeder and the latest insights into genetics. Between 1939 and 1945 he had drawn up a progress report of more than 1,000 pages, which was kept in a massive archive in Freiburg under the title *Rau-Berichte*. Brandts had photocopied it and bludgeoned his way through, keeping an eye out for information about the military depot at Draschendorf, where he had grown up.

One of the first reports described the chaos shortly after the Polish capitulation in September 1939:

> While fleeing eastward, the Racot stud in Posen province, known traditionally for raising Berbers, was bombed by our planes because of the Polish stablemen's mousy-grey uniforms. The director of the stud farm was killed, the herd scattered . . . After resuming their flight, they were once again strafed by our pilots. Many horses killed . . . The prize stallions Indogermane and Centurio, both Trakheners, were killed by machine-gun fire . . . The celebrated German pure-bred stallion Rheinwein drowned while swimming across the Vistula.

For six whole years Rau travelled from stud farm to stud farm, first in a chauffeur-driven car and later, when the Ukraine became his responsibility as well, in a little three-seater aircraft that could land and take off almost anywhere. His headquarters was the confiscated villa of a Jewish textile baron in Lódź/Litzmannstadt, boasting luxurious bath-rooms and a view of the barbed-wire fence surrounding the local ghetto. Rau, a meaty fellow, knew no shame, not even when it came to his stoma: on warm days he bathed unabashedly in the Vistula, handicap or no. Out of discretion, Ehrenfried Brandts had in his book used only part of a photograph – inherited from his father – of Rau in swimming trunks: the lower half of the man's torso, with stoma, was cropped out of the picture.

The self-appointed mission of Hitler's equerry was to create new breeds of horses from the best and most diverse genetic material that the genus *equus* had to offer. Just as Poseidon had given the horse to mankind, so Rau planned to bless the German people with *das ideale Soldatenpferd*, the ideal warhorse. Such a horse, he wrote, would possess the heart and temperament of a cross-breed, the musculature of a medium-sized underbred, hooves tough as steel, a broad chest and, last but not least, great stamina on a diet of grass and hay alone. This last consideration addressed the traditional disadvantage of hereditary refinement: without oats, even the noblest of horses, including the Lipizzaner, became finicky animals that simply lacked the stamina to forge on. Rau quoted a letter from a soldier on his way overland to the Caucasus: 'We have seen so often that fatally exhausted horses hang in the harnesses, their heads bowed, until they are unhitched. Then they kneel, never to rise to their feet again. We have crossed mountain roads that we called "the path of dead horses".'

The digestion and metabolism of most 'modern' horses was accustomed to run on feed concentrate. If these happened to be unavailable, they collapsed on the spot.

At the table in the serene, almost sterile Intercity Hotel, Brandts drew my attention to Rau's background – which he felt was important. As a member of the heavy cavalry under Kaiser Wilhelm, he had been wounded in action on three occasions. 'He who has rushed the enemy wielding a lance', Rau advanced in his *Buch der Kavallerie*, published in 1936, 'has at least made something of his life.'

He wore his scars like medals. He despised automobiles and resisted motorization and mechanization with the zeal of a knight errant. An officer should view the theatre of battle from the back of his Rosinante, openly and without obstruction. Hiding between armoured plates he became listless and dull. He insisted till the day he died that 'No army will ever succeed without its cavalry.' Rau did admit, however, that the mounted charge was a thing of the past. Western military science had long depended, perhaps for too long, on its standard formula for success: galloping straight at the enemy in tight formation, so as to drive a wedge in his defences. Since the time of Alexander the Great, the use of horses as shock troops had proven superior to the tactics of the mounted Asiatic hordes, who were faster, more agile and more flexible, but who ultimately excelled only at trampling underfoot the settlements they came across. Other special 'oriental' tactics (such as Moorish units who crept up on hostile camps on the backs of mares, because they make less noise than stallions) had never amounted to much either. Until the early twentieth century, therefore, most European commanders had clung to the romantic image of the 'sporting' war on horseback. As commander-in-chief of the German forces, Kaiser Wilhelm did not sit in a chair at his writing desk, but on a saddle mounted on the legs of a stool. And no one dared withdraw the horse from the front lines of the First World War, even though the animal was helpless in the face of machine-gun fire. When poison gases were introduced, a special mask was designed for quadrupeds. One still came across the pictures: rider and mount, each breathing through their own rubber tube. And meanwhile, out of the haze of gun smoke over Flanders' fields, there arose the proto-type of the horse's usurper, the tank.

More than one million horses died in battle between 1914 and 1918. 'A huge sacrifice on the part of this mute creature,' Rau noted, 'and in unheard-of numbers.'

The role of the cavalry had changed, but was not yet over. In this new world war, Rau had wanted to outfit the German army once more with four-footed diesels. But the generals placed their faith instead in motorcycles, jeeps, trucks and fighter planes. The curtain fell on what remained of the cavalry in the autumn of 1941: on its way to Moscow, the last German mounted unit was ordered to merge with an armoured division.

Rau: 'Each step forward along the path of technology is a step backward for the forces of nature.' Horses could press on at twenty degrees below zero – they were an all-weather means of conveyance.

The disbanding in 1942 of the last US Army mounted unit, Rau felt, was due to pressure from General Motors – with its vested interest in motorized weaponry. Yet certainly in the Eastern mud and snow, practical warfare remained heavily dependent on horses as pack and transport animals. For the care of the animals' hooves alone, the *Wehrmacht* employed 3,700 blacksmiths. The breaking-in of the three-year-olds was entrusted to women between the ages of eighteen and forty. The German army owned more than one million horses, and required 6,000 new animals each month to compensate for fatalities.

'Rau wanted to deliver quantity and quality, without ever bowing to compromise,' Friedel Brandts explained.

He planned, at one fell swoop, to breed the ideal farm horse, 'an animal whose stature will cover much ground', *and* the world's best jumping horse for equestrian sports.

When necessary, Rau made use of the shrillest of National Socialist rhetoric – extending his arm in the Nazi salute, talking about the way the Führer principle was applied at his stud farms, or wishing his helpers 'a glimmer of Goebbels' genius'. But niceties were foreign to him. Brandts told me that Rau had once summoned his father with an unmilitary: '*Heinz, komm mal hierhin!*)' (Heinz, come over here!) – and that his father had taken a great risk by replying: 'For you, Herr Oberst, and for you at all times: Herr Major.'

I wondered aloud how Rau might have felt about the Brothers Heck – with their goal of resurrecting pure-blooded primal horses and oxen.

Friedel Brandts dabbed at his lips and said there was a world of difference between them. Rau was interested in purpose, in utility. English and Arab thoroughbreds were the primary colours on his palette; he needed them to paint with, but would not have wanted them to be seen as the painting itself. Hitler's chief equerry, Brandts told me, also made pronouncements that were at complete odds with Nazi doctrine. 'Thoroughbreds do not perform any better than cross-breeds.' And: 'Build is more important than breed.' While the ultimate racial segregation was being carried out in the world of *Homo sapiens*, Rau was mating horses of the most diverse breeds possible. The coldest coldblood with the warmest warmblood, for example – that was one project on which Brandts' father had been expected to assist. 'At the stud farm we had a Noriker mare, a really heavy-limbed Shire horse, and we had to cross her with a Lipizzaner stallion that was staying with us temporarily.' The result was a rather lumpish foal with bones that seemed almost too big for its skin, but Rau considered it 'a successful hybrid'.

I found it strange to hear that such experiments had been carried out with Lipizzaners under Nazi supervision.

'*Zuviel Vollblut macht verrückt!* So much pure blood ruins everything!' Brandts said all of a sudden. It had just popped into his mind, perhaps he had once heard Rau say that, that was quite possible. In any case, it clearly showed that the chief equerry was a man of practical considerations who wanted to produce horses that could be put to use, who had no interest in nonsensical conventions. Rau tinkered with the very building blocks of the ideology he served. Viewed rationally, of course, the notion of pure blood was not at all clear or easy to delineate. Racial purity was an arbitrary concept. The Lipizzaner itself had been moulded from Danish (Pluto), Italian (Conversano and Neapolitano), Egyptian (Siglavy) and Czech (Maestoso and Favory) forefathers of divergent breeds. One could just as easily claim, therefore, that the Lipizzan was a bastard, the product of a mixed-blood herd from which breeders had distilled a certain racial line, and which people had – for lack of a better term – subsequently begun referring to as 'pure'.

Brandts, too, had been surprised to see how arbitrarily the Nazis had enforced their own biological tenets. He recalled a limerick he'd had to learn by heart at his Germanized school – to give the students a feeling for English, *and* for Mendel's laws:

> There was a young lady named Sharkey
> Who had an affair with a darkie.
> The result of her sins
> Was quadruplets, not twins,
> One white, and one black, and two khaki.

Leaning on the edge of the table, he looked round the restaurant, which was empty but for the waiter.

As a child, he said, lowering his voice, there was one thing he had never realized: his father was also in charge of the horses at Auschwitz, which was quite close to the Draschendorf stallion depot. Originally, the task belonged to Gustav Rau himself, who had visited Auschwitz in June 1941. In the report he wrote afterwards, he said that 8,000 prisoners ('ninety-four per cent of them Poles') had been put to work there. 'It is going to be a huge farming operation of almost 4,000 hectares, and will include breeding programmes for horses, cattle and pigs.' The agronomist and former poultryman Heinrich Himmler, head of the SS, had agreed to set up a stud farm at Auschwitz with seventy mares, half of them cold-blooded, the other half Holsteins – each with its own stallion. Rather than see to them himself, though, Rau decided that Major Brandts should have this additional responsibility. Suddenly, the task of training horses for the camp's guard units, the mounted SS Death's Head brigade, was in his father's hands as well.

'He called and spoke to camp commander Rudolf Höss a few times,' his son said. 'But as far as I know he never went to Auschwitz. Probably because they weren't eager to have people looking over their shoulders.'

☡

Years ago, on Radio Noord-Holland, I had heard an excitable DJ pose the following question in a quiz: 'Which gas was used to kill Jews at Auschwitz? Was it a) mustard gas, b) Zyklon B, or c) carbon monoxide?'

The first listener to call with the right answer would win two tickets to a pop concert. The person who had thought up that question, the DJ and the caller ('Mustard gas!') all belonged to the 'why the hell not?' generation. Discernment was sorely out of fashion. As I listened, I had asked myself: can you hold someone to account for being wilfully stupid?

Now I was hearing uncomfortable facts about which I myself had no clue, and which shed light on the degree of my own ignorance: Auschwitz as stud farm. So there, under the smoke from the crematoria, they had performed stirpiculture with all the precision and dedication that required. Nor had I known that botanical experiments were carried out within the camp grounds, nor that Himmler was greatly interested in homeopathic medicine and medicinal herbs. The SS, it turned out, had even had its own Institute for Phylogenetics. In addition to a human slaughterhouse, the largest ever, Auschwitz was also an experimental farm and an industrial estate. Before his execution in 1947, Commander Höss stated at Nuremberg that he had been in charge of a 'huge agricultural research station'.

There had been a rigorous method to the way the Nazis dealt with flora and fauna – including human beings. *Generalplan Ost* involved the ethnic cleansing and colonization of half a continent, with the supposedly inferior genetic material replaced by the supposedly superior. At Auschwitz, where that all came together, humans categorized as inferior were – before being exterminated – first put to work improving the traits of horses. And in the fields at Raisko, a part of Auschwitz, they had experimented with raising dandelions for the production of rubber.

At the same time that it disbanded its mounted cavalry in 1941, the *Wehrmacht*'s bureau of statistics had announced that the 'supplies of rubber for shoes and tyres' would last for no more than a month. No one had bothered to heed Gustav Rau's warning ('horses are the most reliable means of transport'). The network of German autobahns had indeed proved useful, but the Allied blockade at sea was now forcing the Germans to find sources of rubber other than the tropical plantations. Hitler and Himmler thought they had hit upon just such a source in the milky-white substance found in the stem of *Taraxacum officinale*: the common dandelion. Stalin's Soviet Union had already developed an extraction method using a variety substantially richer in latex: *Taraxacum koksaghyz*, also known as the Russian or rubber dandelion which, thanks to the intervention of the Führer himself, an SS commando unit of Nazi biologists went on to track down successfully. Code name: 'Plant 4711'.

All the confiscated genetic material was promptly labelled necessary for the war effort. Some 350 prisoners at Auschwitz, most of them Jewish women and some with doctorates in biology, went to work on the various varieties of *Taraxacum* with nail clippers and paintbrushes, in order to improve the latex crop by means of manual cross-pollination. The methodologies and results were written up in a scientific publication. Nearby, at the Buna factory, also at Auschwitz, the harvest was processed into rubber.

On the occasion of the 120th anniversary of Gregor Mendel's birth, in July 1942, the chairman of the German Federation of Biologists wrote: 'Anyone attempting to measure the range of what has been achieved in this country using the laws of genetics would be struck dumb with awe at the grandeur of what has already taken place and the objectives already established.' The task of the German people, an NSDAP pamphlet dedicated to Mendel advised, was the same as that of the plant or animal breeder: 'promoting the useful, and rooting out the undesirable'. The decision to implement the Final Solution had been reached earlier that year; the freight carriages were already criss-crossing Europe in accordance with an ironclad timetable. While what Himmler called the 'weeding out of inferior racial elements' was being enacted with increasing vigour, the SS devised a plan to loot the world's largest collection of germ plasm: Nikolai Vavilov's seed banks.

Within the Soviet Union itself, Vavilov's collection had been virtually forgotten once Mendelian genetics had lost out to Lysenko's theory of the 're-educability' of species. Not one of the eleven seed banks containing Vavilov's collection had been withdrawn to beyond the Urals, as most strategic facilities had – entire factories had been dismantled, put on trains and reassembled in the Siberian wilderness. The SS Institute for Phylogenetics drew up a list of Vavilov's most important field stations in the various climatic zones between Murmansk and subtropical Baku on the Caspian coast. For the purposes of this mission, a brilliant botanist, Dr Heinz Brücher – barely twenty-seven at the time – was given an interpreter, a dozen soldiers and two army trucks. He took 3,000 varieties of wheat, 1,000 of barley and 500 of oats from Vavilov's depots in the Crimean and the Ukraine interior, and his *Sammelkommando* (Collection Unit) also went searching for a variety of geranium from which the Soviets extracted a lubricant that resisted coagulation even at extremely low temperatures, a by-product of the latex-bearing shrub *guayale*, once brought back from Mexico by Vavilov himself and tested at an alternative-rubber plantation in Azerbaijan.

The loot was stored in the hills west of Graz, at Lannach Castle, which had 120 hectares of test plots for crop improvement; the most frost- and mildew-resistant grains were taken from there and sowed in fields between the Oder and the Volga.

Gustav Rau had done the same with horses. Friedel Brandts told me that in 1943 Rau had sent the most capable members of his staff to southern Russia, with orders to retrieve hundreds of Kabardin horses. The herd had originally belonged to Cossacks who, in their heart of hearts, had always remained loyal to the murdered czar. Whilst the Red Army commanders in Moscow had ordered them to take their animals across the Caucasus to Georgia, they instead defected to the enemy, bringing as a peace offering almost the entire Kabardin breed. Rau's envoy in charge of transporting this equine material was Dr Frielinghaus, the same man who had purchased the Lipizzaners of Vukovar.

Operating in the spirit of *Generalplan Ost*, Rau applied his pool of Lipizzaners in Hostau for the dissemination of new genetic material. He stationed breeding stallions at remote stud farms so that they might spread their seed; at Draschendorf on the Vistula in 1944, these included two Conversano sires. To expedite the colonization of the Ukraine, he also set up a Lipizzaner stud outpost in the town of Dembina, along the railway line towards Lemberg, with two stallions and thirty-three mares from the Hostau herd. They were given shelter at a deserted farm 800 kilometres east of Hostau – not far from the crumbling Eastern Front.

∪

It had taken Ehrenfried Brandts half a century to return to his childhood home. He had never dared to before because his father had once worn the oppressor's uniform. When at last he found himself standing there, in 1986, he saw that the poplars along the Vistula had shrunk. The beech tree in the garden, under which he had taken cover as the bombers filled the sky, was also smaller than he remembered .

'Apparently I had grown faster than they had.'

His sister Beate had never dared to confront the past head-on. But she had also endured more than he had – the violent interrogation of the Polish gardener in the greenhouse, for example, by two Gestapo agents who thought no one was at home. The gardener was taken away to Mauthausen and never heard from again. Friedel had asked his sister to contribute to his book, 'Reminiscences about Mother', but that was beyond her.

He was not out to clear his father's name but, in the absence of a headstone, he did hope to erect a memorial to him. On paper, in this case. In his book, I read that Major Heinz Brandts had sent a Polish stableboy to Auschwitz in 1942 to tame a wild horse belonging to the SS Death's Head brigade. The boy succeeded, and even came back alive. On another occasion, the head of the stud farm before the war, a Pole by the name of Kayetanowicz, was released from Auschwitz after Brandts, Sr had mediated on his behalf. 'He has a lot of experience with horses, we need him here,' he told Commander Höss. Kayetanowicz's discharge papers – after three years' forced labour – had been preserved for posterity. A rare document: very few prisoners ever walked out of the *Arbeit Macht Frei* gates.

Friedel Brandts' particular obsession was the evacuation of the Draschendorf stallion depot, with his family, in the winter and spring of 1945, a route he had retraced many times after his retirement. Reconstructing the first leg of the journey to Czechoslovakia, which had taken place in the freezing cold, was no problem. He found his way almost blindly to the gate of the women's clinic at Olmütz, where he had sat in his father's car until word came that his mother was dead. The only complication was that Olmütz was called Olomouc these days.

It had been more difficult to trace his father's wanderings after their final, hurried farewell in early April, the Saturday before Easter. Late that afternoon, with more than one hundred stallions loaded into livestock carriages, his father had left in a westerly direction and vanished from his life. On 7 or 8 April 1945, Friedel Brandts discovered, the convoy had arrived at a field hospital for horses on a hill outside Dresden, but was unable to stay there. The city itself was one vast char, still bearing the imprint of its former network of streets like a chequered trellis. The bridges over the Elbe had been destroyed as well, and the Bolsheviks had already reached the Neisse. Major Brandts was forced to hand over sixty of his breeding stallions to the corps of engineers, to help drag tree trunks. 'Sixty horses are going to the troops, uncastrated', he wrote in a letter that day. 'That means they will first be beaten till they are crippled and then killed, supposedly because they are unmanageable. All my work of the last five and a half years is gone like dust in the wind.'

With the paltry remains of the herd, Brandts' father followed the valley of the Elbe south in search of a bridge or a fordable spot. On the afternoon of 17 April they were attacked from the air. They took cover, but two stallions and two Polish stable attendants were killed when a wall collapsed.

On 1 May 1945 the day that Joseph and Magda Goebbels killed their six children in the Berlin bunker and then followed their Führer by taking their own lives, Brandts Sr was informed that he had been promoted to the rank of lieutenant colonel. 'As a military man to the core, that must have pleased him,' his son surmised. 'Even though, by that point, all was lost.'

Four to five days' march from Hostau, the convoy ground to a halt in a village north of Prague. The Russians were too fast for his father, and forced him to surrender. It was 9 May, the day of the general German capitulation. After Brandts and his men handed over their weapons, the Soviet soldiers turned to the horses. One of the non-commissioned officers took pleasure in submitting Brandts' mount, the Anglo-Arab

Hildach, to a test. To the loud shouts and cheers of his men, he urged the horse on, jumping fences and low walls – until the animal fell. Eyewitnesses said that Hildach had scrambled to his feet, but limped so badly that he was put out of his misery on the spot.

After being forced to watch this, Lt Col. Brandts declared the Draschendorf stallion depot to be disbanded and removed his uniform. The Russians left, taking the rest of the horses with them. When Brandts realized that no one was going to try to arrest him, he went off as a free civilian in search of his children. He hoped to save them from the chaos of the moment, but got no further than a railway station on the outskirts of Prague. While changing trains, he was arrested by Czech militiamen and taken to Pankrác prison. Three years later, in April 1948, a two-line telegram arrived from the Red Cross, stating that Brandts Sr had been shot, presumably as early as the summer of 1945, after having reportedly attacked a guard.

U

Concerning his own attempt at escaping with fifteen stallions to unreachable Hostau, Brandts Jr had little to say. He referred me instead to the day-by-day account he had put to paper in late 1945 as a Christmas present for his first foster parents.

Friedel Brandts rubbed his forehead with his fingertips.

I asked whether, later on in life, he had ever done anything else with horses. Did he own one? Did he still ride?

'No, but I often sit on the coach-box. I enjoy driving.' During the years he had spent charting the routes of horses in wartime, he had also attended a course in coach-driving at Szilvásvárad, Hungary.

'At the famous Lipizzaner stud there?' I asked.

He nodded. 'In Hungary, they breed Lipizzaners as carriage horses.'

Now it was my turn to nod. I thought I understood what was not being said: Friedel Brandts was still trying to excel in what he had failed at as a ten-year-old boy – driving two Lipizzaners before the cart, trying to escape from *der Iwan*, the archetypal Russian conscript, even when he had the almond eyes of female Uzbek soldiers.

SUMMONED TO
MILITARY SERVICING

THE CLICK-CLACK OF INES Hubinger's high-heeled boots echoed through the monastery courtyard. On all four sides were arched cloisters, painted a Wedgwood blue. I followed Frau Hubinger across the stone tiles, which were laid out in circles across the square patio. The Alpine air crackled with cold, our breath appearing in little clouds.

'I'm going to let you go about your business on the top floor.' We arrived at a modern staircase and a lift with a cage of glass and metal. 'We trust you. I'm going to bring you some coffee in a moment, but otherwise I'll leave you to your own devices.' My hostess was the 'stud-farm secretary' of the Bundesgestüt Piber, in the south-eastern foothills of the Alps. Her jet-black hair and fashionably tight designer jeans were probably an advantage when it came to her main duties – attracting prospective buyers for those Lipizzaners that did not go to Vienna. Her sideline was managing the archives of the Royal Spanish Riding School, but they had been moved so often that no one could make head or tail of them any more.

There was not another living soul in sight, inside or outside the monastery walls; the season for visitors began only after Easter. Ines Hubinger led me across the parquet floor on the second storey, sliding aside curtains and turning on radiators – like an estate agent. I looked around at what seemed to be a two-room apartment with furnishings from the 1950s; racks, sideboards, reproductions of paintings of famous Lipizzaners and, on the floor, piles of unopened removal crates. In one corner, behind a floor lamp, was a door. Ines rattled through her key ring and unlocked it: directly behind it was yet another door, also white and equally unobtrusive. The second, however, was made of steel, and served to protect a bricked-in safe. 'Fireproof,' Inez said, swinging it open.

The shelves at stomach height were lined with antique books bound in cognac-coloured leather: the original stud books for the Lipizzaner breed since the year 1822.

Frau Hubinger removed one of the volumes and carried it to the table in the middle of the room. I had never believed I would be allowed to handle them without white gloves, but she let me open the book myself. The nineteenth century wafted up from the paper. I looked at the page relating to the mare Palerma from the Imperial and Royal Stud at Lipica, with the preprinted categories: head, neck, shoulder, hooves, physical proportions in general, gaits, character and, lest we forget: lineage.

For years, Slovenia had been pressing a claim to gain possession of these stud books. Were I later to tuck them under my arm and carry them across the border, I would unleash an acute diplomatic crisis between Vienna and Ljubljana. The Austrians so feared the Slovenians' demands relating to every aspect of the Lipizzaner tradition that they had arranged a diplomatic give-and-go with Italy: in 1998, in exchange for Austrian support protecting Italian wines in the European marketplace, Rome had formally recognized that there was only one 'country of origin' for the Lipizzaner: Austria.

'Fantastic,' I said, pointing at the quill and nib handwriting, graceful but illegible to me.

'I'm not sure I find it as fantastic as you do.' Ines tossed a dark lock over her shoulder. 'It's sheer drudgery, trying to keep it up to date.'

Thousands of double-barrelled names pranced in fine handwriting across the pages. And to think that this noble family register was actually incomplete. It did not go all the way back to the year of inception, 1580; the older stud books had been lost in the wake of looting under Napoleon, or had at least disappeared. From 1822 onwards, the Viennese court had ordered that two copies be kept, one at Lipica and the duplicate in the imperial capital. After the First World War, Italy had taken not only 109 Lipizzaners, but also a stud book – the Viennese duplicate, the Austrians claimed. What I was now holding was said to be the original, and the object of Slovenia's desire.

These days, Ines told me, she entered data about the foals directly into her computer, but she also had to register the animals by hand. 'The law requires it.'

I asked what law that was.

'The Royal Spanish Riding School law,' she said.

ʊ

As soon as Frau Hubinger had left me alone, I tossed my coat over the back of a chair. Feeling a bit surreptitious, I pulled out my floor plan – a sketch I'd made at home, based on information from the Secretary General of the LIF: the International Lipizzaner Federation. The Secretary General was a Dutchman by the name of Atjan Hop, a businessman's son who – during office hours – did the administration for stem-cell transplantations at Leiden's academic hospital. I had come into contact with him rather late in the game; a pity, seeing as he had a hand in all things Lipizzaner. When a meeting was held at the Hofburg concerning 'the Spanish School', Atjan was in on it. Whenever a prize stallion died in Vienna, it was he who wrote a glowing *in memoriam*. And when the veterinary manager at Piber was in a quandary concerning breeding guidelines, it was Atjan Hop who whispered suggestions in his ear.

I compared the room's layout to my sketch. In the bookcase in Room 1, at right angles to the windows, I found – just as the instructions said – the row of six loose-leaf binders for each of the six stallion lines: Conversano, Favory, Pluto, Neapolitano, Siglavy and Maestoso. As volunteer registrar, Atjan Hop had put them there himself; he had come here for years, often during his holidays, to help bit by bit in organizing the documentation on the history of the Lipizzaners. On the phone before I left, he'd told me about some correspondence from the years 1940–5, in which the Lipizzaners from the Balkans were referred to as *Beutetieren*, literally 'animal spoils of war'.

'I filed those letters away neatly, but when I came back the next time they were gone. You'd almost think they'd been hidden, to avoid claims.' For six years, under the former director, he had been denied access to the archives. 'I was *persona non grata* there for a while, that's what it amounted to.'

Atjan had piloted me in here by remote control at a moment – though this was a coincidence – when the inapproachable director, Frau Elisabeth Gürtler, was in New York. Her personal presence turned out to be entirely unnecessary; she was the kind of manager who could delegate responsibility, and in addition someone who had shocked conservative Austria by opening the Royal Spanish Riding

School to female pupils: running counter to the current of tradition, she had announced only a few weeks ago that two women had been admitted to train there as riders.

In the drawers of the filing cabinet, also following Atjan Hop's directions, I found the 'foal cards' for the last half-century, arranged by date of birth. I extracted Conversano Primula's card and read that the birth on 20 January 1967 had been 'easy'.

Colour of the umbilical cord: *Yellowish-white.*
Placenta: *Bordeaux red.*
Appearance on second day: *Small but symmetrical build, noble and very attractive: lovely aristocratic head, well-formed neck, very good shoulders.*
Height at withers: *92 cm.*

After four months, at the time of weaning, his 124 centimetres rendered him 'still rather small'. In his evaluation as yearling and two-year-old, his 'limited height' featured again, in addition to his 'restless' character and 'outspoken stallion temperament'. In conclusion, the entry for the spring of 1970 read: 'Earmarked for sale, due to failure to reach the required measurements.' Below that: 'Sold on 27/5/70 to Mr P. C. Bakker, Holland.'

To my surprise, there was another page attached to the foal card: the programme for the 'National Lipizzaner Day' at the Tarpan riding school, seventeen years later, in October 1987. The then director of the Spanish Riding School, cape draped over his shoulders, had stood beside the Deurze Stream that day and inspected a handful of Lipizzaners. One of the high points had been Piet's performance with Primula on the long reins. I laid the programme on the table and took a picture of it. Ines came in with a tray of biscuits, fruit juice and coffee. She must have seen the flash, but said nothing. The restaurant downstairs was closed, she told me. If I needed anything, she would be in her office.

I put on my coat again and wrapped my hands around the coffeepot; despite the excitement of the first discovery, I was cold to the bone. The heating was obviously on the blink. I drank some coffee, then flipped through the folders mentioned on Atjan's list. Reluctantly (for there were too many), I opened at random a number of the closed removal crates. They were full of veterinary dossiers. But then I stumbled upon a box of a different shape; written on it, in felt pen, was the date '1943'. 1943: the year Goebbels had asked a packed Berlin Sportpalast: *'Wollt Ihr den totalen Krieg?'* (Do you want an all-out war?) – the answer to which had been an orgiastic *'Jaaaa.'* I went back and looked through the other piles, but there were no similar boxes marked '1941' or '1944'. I texted Atjan about the '1943' box – did he know about it?

Less than a minute later, my phone buzzed. NO! YOU'VE GOT ME CURIOUS. CAN YOU TAKE PICTURES?

I forgot all about eating and drinking and fished out a memorandum about a new Lipizzaner statue in Vienna, the choreography of the obedience test (the same test that Conversano Savona had completed in front of the cameras in 1939) and an announcement of a visit by the Hitler Youth: 'In conclusion, we rely on the fact that you will provide a capable guide – Heil Hitler!'

The more papers I unearthed, the clearer it became that the Royal Spanish Riding School had prospered under the pan-German authorities. Alois and Verena Podhajsky were allotted a staff residence in the Hofburg. An antechamber for special guests had been decorated with period furniture and paintings of Lipizzaners, and the riding hall itself was fitted out with three chandeliers the size of the bells in St

Stefan's Cathedral. All the riders received new uniforms, their mounts new, gold-braided saddlecloths. They performed each year at the great 'Day of the *Wehrmacht*' and at benefit performances for the war effort and the German Red Cross. In April 1944, Colonel Podhajsky was decorated with the War Service Cross First Class (with swords).

'The pan-German Empire possesses the world's most famous riding school', I read in a brochure. In Gothic letters, the author expressed his gratitude for the 'protection as cultural treasure' given to that institution under German rule.

The old lustre had been revived. Downstream along the Danube, a sister academy was set up in Budapest. Hungarian hussars had in the past taken hesitant steps towards establishing a dependency of the Royal Spanish Riding School at the Lipizzaner stud in Bábolna. In 1938, however, the academy was moved to the riding hall of the castle in Buda, where the governor of Hungary, a Nazi-sympathizer, had his residence. Twenty-two pure-bred Lipizzaner stallions received training in classical equestrianism there. In 1941 there was sufficient funding to have them brought to Vienna for a guest performance – the brochure mentioned that too.

Like everyone else, Commander Podhajsky furnished his letters with swastika stamps and Heil Hitlers – followed either by an elegant P or his full signature. In a report he characterized Oberbereiter Lindenbauer as 'unequivocally loyal and dedicated to the National Socialist government'.

MY FLASH IS WORKING OVERTIME, I texted back.

I found lists of the inhabitants of the Stallburg, updated yearly, which showed that in the period 1940–3 the number of Viennese stallions had grown by more than fifty per cent: from forty-two to sixty-eight. The 1940 review included both Conversano Savona ('*levadeur*') and his son, Bonavista ('a sterling high-school stallion, who excels at the long reins').

But the father was not on the list that next year. Old Savona from the imperial Lipica stud must by then have reached the age of thirty. No mention was made of precisely how he met his end, which could mean that he had died amid the pillars of the riding hall – in harness.

Bonavista had taken over from his sire as the number one performing stallion of the Conversano dynasty. He topped the lists in 1941 and 1942, but was missing in 1943. That was strange. According to the inscription on the wall of the Stallburg, Bonavista had only died in 1953.

I turned to his page in the stud book, which gave the date on which he was selected for a career in Vienna (13 September 1929), but made no mention of any time on the sidelines. Had he been injured? His veterinary dossier offered nothing, and his unexplained absence bothered me. Bonavista was Oberbereiter Lindenbauer's regular and favourite mount, and in 1943, as an eighteen-year-old stallion, must have been at the pinnacle of his abilities.

∪

After a lunch of biscuits, sugar cubes and apple juice, I found a bundle of orders from Berlin. One came directly from Hitler's office and was dated 26 June 1943: the instruction henceforth to use only the term of address '*Der Führer*'. Or, for German subjects: '*Mein Führer*' – in either case without the till-then common addition '*und Reichskanzler*'. The bundle also contained the minutes of meetings confirming that the breeding stock from Piber, 103 animals in all, had been sent by transport to Hostau on 4 October 1942.

In his memoirs, Podhajsky made no bones about how disastrous he felt that move had been. During his lifetime he had seen Austria shrivel from an empire to a German province, and on top of all that there was now the loss of the 350-year-old tradition of Lipizzaner breeding. Hostau not only lay outside the borders of the new province, but the landscape there was also too gentle, the climate too mild. As the principal customer for young stallions, the leader of the Royal Spanish Riding School warned against pampering the breed. The Lipizzaner, he argued in a letter to Berlin, had been shaped on the rocky Adriatic coast and on the intemperate, high pastures above the monastery at Piber – stormy winds and harsh ground had made it tough. In the low-lying Sudetenland, the breed would soften and ultimately meet its demise.

The Berlin high command had passed his letter to Gustav Rau for comment. He sent it back with only one remark in the margin: 'It has not been proven that the horse is a product of the soil.' With that single sentence he laid his finger on the essence of Nazi biology: anyone claiming that environment affected heredity was guilty of 'Lamarckism' or 'Lysenkoism' – which was tantamount to Judaeo-Bolshevik propaganda. Cut the tails off twenty-two successive generations of mice, as the German August Weismann had done, and the twenty-third generation would be born with tails. Jewish babies, by analogous Nazi reasoning, were at birth as cunning as their parents. That's how heredity worked.

In October 1942, Gustav Rau visited his model stud farm at Hostau to inspect the Lipizzaners one by one. He was particularly pleased with the Croatian mares, but those bearing the Piber brand, the master said, were 'too deeply inbred'. He found some so defective that he ordered Major Rudofsky to sell them on the local livestock market. In late 1942, as soon as Podhajsky heard that Piber mares were being auctioned off at Hostau, he too travelled to the Sudetenland, where he complained about the mares looking too plump and cuddly. The high command, clearly irritated by the running feud between the two colonels, summoned both Rau and Podhajsky to Berlin in January 1943.

As Hitler's 6th Army reached the Volga and was being surrounded by hardened Soviet troops, Podhajsky travelled to *Wehrmacht* headquarters to air his grievances. At the conference table in the command bunker, he employed fresh ammunition: Rau was having the mares at Hostau covered at the age of three, even though the Lipizzaner by nature matured slowly.

'Ah yes, the three-year-olds,' Major Rudofsky is rumoured to have told him, 'in fact they are still only children.'

Rau was not impressed. 'The methods applied with Trakheners', he remarked, 'can also be applied to Lipizzaners.'

During the face-off in Berlin, Chief Equerry Rau did not budge an inch. Podhajsky left after entering a plea to protect the breed from 'unusual experimentation', and if that protection were not forthcoming, he predicted 'an untimely end to the Lipizzaner as we know it'.

Looking up from my papers, I saw that the sun had disappeared behind a veil of clouds. I moved the floor lamp to the table in the middle of the room, on which I had spread out the documents. Amid a sheaf of trivial correspondence I found a letter from the high command, signed by a certain Colonel Stein, in which Podhajsky was told to lend out a 'high-school stallion, not too advanced in its dressage training', to the stud farm at Hostau. Behind that letter I detected the hand of Rau, whose inclination was to requisition his Viennese studs by way of Berlin.

At that same moment I received a text message:

JUST RECEIVED EMAIL FROM INES: 'HEY, ARE ALL YOU DUTCH PEOPLE SO FANATICAL? TOOK HIM UPSTAIRS AT 10 AND IT'S ALREADY 4 IN THE AFTERNOON ...' EVERYTHING OK?

I grinned, poured myself a glass of water and emptied the last sachet of sugar into my mouth. Suddenly, I had a glimmer of what might have happened to Bonavista.

In 1943, Rau had attended a gala performance for Nazi high officials at the Royal Spanish Riding School; Podhajsky had written about that in detail. Afterwards, a glass of sparkling wine in hand, the German chief equerry had praised him to the skies. What Podhajsky had showed the world with his Lipizzaners bordered on perfection. The praise, however, was followed by a venomous 'but'. In a voice audible to all, Rau had apparently added: 'But you would, of course, establish your reputation once and for all if you succeeded in developing classical dressage at the Spanish Riding School with the use of Hanoverians.'

I believed I knew what Rau had come to do in Vienna. My hunch was confirmed by what I found at the bottom of the letter from Berlin. I had read it hastily, confident of what it was going to say. On Rau's behalf, the high command was summoning the two best 'school' stallions of the day to servicing in Hostau:

1) FAVORY AFRICA,
2) CONVERSANO BONAVISTA.

THE BREEDING STATION

THE STABLES ARE HALF-HIDDEN from view by a waist-high screen of stinging nettles. Four long buildings, running parallel along a gentle slope and marred by large holes where the windows once were. The haylofts, where they have not collapsed completely, are roofed with flat pieces of slate. To the left and right are cart tracks that wind across the fields in the distance and disappear into the cover of the Bohemian Forest. For half a human lifetime, the ridge on the horizon marked the 'Border of Socialism and Peace' – also known as the Iron Curtain.

'Liberation Street,' Martina reads aloud from a little sign bolted to an electricity pylon. 'Well, I guess it depends on what you call liberation.'

Side by side, we wade through the sea of nettles with our hands held high – like prisoners at an exchange. A striped tomcat perched on the breeze-block sill begins to meow. 'Sssst,' I say. Less lithely than the cat in its escape, I clamber up to its perch and jump down from the wall on to the concrete floor. Martina follows, refusing a hand down.

Spread out across the floor is the carcass of an Eastern Bloc computer, a pile of cokes and a non-biodegradable toy wheelbarrow made of bright red plastic. Only the troughs along the walls and the manure drain in the floor speak of the former presence of animals. The roof over our heads once sheltered Europe's most expensive horses: the confiscated black Lipizzaner stallion of King Petar II of Yugoslavia, Minister Ribbentrop's thoroughbred, and Favory Africa, the Viennese grey once singled out, not only as breeding stallion, but also as Hitler's never-delivered gift to Emperor Hirohito.

How can I explain to Martina exactly what is so sensational about this dump?

In my bag I have the complete series of 'Rau-reports' dealing with Hostau: Ehrenfried Brandts had selected and copied them for me and festooned them with yellow adhesive notes with comments. They even contain a report on the 'reproductive career' of Conversano Bonavista. In the spring of 1943 he covered twelve mares for a total of thirty-five acts of coitus, resulting in five pregnancies. His degree of fertility came out to 41.7 per cent. Gustav Rau looked at the figures and, going against Major Rudofsky's advice, summoned Bonavista for a second try during the 1944 foaling season.

Martina calls to me. She is standing beside a low brick wall, behind which she has discovered a pen for piglets. On a carpet of hay beneath a heat lamp, a row of bristly little sausages are cuddled up together. The cord disappears around a corner, where we find a chopping block with an axe in it. There is no wall plug, the cable runs further through a crack in the outside wall: from the looks of it, the electricity is being tapped illegally from the nearby pylon. Beneath the eaves is a rain barrel, the stinging nettles make way here for little plots of chives and beans, and suddenly we realize that this end of the biggest Lipizzaner stud farm in history is inhabited by people. The bright red wheelbarrow belongs to a Czech toddler who is growing up in a stable.

∪

Across Liberation Street, behind the former brewery and the Church of St Jacob, is a home for young offenders. We had gone there for a look earlier in the day with the mayor of Hostau. 'No murderers or rapists, just thieves and drug addicts,' the mayor said. During our tour of the village he had avoided the stalls, which he felt were in no state to be seen. The minimum-security reform school, however, was neatly fitted with rain pipes and aluminium window frames. During the Second World War, this renovated country house flanked by stately old trees had served as the administrative office for the stud farm.

The mayor drove his Volkswagen over the hissing gravel to the front steps, where sixty years earlier Commander Rudofsky had reined in his Lipizzaners each morning. His orderly, standing ready to take his carriage whip, had by then polished his spare boots and would deliver a concise report on the birth of a foal or whatever else had happened during the night.

The mayor raised his hands helplessly: sorry, he didn't know the details. 'Why don't you two tell me what happened here?' he suggested. Like me, he was born in 1964. Trained as an agricultural engineer – that, too, we had in common. The mayor pointed a hairy hand at the gardens of the correctional institute: two wings of the building had once stood there, which meant it had been a true manor house: Schloss Trauttmansdorff.

The Trauttmansdorff family, I told him, had been nobility under the Danube Monarchy – a house of equerries to the court at Vienna. Their fortified castle stood downriver at the district seat of Bischofteinitz, where the aristocratic Rudofsky also came from.

'Please, tell me more!' the mayor urged. All he knew was that, before the revolution, Count Trauttmansdorff had owned 'everything around here that even looked like a pasture'.

'The revolution?' I ask.

Martina elbows me in the ribs: that's what they call the communist coup in Czechoslovakia.

The mayor tugs at the tails of his lumberjack shirt. 'After the war, this manor house was occupied by Russian border guards and became completely run-down,' he went on. 'Until 1990, this was their barracks.' His municipality ran all the way to the border zone, a strip of land about ten kilometres wide where only the villagers were allowed to go – to graze their cows or gather hay. Beyond that buffer you had no-man's-land: two kilometres of untrammelled nature all the way to the actual line of demarcation between communism and capitalism. When we met at the town hall, he had shown us the only history book about Hostau: a photographic chronicle dealing with the years 1948–89. It turned out to be a commemorative album in black and white, showing the annual May Day parades with Soviet soldiers driving jeeps down Liberation Street, sometimes with a decorated combine harvester out in front by way of a festive float. COMMUNISM IS OUR OBJECTIVE! the placards cried. The International Day of Labour had rolled around year after year, with such complete interchangeability that all sense of chronology was lost.

As we leafed through the book, the mayor fidgeted in his leather armchair. What else could he show us? Oh yes, there was a recent aerial photo of Hostau that hung at the foot of the stairs, and there were also the brochures put together in the last few years by the *Heimatkreis*.

The word *Heimatkreis* didn't immediately ring a bell with me. I looked at Martina, but she simply straightened her glasses and asked him something in Czech, then translated his answer for me: each village in the Sudetenland had an active circle of residents-in-exile. Members of the original German population, in other words, who had all been driven out after 1945. '*Odsun*, they call that,' Martina explained, 'literally something like "relocation", but in the Czech Republic that's something we don't talk about much.' What it came down to was that the Czech victors had collectively sent the Sudeten Germans packing to Germany, almost to a man. They, after all, had been the ones who'd cheered '*Ein Volk, ein Reich, ein Führer!*' back in 1938 – so now, with no exceptions, they had to get out. Each individual was allowed to take fifty kilos of baggage. Jewels, watches, precious metals, foreign securities and savings deposit booklets were confiscated. Then the Germans were deported across the border in boxcars.

I looked out the window, across the chimneys of Hostau, and thought about how the villagers had been forced out of their homes in two separate sweeps, first the Czechs to the east and then, seven years later, the Germans to the west, obliterated by the ethnic broom of war that always sweeps twice, like the eraser in a child's magnetic drawing toy.

During the entr'acte, there had been more horses than people in Hostau. Of the modern-day population of 1,000 souls, there was no one – the mayor was willing to bet his chain of office on this – who remembered the period October 1938 to May 1945. Of the original Czech population, only Mr Váchal had come back. Holding his mobile phone at arm's length, the mayor thumbed quickly through his list of contacts and dictated Mr Váchal's number. 'He can tell you about the time before the war, but he wasn't here during the German occupation.'

The Rau-reports in my bag dealt precisely with those blanked-out years. They described how, in the stalls behind the church, a bold genetic venture had been carried out with the Lipizzaner breed. The regal white animal, Hitler's chief equerry felt, left plenty of room for improvement. In terms of temperament Rau found the Lipizzaner to be in a class apart: eager to learn, intelligent, high-spirited yet friendly towards humans. But in Rau's judgement, the animal's loco-motion was too stiff. A 'foursquare horse', not fast on its feet or much of a jumper. Its charm was undeniable, and was due in part to a fortuitous inbred trait: the breed possessed rela-tively straight forearms (at forty degrees, rather than forty-five), which caused the Lipizzan foal to lift its legs higher and therefore frolic more gracefully than other breeds. Rau was not out to do away with this noble trait, but he did hope to release the Lipizzaner from its 'old-fashioned shackles' and give it a 'more military' bearing. As I followed the signposts of Brandts' Post-it notes, I had encountered one surprise after another. In order to achieve post-haste his breeding objective of a stockier, more supple Lipizzaner, Rau instituted contro-versial breeding schemes. And he had covered his back by reporting in advance to Berlin that 'crossing full brothers and sisters was not unusual in the context of the most recent, authoritative studies into genetics'. At Hostau, with the same bravura with which he had crossed coldbloods with warm-bloods and draught horses with saddle horses, he set about crossing stallions and mares closely related by blood. Using the Lipizzaner, Rau tested the method known as 'line-breeding': the intentional use of inbreeding.

He ordered Rudofsky to have nieces covered by nephews,

and even daughters by fathers. Amongst humans this was called incest, and was subject to taboos all over the world, but led by the *Herrenvolk*, the noble race, the German Empire sought supremacy precisely through selection and cross-breeding, and would be held back by no obstacles in its drive to experiment with racial upgrading. Rabbit and poultry breeders used inbreeding to put the finishing touches to their product. *Blutanschluss*, the annexation of blood, was what the Germans called it. Once the breeders had moulded the desired form from their raw materials, the next step was to accentuate the traits and perpetuate the acquired result. At the same time, linebreeding was an effective method for magnifying certain characteristics. And if it worked with chickens, Gustav Rau must have reasoned, then why not with horses? If one crossed a long-maned father with one of his long-maned daughters, there was a good chance of getting a foal with an even longer mane. The continuous crossing and recrossing of close relatives, paradoxical as it may sound, contributed to the creation of a stable and 'pure' line. Inbreeding promoted the linkage of uniform alleles: the AA and aa combinations slowly but surely displaced the Aa vari-ation, and the descendants began resembling each other more and more. But linebreeding was also a game of roulette: one tried to up the ante, but then at the risk of malformed crea-tures of interest only to the butcher.

Rau to Berlin: 'Have informed Colonel Padhojsky that he is in no way to interfere with the breeding programme at Hostau.'

∪

During our tour with the mayor we had also climbed out at Hostau station, where a diesel train called twice a day. On the far side of the platform was a showjumping field with fences and a set of wooden grandstands. 'That's pretty much all Hostau has left of its equestrian past,' the mayor said. The field was soggy, there were no horses to be seen. Beneath a galvanized tin roof a group of ten boys huddled together, peering over the collars of their coats. The mayor knew them, they lived at the young offenders' institute. They couldn't have been older than seventeen, but their heads were bald and their old-looking faces covered with scars. The tallest among them stared at the piercings in Martina's nostrils, but he too turned away at last, his shoulders exuding hostility.

In the Nazi era these boys would have been classified as degenerate examples of humanity. The inspectors of the Third Reich would have had no qualms about placing them in the *Ausfalltypus*, the rubbish-bin category, as a group society would be better off disposing of. They would probably have been sent to the front as cannon fodder. In the Czech Republic, in 2007, they were given a second chance through the system of probation and aftercare; the commonly accepted notion was that, if they are removed from their unwholesome surroundings and transplanted elsewhere, such boys can be 'resocialized'. Nurture mattered.

It began drizzling. Back in the car I asked the mayor how the people of Hostau made their livings these days.

'I sometimes ask myself the same thing,' he said cheerfully. There was no tourism, no economy. Anyone who didn't have a government position did a few odd jobs on the side, fattened pigs in the garage, received money orders from children who worked tiling bathrooms in Germany. 'Otherwise, everyone hopes to make a fortune one day by finding buried treasure.'

He grinned and paused for effect. Amateur archaeology, he said, was very much on the rise, and had been ever since the fall of communism. All those who could afford to bought a metal detector and went out into the forest in search of jewels that Sudeten Germans had buried there before their expulsion. Every once in a while someone would actually find valuables, boxes containing the family silver, medals, gold cufflinks. Or silver candlesticks. Sometimes the find was a disappointment: nothing but waterproofed cashbooks, diaries or tins containing family snapshots. The mayor made a point of urging treasure hunters to bring in even those discoveries that had no monetary value. Via the *Heimatkreis*, the private effects might make their way back to their rightful owners or their families. 'For them, it does have value.'

At first I assumed that he was our pulling our legs. But he went on in all earnestness about a 'catalogue of missing villages', which the archaeologists used as their guide. Published with German funding, it was an atlas of fifty Sudeten settlements abandoned in 1945 and razed during the Cold War. Back at the town hall, the mayor handed me a copy. 'Here you are,' he said. 'Keep it. In exchange for your book, once it's finished.'

∪

In the bar on the corner, we examined the catalogue. The missing villages went marching by in alphabetical order: Dianahof, Haselbach, Oberhütten, Plöss, Ruhstein, Unterhütten; each of them listed with their Czech name as well, and with a separate page enlivened with old picture postcards, cadastral maps and particulars about a bronze church bell or the decorative woodcarvings in a hunting lodge.

A barmaid in a Bavarian pinafore came to take our order. I looked past her at the tap and saw that, in this stale-smelling barroom, the only brew that flowed was pilsner – the most famous Czech invention of all.

The volume was predetermined as well. With two half-litre mugs within reaching distance, we read about the plundered, ethnically German villages in the shadow of the Border of Socialism and Peace. After the communist takeover, these unattended, half-collapsed structures were a useful hiding place for those wishing to defect or flee to the capitalist hemisphere. So Zemstav, a 'people's' contracting company in Prague with the heaviest of bulldozers, was called in. The comrades from Zemstav let their engines of destruction roar from seven in the morning to four in the afternoon; for every flattened house the demolition service received 40,000 crowns. For a church or a water-driven sawmill, the honorarium was much higher. Zemstav's 1955 annual report spoke of the 'reclamation of usable building materials' – measured in cubic metres. That year, these raw materials came from the villages of Heuhof (ten houses demolished), Schwarzau (six), Schneiderhof (thirty-six), Neumark (four), Maxberg (ten), Fichtenbach (seven), Vollmau (five), Haselbach (thirty-one) and Grafenreid (seventy-one).

The figures had an effect on Martina too, whose own Cold War experiences seemed paltry in comparison with this violent feat of earthmoving. In the late 1980s, at her primary school in Prague, the teachers had instilled in her a fear of the West by means of gasmask drills. 'The alarm would go off and everyone had to pull one of those rigid rubber things down over their face, and above all: carry on playing.' The siren marking the chemical-weapons drill was a final, fainter echo of the general hysteria under which these border inhabitants had truly suffered.

Before the fortifications of the Iron Curtain were raised to full fighting strength – including a *Todeswand* (death fence) with fatal voltage running through its wires – thousands of Czechoslovakians had scampered like mountain goats across the ridge of the Bohemian Forest. According to the atlas, that human migration had lasted six months, from February 1948, when the communists seized power, until the late summer of that year. Only then were border troops finally able to halt the flow of refugees by means of intensive patrolling. To staunch the final dregs as well, the Czechoslovakian Stasi, the StB, came into action. StB agents pretended to be frontier-runners who knew unpatrolled escape routes through the wilderness. For pay, they would bring 'defection-sensitive' individuals to a quiet path in the forest, with a barrier at the end: the promised 'outpost' of an American army base on West German soil. The final steps to freedom they had to take on their own, until stopped by a silent 'Yankee' who led them to a canteen. In that bare room they were presented with a form for requesting political asylum – complete with questions concerning the reason for their flight. As soon as the form was completed, the asylum-seeker was handcuffed. The damning evidence was there in black and white, written in his own hand.

One of these StB traps, replete with American flags, was pictured in the catalogue: a little house in the forest not far from the glassblowers' settlement of Fichtenbach, also razed in the 1950s.

∪

A watery sun has reappeared, but the landscape around Hostau seems grimmer. The air has grown colder and smoke is curling up from the chimneys, the characteristic odour of the Eastern Bloc is everywhere: on this side of the dividing line, coal is still the standard heating fuel. As we wait for Mr Váchal to come home, we climb to the top of a hill. His son had answered the phone: his father, he said, had gone to

Bischofteinitz but would be home in half an hour – they have no doorbell, after five o'clock we could simply let ourselves in through the garden gate.

At the edge of the forest is a little chapel. Virgin, baby Jesus, tea-warmer. The furnishings are brand new. We have a view of the valley of the Radbuza, the rolling pastureland and the little huddle of houses around St Jacob's Church. Atop a hill in the distance, a spindly border-patrol radar mast peeks over the treetops. Martina says this landscape reminds her of a novel by Bohumil Hrabal, set in the Bohemian Forest amid the wreckage of Sudeten–German history.

Back in Prague – at the literature festival in the theatre reclaimed from the waters of the Vltava – we had talked about Hrabal too, and about his most famous work, *I Served the King of England*, written in 1971. I had seen the film based on the book, and then read the novel. What had struck me was a parallel with the model stud farm at Hostau. At the time of the German invasion, the Sudeten girl Liza initiates the hero of Hrabal's classic, Jan Ditie (Ditie means 'child'), into the secrets of pure blood. Through her, he – as a Slavic boy ('flaxen hair and blue eyes') – is able to work his way up to the position of waiter in an idyllic mountain hotel with a statuary garden full of Teutonic warriors and other pure-bred Germans in horned helmets. 'Liza explained to me that this was to be the site of the first European breeding station for the improvement of the human race.' Jan Ditie serves beakers of milk to buxom country wenches and Rhine and Mösel wine to the thoroughbred soldiers of the SS. Then he realizes that the girls retire to the hotel rooms for the same reason that 'the heifer must go to the bull, and the goat to the village billy'.

This was no grotesque fantasy; the grotesqueness was in the reality Himmler had created, in the special leave he had instituted for SS officers to go to fancy hotels in the mountains and reproduce. 'All wars constitute a letting of the best blood', Himmler had written in his 'siring order' in October 1939. The losses of male soldiers had to be compensated for, and the most intensive participation in sexual intercourse was the due of Germany's racial elite: the SS.

Along the same lines, it was Hitler who declared a *Kleinkrieg* (an offensive) against contraceptive devices and abortions. 'Sex lives are our concern,' the Führer said. And: 'A people will not die out due to the loss of men, but it will when there is a shortage of women.'

The mares were more important.

U

Of course, all these motherhood premiums and the medals received by women surpassing the propaganda goal of four children per family were ridiculed. 'May you be as fertile as Hitler!' the whispered joke went. But Magda Goebbels, with her six children, did fulfil the exemplary role of super-mother. And unwed mothers within the SS's Lebensborn programme, who were referred to as 'the Führer's brides', were given all the room and rest they needed to nurse and care for their babies. The obsession with blond hair and blue eyes meant that Scandinavia had the densest network of such SS clinics: 12,000 Lebensborn children came into the world there, and were often 'baptized' during a ritual with the ceremonial SS dagger.

Martina saw where I was heading with all this: the breeding of Lipizzaners under Rau as a mirror to Himmler's birthing clinics.

Like the Lebensborn houses, the chief equerry's stud farms, with their peacefully grazing mares flanked by a playful foal, focused on the expansion and improvement of the chosen race. The *Wehrmacht* expected Rau to supply them with 6,000 new horses each month to replace those killed, but his ambitions went further: the creation of the ideal warhorse. In his model stud farm at Hostau, the most intensive participation in sexual intercourse was the due of the elite Viennese stallions. As soon as their progeny reached the age of six months, they had a sign burned into their hide with a glowing staff: an H with a dagger struck down the middle, through the horizontal bar.

U

We find Mr Váchal in his shed. His cheeks are criss-crossed with purple veins and he wears a knitted cap with a white stripe down the middle. His son, as it turns out, didn't tell him we were coming, but that doesn't matter – he always has time to answer a question.

Mr Váchal nods: that's right, he is the only surviving inhabitant of Hostau who also lived here before the war.

Horses?

He nods again. Horses, of course. Mr Váchal stands there, surrounded by his long-necked geese, and submits to the conversation like an interrogation. He makes no move to invite us in, but after a while he asks a question of his own: had we seen the village school at the edge of town?

Not that we can remember.

'It looks out over the stud farm. If only you knew how often we saw soldiers fall off their horses!'

Before the Germans came, Mr Váchal says, the Czechoslovakian army bred and trained its cavalry mounts here. Between Schloss Trauttmansdorff and the school was a field with a wooden fence around it where the young animals were broken in. First they had a dummy tied to their back, then they were mounted by a recruit. He had watched scenes that resembled a rodeo, and he wasn't the only one – even the teacher sometimes lost track of what he was saying.

After the formal, slightly hesitant start, Mr Váchal proves more talkative. As a ten-year-old boy, he tells us, he heard the leader of the Sudeten Germans cursing and ranting at a rally. On 1 October 1938 the Germans pulled into Hostau, just after the school year had begun.

'There were parades with swastikas, I went to the square in front of the church with my parents, to watch. The boys from my class screamed at me: "*Tschechischer Hund!*" Czech dog!'

I ask whether he speaks German.

He had, once. Fluently. Like everyone else. But he refuses to speak it ever again. 'I wasn't allowed into the classroom any more and had to go to a little school for ethnic minorities. That lasted all of two weeks, then we were deported.'

Never in all his life had he seen a Lipizzaner. The Lipizzaners' 'German' years were precisely the ones he had missed.

Mr Váchal steps into his shed to put away a rake and a spade.

That's all he knows. 'You can do the arithmetic yourself,' he says. 'My father was born in 1898. Yesterday would have been his birthday. He joined the partisans, and took part in the liberation of Hostau. He arrived here along with the Red Army on 17 May 1945. The horses were gone by then.'

OPERATION COWBOY

I N THE END, IT was not the *Heimatkreis* who put me in
touch with a stray member of the Rudofsky family, it was
the Church of Latter Day Saints in Utah – thanks to the
tentacles of their genealogical web. One of the Mormons'
family-tree sites showed a query posted by a man by the name
of U. Rudofsky, under the heading 'Bohemia'. My response –
'Are you by any chance related to Major Hubert Rudofsky?' – hit
the bullseye, a lucky shot if ever there was one.

Dear Mr Westerman,

Major Hubert Rudofsky, commander of the military
stud farm at Hostau from 1943 to 1945, was my uncle.
He was my father's eldest brother. I inherited all his
papers. If you're interested, I would be pleased to run
through them and share them with you. Greetings and
all the best,
     Ulrich Hubert Rudofsky
     Delmar, New York, USA

PS: For some reason, your email ended up in my spam
folder, but my eye fell on the word 'Bohemia'.

Of course I was interested, but I was also looking for an eyewitness – someone who could give me a first-hand account of the final hours at Hostau. The next day, as soon as the American East Coast had finished breakfast, nephew Ulrich Rudofsky checked in again:

> Of course I also have memories of my own concerning the Lipizzaners and the war. But please bear in mind: I was only ten at the time. I liked to visit Uncle Hubert at the stud farm. My favourite animal was a baby Lipizzaner with a reddish coat. When you blew on his hair you could see his pale skin shining through. All the other foals were either black or grey. And I remember their intriguing names: Maestoso, Pluto, Africa.
>
> But before I go on: I'm on Skype, with a webcam connection. Are you?

I had Skype, but no camera. I asked Mr Rudofsky when the best time would be to call.

Not right away, he replied, he had to go to the hospital that afternoon for an oesophageal endoscopy. He would probably have trouble talking after the examination, but he suggested we try later in the week. 'PS: You may wonder why I'm so eager to tell you about all this. I'm seventy-two and have a strong feeling that I should talk to someone about my past. My own children aren't particularly interested.'

In preparation, I watched and re-watched *Miracle of the White Stallions* – the 1963 Hollywood movie of which Hans Brabenetz had been so critical. The title wasn't hard to find, and it was even easier to order the DVD online. The cover showed a poster along the lines of *Doctor Zhivago*: 'Louis' Podhajsky in his colonel's uniform, with his wife Verena clinging to his chest – surrounded by galloping white horses

being herded by American tanks. 'The day the war stood still
. . . for a daring man, a devoted woman and 1,000 magnificent
stallions.'

It was a peculiar film, one that suggested that the life of a
horse, or at least that of a Lipizzaner stallion, was worth
more than a human's. Yet this, in fact, was true: history, and
this particular history especially, confirmed it.

The opening scenes were set in Vienna in March 1945 and
based on Podhajsky's own memoirs – about the Allied bombs
raining down on the city despite the anti-aircraft guns on the
Flaktürme, about his repeated requests to evacuate the
performing horses (requests which met time and again with
a *'Nein'* from his superiors), about his preparations to flee
the city regardless, followed by a chaotic trip with the stallions to a train station overrun with refugees and the journey
by livestock carriage, with repeated bombardments along the
way. Ultimately, the horses found shelter at Sankt Martin,
only a stone's throw from Hitler's birthplace.

There were lots of aspects with which one could find fault
(Robert Taylor's rather wooden acting, the screenplay's lack
of nuance), but it was not an outright falsification. Alois
Podhajsky and his wife Verena really had fled Vienna with
the stallions (including Conversano Bonavista, returned from
his tour of servicing duty). Bombs had fallen on
Michaelerplatz, and damaged the Stallburg. Fear of the
advancing Russian army was justified, especially in view of
the fate of the stallions recently evacuated from the Riding
School's dependency in Budapest. At first, the Hungarian
evacuation had seemed to progress successfully and on time:
the horses arrived at their haven on the puszta just before
the Red Army besieged Budapest and then took the capital
on 13 February 1945. Riding-school commander Géza von
Haszlinszky, with his greys and his hussars, had moved

westward in stages, from one stopover to the next. At last he sent one of his men ahead to Vienna to act as quartermaster; Podhajsky offered the Hungarian envoy the use of the entire Stallburg, given that he was himself about to leave with his own animals. The hussars of Budapest, however, were not fast enough. On 24 March 1945, their convoy of Lipizzaners – barely an hour's march from the Austrian border – was overtaken by Soviet tanks. Eighteen of the stallions proved so high-spirited and unmanageable that they were butchered on the spot; the four remaining horses allowed themselves to be harnessed and were put to work pulling ammunition wagons towards Vienna.

In the film, Verena Podhajsky (played by Lilli Palmer) is more quaky and impetuous than her real-life counterpart, but the events themselves accord with historical fact. In real life, as well as in Hollywood's version, Podhajsky/Taylor removed his uniform just in time to meet the enemy in civilian clothes.

By now the script was moving towards its first climax: the hasty preparations for a performance on 7 May 1945, for General George Patton and his men. As commander of the US 3rd Army, the tank-strategist had forced a breach across the Rhine, opening up southern Germany and Austria to an Allied advance. On the penultimate day of the war, however, he attended an improvised performance by the riding school in exile, with music selected by Podhajsky, a *pas de deux* act, exercises on the long rein and high-style exercises 'above the ground'.

Conversano Bonavista put in an appearance in the ring as well. Just as he had danced shortly before the war for Hitler's most loyal Austrian, Arthur Seyss-Inquart, so he danced now for the victors who would soon put to death Seyss-Inquart and his ilk.

At the end of the show, Podhajsky himself, astride Neapolitano Africa, asked the American commander to grant protection to the Royal Spanish Riding School – and not only to the Lipizzaner stallions themselves, but also the mares and foals in Hostau, Czechoslovakia. 'Without the mares, the breed will die out,' he said.

Photographs of this solemn moment still exist. General Patton had risen to his feet when Podhajsky addressed him, and tapped his fingers against the brim of his helmet.

The entry in Patton's diary on that seventh day of May read: 'It struck me as rather strange that, in the midst of a world at war, some twenty young and middle-aged men in great physical condition ... had spent their entire time teaching a group of horses to wiggle their butts and raise their feet in consonance with certain signals from the heels and reins.'

In the film, he says more or less the same thing out loud. But then, with the cinematic clock at fifty-eight minutes and with half an hour still to go, script and reality part company: in the silver-screen version, Patton honours Podhajsky's request by immediately ordering the liberation of the mares and their foals from Hostau.

'They Disneyfied the truth,' Hans Brabenetz had warned me.

∪

Hubert Rudofsky had turned forty-eight on that same seventh day of May. In a report drawn up by Hitler's chief equerry, Gustav Rau, in April 1945, one reads that Rudofsky, as the most senior German officer for miles around, has been charged with defending Hostau. Geographically speaking, as an obscure pinpoint on the map, the Lipizzaners' haven at

Hostau was far away from the front lines. In the spring of 1945, however, the Russians were closing in from the east and the Americans from the west, rendering the Sudetenland an increasingly narrow corridor of German occupation. Hundreds of prisoners of war had been put to work at Hostau and the Gestapo was investigating the loyalty of local nobleman Count Trauttmansdorff, but there was no fighting going on.

It was in the summer of 1944 that the shockwaves from the German defeats on the Eastern Front first reached the stud farm. Only a single season after it had been established, Gustav Rau found himself compelled to dismantle his Lipizzaner outpost in the Ukraine. The thirty-five horses with their foals, originally dispatched as a part of *Generalplan Ost*, now returned to Hostau after an 800-kilometre march. Two of the mares, Basta and Batista, succumbed on arrival to the highly contagious disease glanders. Rau ordered the entire herd quarantined. But once the risk of an epidemic had blown over, a new problem presented itself: where were all these horses to be quartered for the winter? On 18-20 October 1944, Rau and Rudofsky inspected the entire Lipizzaner herd of close to 500 animals and singled out seventy-three to be sold at the *Rossmarkt* on the square outside the Church of St Jacob. 'Everything with a bad temperament must go.'

In his dispatches, calmly, as though the pan-German Empire were not about to collapse, the chief equerry aired his views on the new and in his eyes highly promising field of animal psychology. Rau's more mundane entries were interspersed with philosophical ramblings about the extent to which the *behaviour* of both man and animal was genetically determined – and the far-reaching effects such an insight might have on breeding activities. Without naming names, he appeared familiar with the pioneering work of Austrian

zoologist Konrad Lorenz, who in 1942 had helped the authorities in Poland to test individuals for their ' German-ness',
and who reported that in 'half-breeds' of mixed Polish and
German parentage, 'the German aptitude for efficiency is
largely negated by hybridization'. Rau seemed well informed
about the central tenet of animal behavioural studies, as
advanced by Lorenz and a handful of others ever since the
1930s, that in addition to physical traits such as blood type,
eye colour or shape of the nasal profile, certain behavioural
profiles were also fixed by genetic predisposition.

Newly hatched Greylag goslings, for example, automatically went waddling after the first moving object they saw
– normally speaking the mother goose, but in Lorenz's experiments the Austrian ethologist himself. Some behaviour, in
other words, was not learned but genetically 'preprogrammed'. In this way, like Mendel before him, the future
Nobel Prize laureate Lorenz won a major round in the 'nature
vs nurture' debate, to the benefit of nature and, indeed, of
Nazi ideology. With a clarity of mind striking amid the
doomsday events of 1945, Gustav Rau understood the signs
of the times and coolly conceived a plan to apply these latest
insights to the breeding of Lipizzaners. From now on, his
inspectors were required to select more often for traits such
as inquisitiveness, obedience and intelligence, since such
intangible characteristics were now understood to be genetically determined to a far greater degree than had previously
been supposed. In the same entry, Rau reported his plan to
recruit black Lipizzaner stallions for siring. The semblance
of normality continued for a long time. Yet seeping in
between the lines one saw more and more bad tidings. In
early 1945 a stud farm in eastern Poland was overrun by the
Soviets: 'Major damage caused by gangs of Red Cossacks.
They spare nothing, and seem to have specialized themselves

in the stealing of horses.' Rau ordered the immediate evacuation of the Polish stallion depot at Racot ('on 21 January at 10 a.m., in four convoys') across the Oder to Hostau. The next to last set of my photocopies bore one of Brandts' yellow Post-its: 'The Rau Network disintegrates. Dramatic!'

I read about stable attendants who cut and ran, severed telephone connections and a stampede by a group of Arab horses strafed by a swarm of Allied planes near Dresden: 'Because some of the attendants released their horses during the attack, the stallions Allegro, Lampas, Dar II, Zeus, Adagio, Königspage, Omega, Einerlei, Krokant and Liwiec were able to escape. The stallion Atlas was later found dead. Minorit suffered a broken coffin bone and had to be shot, as did Ikarus.'

Finally, on 14 March, the horses from Racot arrived at Hostau 'without any loss of breeding material'. The herd, when it arrived after a gruelling march of more than 1,000 kilometres through the snow, turned out to comprise no fewer than 170 animals: the Kabardins and Don ponies taken to Poland one year earlier by Dr Frielinghaus. Now, along with a band of Cossack deserters, they were at Rudofsky's doorstep. What was he supposed to do with them? The Cossack chieftain, a man who styled himself 'Prince' Amassov, was determined to stay out of the hands of the Russians. He and his men offered to assume the work of the stableboys who had deserted, which turned out to be a blessing in disguise.

Brandts' stick-it note on the next set of reports read: 'The last!'

The siring was in full swing. During Rau's last visit to Hostau, on 3–5 April 1945, he ordered three new school stallions brought in. For lack of rail or road transport, they were to be 'led or ridden from Sankt Martin, where the Viennese

Royal Spanish Riding School is now present'. With military concision, he also confirmed the appointment of Lt Col. Hubert Rudofsky as 'commander-in-arms of the base at Hostau'.

The final report was dated 25 April 1945, and dealt with two mares, Marschmusik and Dragonerliebchen, that Rau had been forced to turn over to an infantry division.

The rest of the page was empty.

On it, in pencil, Ehrenfried Brandts had written: 'Rau met the British officers in civilian dress. He was not taken prisoner.'

☽

Swallowing was still painful, but talking wasn't much of a problem for Ulrich Rudofsky. Every once in a while he interrupted our transatlantic conversation for a sip of water.

'So you were not only in Hostau, but also in Bischofteinitz. Well then, when you walked along the castle wall from the church square, you must have seen a pharmacy on the corner opposite the bridge. That's the house where I lived until I was ten.'

Ulrich spoke English with an American drawl, and not a hint of a German accent. His grandparents' house, he told me, was a neo-Roman villa that now served as a catering college. His father, a general physician with a practice of his own, had left for the Eastern Front and never sent word home. Then, after the war, he suddenly materialized again. Shortly afterwards, he took his own life. Ulrich had barely known him.

'So, from a very early age, therefore, I considered Uncle Hubert my foster father. I called him "Onka Hu" or just plain "Onka", and he always called me "Matzl", even after I'd turned fifty.'

I asked about his uncle – did he remember anything from the days of Hostau and Bischofteinitz?

'I can still picture him driving by with his team of Lipizzaners. He always passed under our window, and if I didn't have to go to school I was allowed to go along. After the war, when my mother and sister moved to America, he paid my college tuition. I've always been grateful to him for that.'

Our conversation was ricocheting back and forth like a pinball. But all I had to do was mention a name, and the machine invariably lit up.

Gustav Rau? 'Of course, he used to come to the house for tea. Onka would be there too, and whenever I came in he would make me recite the seven-times table. Or spell some difficult word. I hated that.' He knew the Cossack Prince Amassov, too. 'He picked me up once and put me on the back of a big, black horse. As the story goes, I shouted in a squeaky voice: "*Onka Hu, es ist heiss hier oben*. Uncle Hu, it's hot up here."'

Ulrich was an altar boy at the church in Bischofteinitz. The church had a stained-glass window donated by his grandparents on the occasion of Uncle Hubert's safe return from the First World War, during which Hubert had fought as a dragoon in the Piave valley. On the other shore, Ernest Hemingway, still beardless and only eighteen, was driving an ambulance for the Italian wounded – and was finally wounded himself while distributing mail and cigarettes.

'Uncle Hubert never missed Mass on Sunday. He would arrive still wearing his *Wehrmacht* uniform. I now have his soldier's logbook, in which he wrote that he was a Roman Catholic and, if mortally wounded, wished to receive extreme unction.'

Ulrich's Aunt Brigitta lived further down the main street.

'She was the boss of all of the Nazi women in Bischofteinitz. Her husband was cut from exactly the same cloth. Not Uncle Hubert, though. Deep in his heart he remained an Austrian monarchist – k.u.k., does that term mean anything to you?'

I wondered whether the Rudofskys saw themselves as members of any particular ethnic group, but didn't quite know how to broach the subject.

Ulrich himself had no problem with that: 'We're Germans, with Polish roots. Driven out of Silesia in the sixteenth century during another wave of ethnic purification.'

Sitting at his computer in New York State, I could hear Rudofsky start to cough. He said his throat hurt. Bischofteinitz, he went on, had survived the war almost unscathed. At the very end, though, a stream of refugees had passed through the town, pulling and pushing carts containing everything they owned. They were heading west, away from the Russians. Roadblocks of telegraph poles and wire were thrown up across the street. 'There was one opposite our house, at the bridge. That was exciting. The members of the *Volkssturm*, the civilian militia, and the Hitler Youth took up positions behind the wall of the castle and between the tombs in the cemetery. A gun was put in my hands as well; my school-teacher was the local militia commander. But when Uncle Hubert saw me, he took away the gun and sent me home. I was still only a child, he said.'

On the day Bischofteinitz fell, Onka Hu was at the stud farm in Hostau. Ulrich, along with his classmates, took cover behind the castle walls again. Tanks were actually approaching this time, but not from the east. They were rolling across the hills from the direction of Germany. When the first one stopped at the bridge over the Radbuz with its engine roaring in front of the barricade, he saw that it had a star on it. The Americans! It was five o'clock in the afternoon. Then came the repeated pop of gunfire. The barrel of the cannon rotated slowly towards the cemetery, followed by a dull boom. Ulrich felt the earth – and his boyish legs – tremble. Then everything was quiet. A minute later, led by the teacher, they came out of hiding, waving a white sheet.

'It wasn't until much later that I heard what had happened at Hostau, and why it was the Americans and not the Russians who arrived first.'

U

Among the photographs and scanned documents Ulrich had posted me before his endoscopy was a typewritten report entitled 'Fate of the Lipizzaner stud farms during the war years 1941–1945', by Hubert Rudofsky himself. There was also an interview with Rudofsky's chief veterinarian, Rudolf Lessing, and the memoirs of the American commander, Charles Reed, written in 1970.

Using those documents, I was able to reconstruct the fall of Hostau with a reasonable degree of precision.

The arrival of a bicycle messenger marks the beginning of the end. It is 26 April 1945, around one in the afternoon. He is carrying a handwritten message addressed to Lt Col. Rudofsky. The sender's signature is so sloppily written that all Rudofsky can make out is 'Walter H.' This Walter H. introduces himself as a *Luftwaffe* officer who has been taken prisoner by the Americans and who has promptly informed them about the location where Hitler has concealed the breeding stock of the Lipizzaners. There is a chance, he feels, that the animals can be played into the hands of the Americans, but time is of the essence: the Russians may arrive at Hostau within days. All Lt Col. Rudofsky must do is promise not to put up a fight. To capitulate, in other words. The proposal before him, he reads, was drafted with the cognizance and agreement of Col. Charles Reed of the 2nd Cavalry Regiment of Fort Riley, Kansas. By the time Rudofsky reads this, the Americans will have halted at the western edge of the Bohemian Forest. These two men, the vanquished and the victor, have apparently agreed that the Lipizzaner breed belongs to the West, and not to the Bolsheviks from Moscow.

Rudofsky is in a quandary. As a military man of honour, he has sworn allegiance to the Führer and the Nazi flag. On the other hand, rumour has it that the Russians simply eat the horses they capture, regardless of race or pedigree.

Rudofsky confides in Dr Lessing, his chief veterinarian, and sends him across the ridge on horseback to seek more information from the Americans.

Late that evening in the officers' mess – darkness has already fallen – Rudofsky's envoy is given a thorough questioning. Col. Charles Reed, whose regiment switched from horses to tanks only in 1942, is convinced of the value of the prize now within reach. There is only one problem: he cannot take the animals out of Czechoslovakia, for that would be a violation of the Yalta Agreement. On the Crimean peninsula, Stalin, Roosevelt and Churchill – the three men had even posed for the photographer on a sunlit bench – have only recently agreed on the point to which the Red Army will be allowed to advance, and the limits to be respected by the Americans, the British and the Canadians. This 'Yalta line' runs straight along the crest of the Bohemian Forest, the pre-war border between Germany and Czechoslovakia. Colonel Reed proposes that he collect the Lipizzaners once they have been driven to his side of the ridge.

Impossible, Lessing feels. There are too many animals at Hostau, a herd that size could never be smuggled across the mountains unseen. Besides, this is foaling season.

Colonel Reed decides to report the situation to his highest commander, General Patton. Does he have permission, he asks the general, to cross the Yalta line once in order to keep many hundreds of Europe's noblest horses from falling into Russian hands?

Patton is also a cavalry man, who once took part – on a borrowed horse – in the 5,000-metre steeplechase at the 1912 Stockholm Olympics.

The reply is quick in coming: 'Get them. Make it fast. You will have a new mission.'

∪

That same day, 26 April, the first mortar shells – presumably American – fall on Hostau. They blow craters in the pastures and cause the horses to bolt, but the animals remain unharmed. Rudofsky realizes he is trapped. His final orders from Berlin had been to remain at his post and hold position. He and his men are expected to fight to the death to protect an empire that is evaporating before their eyes. In the streets, the Hitler Youth are running amok. Then, suddenly, a *Wehrmacht* general sweeps into the village in a Mercedes. He is on the run and has decided to billet himself in Hostau. The general selects the offices of the stud farm as his command post, edges Rudofsky aside and begins handing out orders to the Nazi faithful.

When Chief Veterinarian Lessing returns in the middle of the night, the situation becomes '*brenzlich*' (volatile), in Rudofsky's own words. Suspecting nothing, Lessing has brought with him Colonel Reed's envoy, Captain Stewart, to arrange Hostau's surrender. The American officer hides in the vet's quarters close to the watermill. No one spots him. The next day, however, the general summons Rudofsky. The lieutenant colonel knows that he is risking the firing squad for high treason, and the thought paralyses him with fear. Plying a series of flimsy excuses, Rudofsky succeeds in postponing their meeting for twenty-four hours. Then, when no further delay is possible, the noose around his neck is loosened as suddenly as it had seemed to tighten: the general loads his bags into his Mercedes and races off.

Meanwhile an armoured American task force is approaching from Bělá nad Radbuzou in the north. 'Operation Cowboy' is the code name for this military foray on to Czechoslovakian soil. At first the Americans meet no resistance, but on 30 April they become bogged down in a five-hour firefight with German units stationed in the hills. Private Raymond Manz, nineteen, is killed. Sergeant Owen Sutton is wounded and taken to the field hospital, where he dies the next day. For the rest, the entry into Hostau goes smoothly: hundreds of prisoners of war line the road and dance.

'More a fiesta than anything else,' Colonel Reed writes afterwards.

U

From the documents it was hard to make out exactly where Rudofsky's loyalties lay. Was it with the Germans, or the Americans? Perhaps it would be fairest to say with the horses. In the administrative offices, Lessing had quickly removed the portraits of Hitler from the walls and destroyed them, to the bafflement of the remaining personnel. Lt Col. Rudofsky did not try to stop him and soon afterwards gave his permission to hang a white sheet from the window. He did not remove his *Wehrmacht* uniform.

Hubert Rudofsky was not a man for the barricades. He had acted circumspectly, almost waveringly. But he *had* sent his veterinarian out on reconnaissance and protected him afterwards, which made him a pivotal character in the end. In the Disney film, however, there is no sign of Rudofsky: it is all about Podhajsky, Podhajsky and more Podhajsky. And about Patton, the general who, despite the wider scope of his mission, risked human lives to save a herd of horses. As obvious as the screenwriter's choices were, they had generated ill feeling among a circle of cognoscenti. Podhajsky had played absolutely no active role in rescuing the breeding mares of Hostau. But after the war it was not he, the commander of the Royal Spanish Riding School, who was taken prisoner: on the contrary, his chest was pinned with the most exotic decorations. The rich and powerful lined up to sing his praises. Queen Elizabeth, Chancellor Adenauer, Prince Bernhard of the Netherlands, Shah Mohammed Reza, Pope Pius XII, General Franco, Marshall Tito, Emperor Haile Selassie, as well as Vivien Leigh and Gary Cooper.

Walt Disney had raised Commander Podhajsky on high with the mere suggestion that Operation Cowboy was launched by his bold initiative – a twisting of the facts that transformed him at once from villain to hero. The film's chronology did not show Patton's troops going into action in late April, but only *after* Podhajsky's request to protect the foals and mares as well. After the historic Lipizzaner performance on 7 May, it showed the American tanks rolling in formation towards the Czechoslovakian border, smoking the Germans out of their lairs and overstepping the Yalta line. Hostau surrendered, thereby putting hundreds of breeding mares and their foals safely into American hands, before the Russians could butcher or steal them.

Had Hubert Rudofsky seen the film?

'I think so,' Ulrich replied. 'In any case, my uncle hated it when anyone mentioned the name Robert Taylor.'

Ulrich himself had often compared his uncle's physical appearance to that of Telly Savalas, alias Kojak, who was bald like Onka Hu. '*Kojak* was his favourite programme, he didn't mind the comparison.'

During the second half of 1945, while in a Czech internment camp for Nazi collaborators, Hubert Rudofsky had lost all his hair. His brother-in-law, Brigitta's husband, had almost died there of tuberculosis. They were released in 1946 and hastily deported to Germany.

Along with his mother and sister, Ulrich emigrated to America in 1951 and lost touch with his uncle for a time. 'But in 1960, while I was in the service, they gave me a choice: either go to the Pacific to help with atomic testing, or go to Germany.'

He had gone to visit Onka Hu in his little flat near Darmstadt. 'The first thing he did was inspect my uniform. Then he said: "How about a Martini?"'

I sat listening and talking to my computer through a headset, like a helpdesk operator. Ulrich told me that he had attended the University of Chicago and become a pathologist. For thirty years he had conducted kidney research using laboratory animals. 'Monkeys, mice, rats, sheep – the things we did back then would be unthinkable these days. I always say to people it's because I come from a family of butchers.'

I didn't understand.

'My great-grandfather was a butcher, my grandfather and my father were doctors. I'm a pathologist. It's pretty much six of one, half a dozen of the other.'

As he grew older, Ulrich had visited his uncle in Germany more often. Hubert Rudofsky had never married, surrounding himself in his old people's flat with drawings and paintings of horses. He cherished his decorations from the First World War, particularly the Silver Medal of Courage he had received from Emperor Franz Josef.

They had never discussed Hostau, not until Colonel Podhajsky died in 1973. For almost three decades he had kept silent, like 'a true officer', but then the stories began tumbling out. 'Saving the Hostau Lipizzaners was not Podhajsky's achievement,' he said. 'That was our doing, Lessing's and mine.'

The high point of his uncle's life suddenly came to pass in 1985, Ulrich said, when Austria prepared a homage to him, with a gala performance by the Spanish Riding School.

Hans Brabenetz, I said, was the man who had arranged that, but the name didn't mean much to Ulrich.

Uncle Hubert received a certificate from the Austrian Minister of Agriculture: 'I am pleased to express to you my THANKS and GRATITUDE for your personal efforts in saving the Lipizzaners.'

'I had to go out and buy all the newspapers,' Ulrich recalled. He had flown over especially for the occasion. 'Onka was beside himself with joy and kept shouting: "Forty years too late, Matzl! Forty years too late!"'

The ceremony was held in Vienna's Stadthalle. Halfway through the proceedings, the master of ceremonies had announced: '*Herr Rudofsky, die Pferden tanzen für Sie.* Mr Rudofsky, today the horses dance for you.' The tears ran down his uncle's cheeks. The performance was filmed and broadcast on television six months later, on Good Friday of 1986.

'He watched it and enjoyed it intensely,' Ulrich said. 'On the Monday after Easter, he died in his sleep.'

Our conversation flagged.

'Here on my desk, I have the porcelain Lipizzaner they gave him during that gala.'

∪

During the final act of Hostau's role as a place of exile for the Lipizzaners, film and reality are once more in synch. The Third Reich collapses. Czech partisans leave their hiding places and try to stem the chaos. They form the Red Guard, recognizable by their red armbands. At Bischofteinitz they drag members of the SS from their homes. At Hostau, their eye falls on the Lipizzaners. During the first weeks of May, Colonel Reed, who has advanced with his motorized cavalry in the direction of Pilzen, is unable to make troops available for the horses' evacuation. Only after Germany has surrendered unconditionally, and after Reed hears that the Czechs plan to move the Lipizzaner herd deeper into the country, does he have the horses of Hostau driven as quickly as possible across the border, into the American zone in Bavaria.

In practice, it turns out to be a major logistical feat. A route is agreed upon – south along the railway and then across the ridges of the Bohemian Forest to Furth im Wald, in Germany. Forty kilometres. Foals younger than two weeks will be taken in trucks, as well as those mares that are still carrying.

Kitty, brought to Hostau from Vukovar, has already foaled and must walk. Of the eight horses from Conversano Primula's family tree who were in Hostau during the war, the mare Soja is the youngest. She makes the journey as a barely one-month-old filly.

Lt Col. Rudofsky, by now disarmed, is charged with preparing the evacuation of the stud farm. 'We'll bring him back to America, as a horse trainer,' he hears an American officer say. Amassov and his Caucasian riders would like nothing more; they are all-too aware of how Stalin deals with defectors. They convince the Americans of their inborn horsemanship and are allowed to assist with the herd.

At sunrise on 15 May, the horses start their trek. They leave in four groups, the young stallions in front. That season's five stud-horses, three Viennese Lipizzaners and two Arabs, have riders. Dr Lessing leads the second group, which includes a small detachment of Americans. US tanks are posted at the crossroads en route. The Cossacks guard the flanks on their Don ponies. To prevent the horses from grazing along the way, they are driven at a non-stop trot. The same goes for young Soja, who covers those forty kilometres at her mother's side.

By late morning the lead group reaches the top of the ridge. But, waiting at an old border post, is a handful of armed Czechs. As soon as they see the strange convoy approaching, they block the road. They don't ask for passports or other documents, but simply drag the stud farm's agronomist – who was riding lead – from his horse and begin to beat him. What kind of unpatriotic attempt at horse-smuggling is this? 'Turn around now,' they order. 'Get out of here!' The Czech partisans with their red armbands keep the barrier lowered and load their rifles. Amid the confusion, the young stallions become increasingly wild and reckless. If something doesn't give soon, the second group will catch up with the first, stallions and mares all mixed together. The impasse continues for perhaps ten minutes, maybe fifteen, until First Lieutenant Quinlivan arrives to see what's going on. Cursing loudly in his thick Irish brogue, he strides up to the Czechs. Dr Lessing's Ukrainian coachman acts as his interpreter. The American says he has not come to negotiate. It is much simpler than that. 'Lt Quinlivan is going to count to three. When he gets to "three", if that barrier isn't open, then something is going to go *booom*!' He points to the barrel of his tank, which is aimed at them, and begins to count.

Once this final hurdle has been taken, the horses trot downhill, into the American zone.

∪

That is how it happened. Except for one detail: at the border between East and West, about fifteen stallions broke out of the tangle and galloped off in ever-widening circles through the surrounding fields. After a while they disappeared whence they had come, back into the Russian zone.

The film-makers did not include this breakaway in the script, but Lt Col. Rudofsky had never forgotten it. He had begged the Americans to be allowed to stay behind in Hostau. That was where he was born, that was where his mother lived. He had escorted the convoy of horses to the gate of his stud farm and watched until they were out of sight. Then he returned to the abandoned offices, where he waited for the Red Guard to come and arrest him. But that evening, before they arrived, a stableboy knocked on the door: four of the stallions had come home. The boy named each of them. They were all waiting in their own stalls.

III

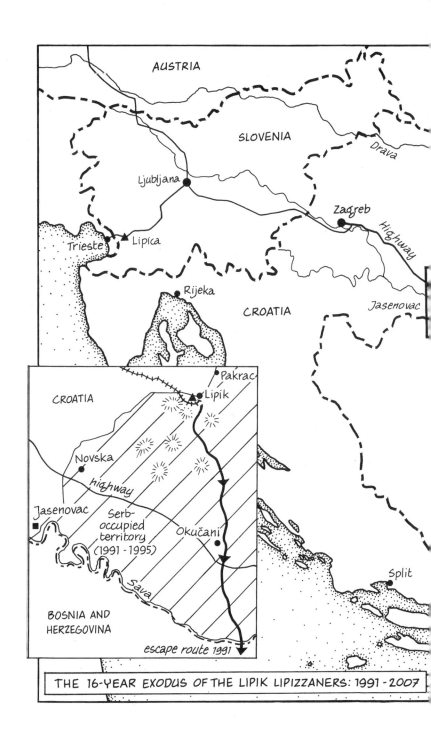

AUSTRIA

SLOVENIA

Drava

Ljubljana

Lipica

Trieste

Zagreb

Highway

Rijeka

CROATIA

Jasenovac

CROATIA

Pakrac

Lipik

Novska

highway

Jasenovac

Serb-
occupied
territory
(1991 - 1995)

Okučani

Split

Sava

BOSNIA AND
HERZEGOVINA

escape route 1991

THE 16-YEAR EXODUS OF THE LIPIK LIPIZZANERS: 1991 - 2007

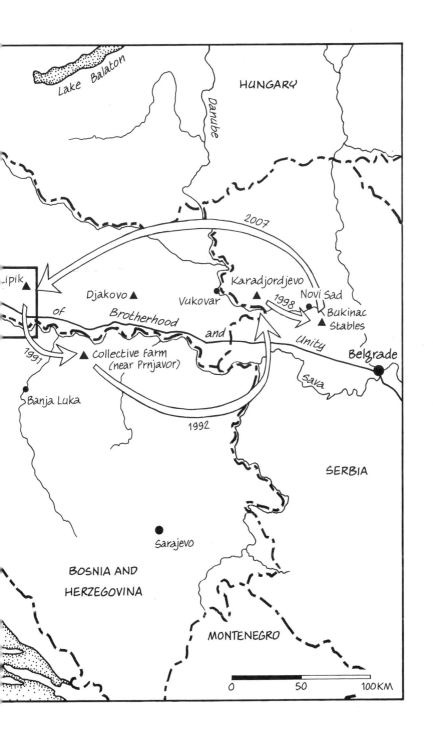

Lake Balaton

HUNGARY

Danube

2007

Lipik ▲

Djakovo ▲

Vukovar

Karadjordjevo ▲

1998

Novi Sad

Bukinac ▲ Stables

of   Brotherhood

and

Unity

Belgrade

1991

▲ Collective farm
(near Prnjavor)

Sava

1992

● Banja Luka

SERBIA

● Sarajevo

BOSNIA AND

HERZEGOVINA

MONTENEGRO

0   50   100KM

BRATSTVO I JEDINSTVO
(BROTHERHOOD AND UNITY)

REFUGEE HORSES DYING

BELGRADE, I AUGUST 2007: A herd of magnificent Lipizzaner horses that survived the bombardments during the war in Yugoslavia in the 1990s are now, in peacetime, faced with death by starvation as neglected 'prisoners of war'.

My reconstruction of the Lipizzaners' wanderings had barely reached 1945 when the story was whiplashed by current events. In the media, reports began emerging concerning emaciated Lipizzaners being detained on the banks of the Danube, in northern Serbia. The horses were rumoured to have gone missing in 1991 when the war in Yugoslavia broke out. A Novi Sad newspaper was the first to publish photographs of these animals, who had surfaced only sixteen years after their disappearance. The international press agencies, with their stringers in Belgrade, larded their reports with descriptions of 'homeless four-footers', 'spoils of war thought missing' and 'majestic Lipizzaners that are only a shadow of their former selves'. Their copy made the pages of newspapers ranging from USA TODAY to the New Zealand Herald.

Again? – that was my first thought.

Between 1945 and 1947, as the clouds of war lifted, the Lipizzaners were spread in small herds across Europe, shuffled like a pack of cards and redealt. But, like the general treaties of Yalta and Potsdam, the divvying-up of the Lipizzaner population also reflected the sentiment of the rapidly accelerating Cold War.

No objections were raised when Colonel Podhajsky was allowed first pick for Austria of the mares bearing the Piber brand: along with their offspring and the occasional stallion, he took 215 animals in all. Nor when the US Army went on to requisition fourteen Lipizzaners, to take back as trophies to the New World. Colonel Reed received a surrey and two Lipizzaner mares with which to promenade, and General Patton was given the exquisite Pluto XX, a stallion that had long been the pride of the Hungarian breeders.

Establishing the new owners of the remaining animals from the Hostau herd was a matter for the American Restitution Commission in Austria. Marshal Tito entered a claim on behalf of the new, socialist Yugoslavia – that, after all, was where the Germans had confiscated them from. The Italian chargé d'affaires, however, also demanded to have the horses, arguing that Lipica was Italian from 1919 to 1943, and that the abducted animals had therefore been born under Italian governance.

In the Piber archives I came across a letter from Dick Weeber, a North Carolina lawyer who was a member of the Restitution Commission.

Pinehurst, 16 March 1970

Dear Louis,
Hope all is well with you and your dear wife.

Weeber, by then in retirement, explained to his friend Podhajsky the lengths to which he had gone between 1945 and 1947 to make sure the communist Tito would get the short end of the stick, to the advantage of the Italians, an arrangement made no easier by Italy's weak status as a former foe. The Russians (who supervised the largest number of districts in Vienna) and the Czechoslovakians ('the Hostau stud farm was on *our* territory') demanded their share as well. 'But it was easy for us to dismiss those claims.' Tito was a different story. His partisans had freed Lipica themselves, and they had been allies. Nonetheless, Weeber recommended that the principal share, five stallions, forty-two mares and thirty-three foals, be granted to Italy, once again with the bonus of a copy of the stud books – a repeat of events at the end of the First World War. The commission had accepted his recommendations. In the end, Yugoslavia received only the thirteen horses that had once belonged to their deposed king.

> For me, dealing successfully with the Lipizzaner claims, and particularly those of Yugoslavia and Italy, was one of the most important things I have done in my life.
> Auf Wiedersehen & in alter Freundschaft,
>
> Dick

If one counted the Lipizzaners on either side of the quickly descending Iron Curtain, the East–West ratio came out at roughly fifty-fifty. The stud farms of Hungary and Romania, Habsburg by origin, had not been cut adrift and so passed seamlessly into the hands of the communists, who at first left well enough alone and merely removed the crown from the imperial brand. The Czechs, in turn, combed out the farmyards around Hostau and succeeded in recovering a few dozen of the Lipizzaners that had escaped or been sold by Rudofsky. Decked out with plumes, their descendants ended up in the state circus at Prague, whose Lipizzaner show ballet formed a folksy counterpoint to the Royal Spanish Riding School.

Lipica, the cradle of the Lipizzaner race, ended up on the eastern side of the new dividing line; its hayfields ran all the way to the watchtowers. Until 1947, British troops used the stalls as barracks and the *velbanca* served as their canteen and cinema. Once they had left, the stud farm started again from scratch with the thirteen 'royal' Lipizzaners that had returned from Hostau. To those were soon added a number of the horses that had been hidden from the Germans in the mountains of Bosnia. Otherwise, Yugoslavia still had the stud in the town of Djakovo, in Croatia, which had been damaged during the war but not plundered. With the normal accretion and some additional purchases abroad, Yugoslav Lipizzaner breeding made a recovery. In addition to Lipica, Tito set up a number of new studs in Serbia, Bosnia and Croatia, some top-down government operations, others worker-run.

Whenever Marshal Tito came on inspection, protocol dictated that he be presented with a stallion. It was a tradition he also honoured: visiting heads of friendly states never left without a Lipizzaner. Queen Elizabeth was given the black mare Stana, and Nasser and Nehru each received a white stallion. In 1955, Emperor Haile Selassie was allowed to select – albeit in return for hard cash – some thirty breeding mares and a few stallions for his own imperial stud farm in Addis Ababa – a daring venture that ended in a tropical failure.

Yet Tito's largesse with Lipizzaners in no way diminished

his passion for them. The president regularly had a span harnessed to the carriage for a ride around his Adriatic island of Brioni. Concerning his own riding horses, two Maestoso stallions, he had a clause added to his will stating that they were to die a natural death and never be put down. Early on in 1980, Lipica's 400th jubilee year, he exercised his influence to ensure that Yugoslavia would soon have its own riding school. Only weeks before the celebrations began, on 4 May 1980 at five minutes past three in the afternoon, Tito died. Despite this setback, the quatercentary marked Lipica's rise from the ashes of the Second World War. Ten years later, the Wars of Yugoslav Secession broke out.

In August 2007, reports about the discovery of the neglected Lipizzaners met with general dismay. The Belgrade action group 'Freedom for Animals' put a film up on YouTube that opened with a black screen and the luminescent words WELCOME TO HELL. Those bold enough to click on PLAY saw a series of photos of emaciated horses in an enclosure beside a brick barn. At first glance, one thought of a ragman's nags – with ribs shining through like ripples in the sand along the waterline. Walking skeletons, wrapped tightly in a tattered, white hide. Most of the animals had their heads raised, their ears pricked up, perhaps having taken the photographer for a caretaker who had come to bring them something edible. There was no narration, but words appeared on the screen, letter by letter, with all the urgency of a rattling typewriter:

PLEASE!
STOP IT NOW!

The soundtrack was Eric Clapton singing and playing 'Tears in Heaven'. The final frame was black too.

Dozens of viewers had left messages:

— 'These horses are more human than the beasts who are doing this to them.'
— 'The story behind this is not clear to me, but does it have something to do with the war?'
— 'Who the fuck said anything about war??? The point is that these animals are being starved to death!'

The most distressing image was of a mare, lying in a bare pasture and using the last of her strength in an attempt to rise to her feet, her bones almost poking through her skin. Looking at this animal, I was struck by the resemblance to a photo that had become an icon of the Yugoslav Wars: the protruding ribcage of a young man behind barbed wire at the Omarska prison camp. The topical picture of the suffering Lipizzaner mare came as an aftershock from the same war, now almost forgotten in 2007.

What had happened? BBC radio was one of the first to report that the herd came from the stud farm at Lipik in Croatia, 'a health resort one hundred kilometres east of Zagreb'. The name Lipik, like the Slovenian Lipica, was derived from the word *lipa*, meaning lime tree. The horses of Lipik were housed in a long set of stables with red roofing tiles from the Habsburg period. Tito had stalled part of his Lipizzaner breeding stock there in 1948. But in the autumn of 1991, Lipik had been blasted to rubble. For eight weeks, hilltop tanks and mortars from the former arsenals of Tito's pan-Yugoslav People's Army, manned now by Serbs, had pounded the Croatians below. Between one hundred and 120 white horses had moved about freely in the midst of this pandemonium, the mares and their foals wandering into the no-man's-land along the railway as moving targets. A mortar strike set the hayloft on fire and was said to have killed twenty-seven – or, in a different account, seventeen – of them. In the end, one foggy day, between eighty and ninety Lipizzaners had been led off behind the Serb lines.

'As prisoners of war,' the Croatians said.

'Propaganda,' said the Serbs. 'The head stableman brought them to us. He saved them!'

The BBC reporter: 'With other reports saying they wandered across the front lines.'

∪

Counting back, I decided it must have been in May 1995 that I had spent a few nervous hours as a correspondent on the outskirts of Lipik. The Lipizzaners from the local stud farm had been missing for almost three and a half years by then, but the row concerning their possible abduction was drowned out by a new clash of arms. In the early hours of the International Day of Labour, the Croatian army had mounted a counterattack – 'Operation blezak' (or 'lightning', an obvious but rather nervy allusion to Hitler's blitzkrieg). The objective was to retake the Highway of Brotherhood and Unity, which in peacetime connected Zagreb and Belgrade. For years, one 23-kilometre section in Croatian territory had been occupied by Serb troops. Operation Blezak was intended to rout them, but the Croatians' ambitions went further than that: they were out for revenge.

My own objective was to travel in the wake of the Croatian army and report what I saw. After looking at the map, I decided to try and reach Jasenovac, the German–Croatian death camp from the Second World War. The killing fields of 1941–5 lay only ten kilometres from the Highway of Brotherhood and Unity, and had been retaken during the initial assaults on Serb positions.

The *logor* (camp) at Jasenovac had no strategic military value, but a clear symbolic one. At Tito's orders, the barracks, machine-gun nests and fences had long ago been ploughed beneath the clay. All that rose above the boneyard now was a ten-metre concrete flower, erected as a monument, and a section of the rails over which the Serbs, Gypsies and Jews had been rolled in like animals to the slaughter. The strong ones were first worn down with forced labour in the brick-yards, but in the final account Jasenovac was an extermination camp where Hitler's Croatian vassals had rid themselves of, above all, Serbs.

Tito had told the Nuremberg Tribunal that 700,000 people were killed at Jasenovac. An unimaginable figure, in several ways, yet any historian who dared cast doubt on that number was imprisoned for sedition. 'The murder of the 700,000' was sharpened into a handy political dagger and used to keep the Croatians in particular in line. As head of state, Tito was forever tinkering with the domestic balance of power. As early as 1948 he had parted ways with Stalin and led Yugoslavia down a road of its own – a task that kept him very busy, for if any one ethnic group were to acquire too much influence, the Yugoslavian ship of state would capsize and sink. It was with good reason then that Tito bore the moniker 'the last Habsburger': like the emperor before him, he – dressed for preference in a white uniform with gold braiding – showed himself able to hold together a nation of many peoples, stretching across myriad ethnic and religious fault lines.

Born in 1892 as a subject of the Austro-Hungarian monarchy, Josip Broz Tito had fought for Emperor Franz Josef as a sergeant major in the First World War. Later, as Secretary General of the League of Communists of Yugoslavia, he was convinced that the political edifice he had constructed would remain standing after his death, as long as the pan-Yugoslav confederation remained robust enough to smother nationalistic outbursts. And so he worked on creating a new people who would no longer consider themselves Slovenian, Montenegrin, Albanian or Serbian, but purely Yugoslavian. The army bases were transformed into training schools, where recruits were administered a ponderous dosage of patriotism. In addition to this nurturing, educational component, the creation of the Yugoslav also had a natural, genetic component: the young conscripts were sent as far away as possible from home. A Hungarian from the province of Vojvodina would be stationed in Macedonia, a Croatian in Kosovo, a Serb in Slovenia – with the explicit intention of having them marry a woman from a different ethnic group. From this ethnic mixture, through state-facilitated marriages, a mixed-breed race would arise that regarded itself, first and foremost, as Yugoslavian.

This was Tito's answer to Jasenovac and more generally to the Holocaust: the mixing of various bloodlines to such a degree that no one could use his 'pure' genes as an excuse for exterminating 'mongrels' or, for that matter, any other individual group.

'This will not be accomplished within a single generation,' the field marshal said of his experiment. 'Perhaps not even within our lifetimes. But our children will certainly see that day.'

∪

In the five dispatches I had dedicated to Operation Blezak in May 1995, the Lipizzaners never appeared. But they were in my notes.

From Zagreb, I had driven towards the front in a rental car with PRESS printed across the bonnet. Beside me sat

Renzo, a short-sighted, dyed-in-the-wool war correspondent from the *Corriere della Sera* who didn't hold a driving licence. Close to the airport we turned on to the Highway of Brotherhood and Unity, built after the Second World War as a seam to hold together socialist Yugoslavia, a set of stitches on behalf of the sorely needed *bratstvo* (brotherhood) and *jedinstvo* (unity). Young volunteers from all over Europe, including a future defence minister of the Netherlands, believed that with their singing and shovelling of sand they were helping to bury the primitive hatred between peoples.

Just past a petrol station with a playground and picnic tables, we arrived at a tollgate. 'Well, look at that,' I said. 'We have to pay to use a dead-end road.' Of the eight lanes, two were still operational. I gave the receipt that the attendant handed me to Renzo, as a memento.

'Aha,' he said. 'Our ticket to the war.'

BELGRADE 374 KM, a road sign read. As a malediction, someone had painted three zeros after the '4'. There was no need: along this road, the enemy's capital was as unreachable as the moon. Somewhere on the horizon ahead was the area known as Vojna Krajina, the 'Military Zone'. In fact it was a buffer instated by Empress Maria Theresia in the eighteenth century to protect her Catholic Croatians from attacks by Muslim Bosnians and their Turkish masters. To that end, she had populated the southern limits of her empire with Serb farmers who, in return for acting as border guards, were allowed to retain their Orthodox faith. As an outsider you noticed nothing of this, despite the hint given by the signs marking municipal limits, which suddenly switched from the Latin alphabet to the Cyrillic. From time to time the earth along this active fault would start to shift, allowing geysers of hate to erupt in the form of razzias, deportations and murders.

We took the last exit before the front; in fact, we had no choice. The motorway was blocked with tank traps and a guard post manned by Nepalese UN peacekeepers in blue helmets. The first column of smoke could be seen rising in the distance, drifting off to the east only when it reached a great height. Along the Sava River, amid tidal forests budding with silver foliage, we passed villages with both a Catholic church, recognizable by their plain crosses, and a Serbian Orthodox one, with their characteristic onion-shaped steeple. Sometimes the rival houses of God stood facing each other, like a pair of mountain goats ready to lock their mismatched horns.

The only horses we saw along the way were beasts of burden, hitched to wagons full of mattresses, jerrycans and caged geese, and topped with entire families, fleeing across a pontoon bridge over the Sava.

At a three-way junction at the foot of a line of hills we came across the carcass of a tank, lying on its side in a puddle of black and brown oil. Easing our way around it we saw that the turret had been ripped from the body of the vehicle. From its gullet protruded a tangle of springs and headsets. There was a sourish, scorched smell in the air, and I feared that strips of flesh were still clinging to the insides.

Past the crossing we took a back road to Lipik, which was rumoured to have been in Croatian hands for the last twenty-four hours. The road was lined with alternating fields of grapes and hops. The road grew busier with refugees on foot and army trucks, which passed us in blue clouds of diesel exhaust and occasionally we felt a heavy thud that echoed against the hillsides. At a junction opposite the first razed houses of Lipik, we were flagged down with a show of military histrionics. Soldiers wearing black headbands had pulled two armoured vehicles across the road as a blockade.

'*Akreditacija!*'

We had to get out and show our credentials. In the yard behind a shed, a dozen prisoners of war were seated cross-legged on the ground. They were being dealt with in accordance with the Geneva Convention, we were told, and we had to watch as they were given a bucket of water, from which they drank in greedy gulps.

We said hello to the prisoners and asked what had happened to them. *Aber nein*, we were not allowed to ask questions. The soldier guarding the group, his Kalashnikov held at the hip with the barrel pointed down, began shuffling his feet.

Why not?

Verboten. And we couldn't enter the town. That was *verboten* too.

Were they still meeting with resistance?

Genug! Absolutely!

The advantage of being in Croatia rather than Serbia was that you could usually get by in German, even if it didn't get you very far. Before they sent us away, Renzo asked what they were going to do with the prisoners.

'We're going to exchange them for the Lipizzaners,' the group commander said. 'One fucking Serb bastard for ten horses – put that in your report!'

That was what my notepad said, including the exhortation to 'put that in your report!'

○

Amid the frenetic events of May 1995, I had missed the gist of that comment. I was focused on Jasenovac, where I spoke to triumph-drunken Croatians in the warm grass beside a low railway embankment, looking out over the unmowed field with its drab concrete flower. 'The real crime carried out here', they said, 'was the falsification of history perpetrated by Tito and the Serbs.' They were referring to the series of jabs and feints that had preceded the Yugoslav Wars. 'The murder of the 700,000' had been jacked up to a million by the patriarch of the Serbian Orthodox Church. By the time the artillery was moved into position, the figure had risen to 1.5 million. The Croatian president struck back with the publication of his own figures on Jasenovac, meant to show that things were not quite as bad as they were made out to be: 30,000 dead, 35,000 at the very most.

During the first weeks of the 1991 war, the Serbs had driven the Croatians out of the village of Jasenovac. The camp museum, they found, had been destroyed quickly before the villagers left. It was in that hall of remembrance that Yugoslav schoolchildren, year in, year out, like it or not, had bent over the display case containing the glove-and-hook implement which the executioners had used to kill prisoners. Afterwards, in the car park, they had thrown up between the buses. But in the end it had not helped: once grown-up, they had gone back to killing each other.

In May 1995, the Croatians were once again on top in Jasenovac. The tables were turned; this time, not a single Serb had been left behind. As a monument to reconciliation, the concrete flower was looking rather forlorn. Soon, the victors bragged to each other, it would be blown up with all due pomp and circumstance. But today, they raised a toast in anticipation.

∪

'*Etničko čišćenje*' was what the acts of aggression were called in Serbo-Croatian: ethnic cleansing – as though something had been left clean once it was over. But no one could show me how a Croat differed from a Serb – in terms of build, behaviour, mentality or even the coarseness of their hair. Let alone explain why one might be inferior to the other. Yet the people of the Balkans themselves, comprised of tangled blood ties, worked like mad to undo the bastardization of Marshal Tito, whose death they had so keenly bewailed. How did they go about it? By ethnically unravelling cities, villages, streets and even families – with a knock on the door and a rifle at the ready.

Speaking to the British journalist Rebecca West, who toured the Balkans shortly before the Second World War, a Serb had said: 'There are things your Western brain can't comprehend, but about which our Serbian blood is sure. We are too rough and too deep for your smoothness and super-ficiality.' Sixty years later I was told more or less the same, by both Serbs and Croatians. By fire and sword they combated cosmopolitanism, the Western idea that all peoples are equal and that they, in the end, all share common desires. I noticed that my own left-leaning opinions, never tested in practice, were taking something of a beating. I met warrior types on both sides of the front who claimed to belong to a Spartan race whose toughness, courage and sharp eyesight was due to the eternal proximity of enemies – the weak, the cowardly and the short-sighted simply did not live long enough to reproduce.

Personally, I couldn't see any difference between them, unless it was that a Croat, when making the sign of the cross, tapped his left shoulder first and then his right, while a Serb did it the other way around. I had a sneaking suspi-cion that both groups were at a far remove from my Western standpoint. Did that mean there really *was* something like a national character? A Balkan Man – a creature with reflexes unlike our own? Out of curiosity, I actually posed that question – but was immediately rapped on the knuckles by my newspaper colleagues. One warned me about 'the pitfalls of racism'. I protested: all I had wanted to do was air the question! – but that didn't get me off the hook. Apparently I had refused to absorb the lesson of the Second World War: that a concept like 'national character' or 'race' was a social myth, and an atrociously dangerous one at that. It was for good reason that, in response to the Holocaust, the United Nations had employed the services of an impressive series of academic heavyweights to root out the tenacious belief that one race was cleverer/more stupid, more volatile/more cold-blooded, harder-working/lazier than another. Such differences existed only in the mind. 'There is no biological justification for racial hatred or prejudice', UNESCO's 1950 *Statement on Race* said. *Homo sapiens* was an extremely homogeneous species; in biological terms he constituted one big *family of man*.

But I was hounded by doubt. Forensic investigations of mass graves showed that an Asian skull could easily be distinguished from that of an African or a European. Medical handbooks stated confidently that most adult Asians were allergic to milk. On the other hand, it was not the done thing to reveal one's amazement that Kenyans and Ethiopians dominated the world's elite of marathon running but were more or less absent from chess championships. Of course one's environment played a major role, but was that any reason to pay no attention whatsoever to genetic differences? Yet any researcher who happened to go ahead and do so anyway was ostracized from academic circles as a practitioner of 'bad science'.

The 1950 UNESCO statement, supplemented and updated in 1951, 1964 and 1967, remained adamant: there are no genetic differences between peoples or groups of people with regard to intelligence, character or temperament. It was not a principle to be tampered with. More than that: it was a principle one shouldn't even *want* to tamper with.

ANIMAL FARM

Saluting Stalin and holding the reins in his left
hand – that was how Red Army commander General
Zhukov returned from the Second World War, astride his
white horse. To the hurrahs of his troops, he sailed at an
easy gallop across the basalt paving stones of Red Square.

As soon as the clatter of hooves had died away, a hundred
Soviet soldiers came marching in with captured swastika
banners, which they carried to Lenin's mausoleum. At the
base of the tomb they stopped, turned ninety degrees and
row by row tossed the swastikas on the ground. A few metres
above them, on the marble gallery, stood Comrade Stalin.
He nodded.

But even more impressive than this victory parade on 24
June 1945 were the ideological fireworks lighting the post-war
sky over Moscow. The moment had arrived to spread the
Marxist egalitarian ideal as the triumphant message of salva-
tion for humanity – to deliver the moral *coup de grâce* to both
fascism and capitalism at one fell swoop. While prosecutors
and witnesses at Nuremberg were revealing the full extent
of the Holocaust, it also became clear that a single, blood-red
line ran from Mendel to Mengele. The Nazis had contaminated the laws of Mendelian genetics, and the comrades'

victory lay within reach: a political system founded on the intellectual heritage of the virtuous Moravian monk from Brünn was, in a word, reprehensible.

'It is a doctrine', George Bernard Shaw said, 'that no state can tolerate, least of all a socialist state.'

To the relief of a broad vanguard of left-wing Europeans, the Kremlin provided an unequivocal response to the Holocaust, one that went further than the non-committal, weak-kneed UNESCO statement against racism.

When I moved to Moscow in 1997 to report on the defunct Soviet Empire, Manege Square was still a bare stretch of asphalt, not yet a half-submerged shopping paradise with fountains full of Russian fairy-tale figures. Zhukov and his white stallion, cast in bronze, guarded the entrance to Red Square. Beneath a fir tree at the foot of the Kremlin wall, Stalin lay in his grave. In the meantime, voices were being raised in rampant-capitalist Russia to remove Lenin's body from its mausoleum and bury it once and for all.

In my Moscow apartment building, built by German prisoners of war, I read breathlessly about the summer of 1948, when Comrade Stalin had charged Soviet scholars with the task of casting biology, the science of life itself, into a new 'proletarian' mould. To that end, he appointed his biologist Trofim Lysenko. From all over the country the most brilliant academics were summoned to Moscow for a meeting lasting several days at the V. I. Lenin Academy for Agricultural Sciences, to examine the state of genetic science.

On 31 July 1948, the first day, Comrade Lysenko, in his provincial Ukrainian accent, read aloud a fifty-page speech peppered with quotes from Marx, Engels and Darwin. Newspaper photos of that event show him staring evangelically towards a point that seems to lie somewhere in the future. His hair is parted neatly, and at the corners of his mouth there is what looks like the onset of bliss. Around him a cult was being built up, emphasizing his sober upbringing, his father's common sense, the *pelmeni* meat ravioli that his mother served with sour cream, and the tender expression that overtook him when one spoke of them.

Lysenko aimed his darts at the fruit-fly researchers. Ever since the Mendelian Thomas Hunt Morgan had mapped the distance between genes on a chromosome in his famous 'Fly Room' at Columbia University, *Drosophila melanogaster* had been the foremost laboratory animal for genetic research, a fact the chairman of Stalin's conference made fun of. In minute detail, he revealed how Comrade Dubinin, by all accounts a world-class scholar, had 'enriched' Soviet science with the discovery that fruit flies in the city of Voronezh during the war exhibited a rare chromosomal anomaly. This was precisely the problem with the teachings of Mendel and Morgan: they were of no practical use to anyone.

Lysenko, who prided himself on being practical, presented by contrast his own neo-Lamarckian experiences. By 'drilling' plants, animals and humans, one automatically created new and useful species. Only from the outside, by means of drastic environmental changes, could one harness the force of evolution. The point was not to mingle, but to graft. Not to breed, but to lead. Lysenko rejected the tenets of Mendelian genetics in favour of 'a true biology in accordance with Marx'. He exhorted everyone to follow his example – academics, agronomists and also animal breeders.

'Hail the great friend of science, our leader and teacher, Comrade Stalin!'

In the hall, one delegate commented: 'It is not that we

disagree with you, Comrade Lysenko, but where you speak of species that change through training or other stimuli, we speak of salutary changes in genetic material. Mutations.'

But that was to no avail. Lysenko drove home his point. Genes? They didn't exist. Had anyone ever seen one? They were a fiction perpetrated by the bourgeoisie, by those who believed that one's origins determined one's future, that one was born with a fixed set of immutable 'vectors of heredity'. Such thinking reeked of predestination and divine will, of Germany and America, of gas chambers and the sweat of slaves.

On the final day of the meeting, Lysenko brought to a vote a resolution calling for an outright *Berufsverbot*, a professional ban, for the followers of Mendel. The grand finale was there, word for word, in the minutes:

'Comrades,' the chairman spoke, 'before I move on to my final conclusions, I consider it my duty to state the following. In one of the notes handed to me, a question was posed concerning the Central Committee's stance with regard to my report. In reply to that: the party's Central Committee has examined my report and endorses it.' (Wild applause. Ovation. All rise.)

Three of the participants wasted no time and asked to be allowed to speak. The first to make his way to the lectern was a prominent expert on chromosomes. 'The speech I gave the day before yesterday was unworthy of a communist and a Soviet scientist. But I say to you today: it was my last speech based on a biologically and ideologically erroneous standpoint.' (Rolling applause.) Then a young Armenian came to the front. 'As from today I will not only endeavour to free myself of my reactionary ideas, but I will also attempt to convince my students and comrades.' According to the minutes, the third and final penitent did not receive any applause, even though his reaction was the most vehement: 'We must assist the party in eliminating the pseudo-scientific rot being disseminated by our foreign enemies.'

Before the summer was over, on 26 August 1948, the Presidium of the Academy of Sciences, the country's foremost academic body, announced twelve steps to be taken to rectify matters. They included: the destruction of all fruit-fly populations used for scientific research; the closure of Professor Dubinin's genetics institute on the grounds of it being 'useless and non-academic'; the replacement of all biology textbooks.

Approximately 3,000 academics were dismissed. One, Comrade Sabinin, shot himself through the head.

On 27 August, *Pravda* announced that the 'party principle' had been restored as the true north of Soviet science. Anyone daring to challenge Lysenko's findings henceforth was obviously an 'adherent of theories popular in Nazi Germany and still advanced by the defendants of slavery and racial discrimination: the Americans'.

The weekly magazine *Ogonyok* (Flame) ran a cartoon mocking such 'fly-lovers/people-haters'. Zealous journalists also called to mind Hermann Joseph Müller, an American fruit-fly researcher who had been brought to Moscow in the 1930s. In 1946 he had received the Nobel Prize for his discovery that mutations could be effected with the use of X-rays, but the scandalous fact about Müller was his plea for eugenics. In his pamphlet *Out of the Night*, he had proposed having as many women as possible inseminated with sperm from a handful of highly gifted men (who would in this manner sire around 50,000 children each) – on condition that race, class and social standing be ruled out as selection criteria. Müller had returned to America in the nick of time. From now on, geneticists of his ilk and other 'disciples of

Mendel' were portrayed in the Soviet press wearing pointed Ku Klux Klan hoods.

And Lysenko? His portrait soon hung in university auditoria across the Soviet Union. At Ostroh in the Ukraine, a statue was erected in a park showing Comrade Stalin and his private biologist, conversing relaxedly in facing armchairs. Young people's choruses added the Lysenko Song to their repertoire:

> Accordion, play a happy song,
> Let me sing of the glory, unrivalled
> Of Lysenko's courage
> That saves us from Mendel and from Morgan.

Surrounded by a small army of ideologists, Lysenko rewrote the history of the natural sciences. Albert Einstein was downgraded; his theory of relativity was too abstract, too far-fetched – for daily life, one required nothing more than Newtonian physics. A far more prominent position was awarded posthumously to Ivan Pavlov. As early as 1900, he had discovered the conditioned reflex: Professor Pavlov's dogs began salivating as soon as he rang a bell five minutes before feeding time. After a period of conditioning, they produced saliva in reaction to the bell even when it rang at irregular times and no food was offered. Insights of this calibre were at least of practical use in the creation of *Homo sovieticus*.

So, the Soviets emerged as staunch behaviourists who attributed all conduct to (influenceable) learning processes – hence their belief in the effectiveness of re-education camps. They rejected the new theories successfully advanced by scientists such as Konrad Lorenz and Dutch Harvard professor Niko Tinbergen, whose emphasis on inborn, preprogrammed behaviour could only lead to 'despicable moral fantasies' – concerning, for example, the biological preordainment of women as mothering animals.

Lysenko reread Darwin as well, and discovered that the great theorist of evolution had been mistaken. Making this claim called for extreme caution, as Darwin was considered one of the founders of 'scientific atheism'. By eliminating God both as creator and arbiter of destiny, Darwin had taken the wind out of the sails of conservatism. Dynamism and change were shown to be part and parcel of nature; Darwin had shown how species produced other species; Marx had shown the same thing with societies. Or, as the leading biologist of the French Parti Communiste had put it: 'Man is merely an element in a huge process of *becoming* that, starting with the amoeba or even lower, will rise above the animal at last in a classless society.'

Lysenko agreed with Darwin that change underpinned evolution, but he dismissed *On the Origin of Species* as 'little more than an adding-up of the centuries-old experiences of plant and animal breeders'. According to him, Darwin had missed the boat when it came to the concept of 'struggle'. Competition *between members of one and the same species* supposedly offered the best chances of survival for the fittest, Darwin argued. But no such struggle took place, not within species. Even a child knew that. 'Wolves eat rabbits,' Lysenko lectured, 'but rabbits do not eat each other. They eat grass!'

Competition was the motor behind *capitalism*. Darwin had casually borrowed the notion of intra-species struggle from Malthus, an economist no less, with harsh theories concerning scarcity, overpopulation and – as a result of famine and food rioting the likely sharp decreases in human populations. That was how events played out on the battlefield of the market economy, but not in nature. The wolf, after all, is not a wolf to other wolves. And so the human race is no wolf to itself, at least not by nature.

This insight, too, lent itself to practical application. Lysenko called on the rubber kolkhozes to sow hundreds of seeds of the latex-bearing Russian dandelion ('Plant 4711') in circular hollows one and a half metres in diameter. From such circular entrenchments, the plants would then automatically close ranks against encroaching weeds. In the field of forestry, Lysenko, on the same principle of 'strength in numbers', advised that saplings be planted close together. Brigades of Komsomol youth sent out on to the steppes in 1949 to plant thousands of kilometres of windbreaks were instructed to place a number of saplings in each hole.

But when they grew, wouldn't they have to compete for scarce water and light?

'No,' Lysenko said, 'at most, one tree will offer itself up in the interests of the forest.'

The Soviet media lauded him as a saviour who could 'turn wheat into rye, barley into oats, cabbage into turnips, pines into spruce'. Sissified pig breeds were transformed by him into sturdy creatures, by re-educating them in Marxist fashion: even in the Siberian cold, the kolkhoz workers were not to shut the stall doors. Not even if the piglets froze by the dozen? Especially not then: their heroic deaths helped the survivors, and their progeny, to become resistant to adversity.

This gene-less theory of heredity flourished from China to Cuba. In East Germany, cattle were subjected to the Lysenko method. At collectivized farms there, 'open stalls' were built: freezing concrete slabs with only a roof, where the weak individuals died to make way for the fit – a process referred to in DDR jargon as 'creational Darwinism'.

And so it went everywhere in the Eastern Bloc. In Budapest,

Hungarian communists celebrated the destruction of their fruit-fly populations like a victory ritual. But Lysenko's heel came down most painfully on the former Habsburg town of Brünn, the city of Gregor Mendel. The abbey was closed and the statue of Mendel in the gardens, fashioned by a Viennese sculptor in 1910, was pulled from its pedestal. The sweet peas in the 35 m × 7 m plot where the monk had conducted his experiments in hybrid culture were crushed and ploughed under.

∪

But what about horses, I wondered – had they too been exposed to Lsyenko's therapies? For years, a stubborn rumour had circulated that, after the war, the Russians had accumulated enough Lipizzaners to start their own stud farm 'beyond the Urals'. The Romanian breeders who worked for the Ceauşescus in the 1970s were said to have received their training there. In the days of glasnost, this perennial rumour had prompted Piet Bakker to write a letter to 'Mr M. Gorbachev, Secretary General of the CPSU' on behalf of the Dutch Lipizzaner Working Group. Was it true, he asked, that the Soviet Union had bred its own Lipizzaners? And if so, was the time not ripe to add these prodigal sons and daughters to the stud book?

Although this suggestion had almost composted into fact, it turned out to be completely unfounded. The Russians had never shown much interest in the aristocratic Lipizzaner. In the 1950s, a Soviet delegation had paid a one-off visit to the Spanish Riding School. First Deputy Premier Mikoyan, inspected the stalls and praised Podhajsky, as protocol prescribed. But no trading ties were established.

That left the Lipizzaners of Romania, Hungary and Czechoslovakia. What had they been through? And what's more: how deep an impact had the anti-Mendel fury had on daily life behind the Iron Curtain? The best informant I could imagine was the geneticist Vítězslav Orel, Mendel's biographer, a Czech from Brno who, as a young scientist, had himself suffered under Lysenko.

Dr Orel led a solitary life. Having turned his back on urban life, he had withdrawn like a hermit to a house on a hill. I had asked Martina to put me in contact with him.

'Dear Madam,' he replied to her. 'I was greatly surprised to note your interest in the subject of Lysenkoism in connection with horse breeding. Please find enclosed several publications that will perhaps be of interest to you. Sincerely yours, Vítězslav Orel.'

Dr Orel had enclosed papers in both English and Czech. Strangely enough, they were about sheep. Merinos. And about Moravian sheep breeders in the nineteenth century.

Martina was puzzled by the annexes too; she sent the documents on to me and added a PS: 'Did you know that Orel hasn't been to Mendel's abbey since 1989?' That was equally strange, since Dr Orel was widely referred to as the honorary head of the 'Mendelianum', a scientific sanctuary dedicated to Mendel which various sources said was located in the abbey itself. The address: Mendel Square 3.

I flew to Vienna and drove my hired car from Austria to the Czech Republic – without being stopped at a single border post. This broad expanse of Danube lowlands at the heart of Europe had, in a way that had long seemed out of the question, once more become one. I drove north along a monotonous road of concrete slabs. Not far from Brno/ Brünn I saw a sign flash by with a pictogram of a battlefield and the word 'Austerlitz' in roadside capitals. Was Austerlitz nearby? To the left and right of the crash barriers were fields of wilted sunflowers, their heads brown and broken. So these were the fields of the notorious 'Battle of the Three Emperors': it was here that Napoleon, in one day, 2 December 1805, had defeated both the Austro-Hungarian forces and the Russian czar's elite troops – with a strategic genius feared so deeply that the herd of Lipizzaners at the edge of the Alps was moved from Slovenia to Hungary, just to be sure.

Arriving in Brno I missed an exit, then another, leaving me to make two full, pointless circuits of the city's ring road. I needed to get to the old city centre, but it was partially closed to traffic: the EU agricultural ministers, as it turned out, were at that very moment paying a visit to Mendel's abbey. When I finally arrived at Mendel Square, police vans were still parked here and there. I checked into one of the rooms along an arched cloister that had been converted into a guest house, splashed some water on my face and went for a walk around the big basilica in search of the world's most famous vegetable garden. The gate I entered led to the court-yard of St Thomas' Abbey. The wings of the abbey were neatly plastered, the tidy garden had the feeling of a park. Half-hidden between two trees stood Brother Mendel in his monk's habit, his arms spread, his petrified, visionary gaze fixed on a point above the visitor's head. Opposite him lay the foundation of his old greenhouse, and beside a stone path his experimental, 35 m × 7 m plot. In the tilled earth there now grew begonias, not peas.

This was hallowed ground, but above all scientific ground.

A few paving stones further was the entrance to the Mendelianum. I was surprised at the glass entryway and the halogen lighting in the foyer. This in no way resembled the photographs I'd seen on the Internet. There was no smell of incense or tallow, nothing to suggest you were in an abbey. Above the door to the refectory I had expected to see Mendel's pronouncement, MY TIME SHALL COME, but what I found instead was an ultramodern counter where one could purchase soup bowls, spoons, little bags of dried peas and other Mendel merchandise. The exhibition that Vítězslav Orel had staged in 1965 under the name 'Mendelanium' had apparently made way for a brand-spanking-new Genetics Museum.

The first exhibition hall was still dedicated to GREGOR MENDEL: THE MAN, THE ABBOT, THE SCIENTIST. I pored over the display case for a better look at his spectacles, his microscope and his cane with its ivory handle. 'Mendel was very tall', a sign above one of the cases read. What I found moving was his dog-eared, heavily annotated copy of *Über die Entstehung der Arten*, the German translation of Darwin's *On the Origin of Species*, published in Stuttgart, 1863.

From the *Jugendstil* case filled with old books it was only three steps to a futuristic room containing a scale model of the DNA molecule. You could walk around it, following its spiral-staircase structure step by step. From somewhere at the back came the murmur of science-fiction-like underwater sounds that drowned out the visitors' footsteps. The cross-pieces, the rungs in the twisted rope-ladder of the DNA, were formed by A, C, G and T, four letters, four different bases, indicated by four different colours. The order in which these letters were arranged determined the life form in question: mouse, ape, human, pea. In a niche in the wall stood a letter dated 2 April 1953, as it had appeared in *Nature*:

We wish to suggest a structure for the salt of deoxyribose nucleic acid (DNA). This structure has novel features which are of considerable biological interest.

James Watson and co-discoverer Francis Crick were aware that, as soon as they succeeded in decoding DNA, their fame would explode across the scientific firmament. Watson, only twenty-four at the time, had composed an immortal first sentence even before they latched on to the trail of the 'double helix': 'Genes are interesting to geneticists' – after which he would proceed to crack the code of life in the form of an austere account of his findings. Watson, as anyone in this abbey could tell you, was made of vainer stuff than Mendel. Once Crick and he had uncovered the blueprint for the vectors of heredity, they also considered dealing at length with the full impact of their discovery: the rope ladders of DNA could detach longitudinally and just as easily be rejoined, which at a single swoop also provided insight into how genetic material could copy itself – in other words, repro-duce. In the end, however, they had stuck to a factual, under-stated account of a single molecule. Only in passing did they note: 'It has not escaped our notice that the specific pairing we have postulated immediately suggests a possible copying mechanism for the genetic material.'

The neglect suffered by Mendel was spared Watson and Crick. They were inundated by adulation, of which the inevi-table Nobel Prize was only a part.

I made an additional round of the molecule that rose up like a pillar of children's building blocks. What a pity that the publication of their 900-word letter to *Nature* had not come a few weeks earlier: if it had, Stalin, who died on 5 March 1953, could have experienced all this as well.

Not that it would have changed his mind. The airtight bell jar of the Soviet system proved impermeable to the revelation that aptitude and origin contained an identifiable, material component. Even during the thaw under Nikita Khrushchev, Lysenko's theories could therefore continue to flourish –

DNA or no DNA. It was only when Leonid Brezhnev ousted his predecessor from the Kremlin in October 1964 that the curtain fell on Lysenko. 'A pseudo-academic' was the verdict rendered only ten days after the takeover, a charlatan who had reduced the Soviet Union to beggary. In America's Corn Belt, a hybrid corn variety was already being raised that produced record harvests, while in the Philippines the finishing touches were being put to a strain of rice that had exceeded expectations in the experimental paddies. And Lysenko? He had shamed the Soviet Union by bringing it to the point where it had to buy wheat on the international market. With the mental contortionism at which Soviet journalists excelled, a propaganda U-turn took place. The same dizzying trapeze act that had dragged Lysenko down returned Mendel to his former pinnacle: in Brno, his statue was returned to its pedestal.

For Vítězslav Orel, this rehabilitation arrived just in time to add lustre to the hundredth anniversary of the publication of Mendel's *Experiments on Plant Hybridization* with a symposium and the opening of the Mendelianum. In August 1965, a seventy-strong delegation of newly rehabilitated Soviet geneticists laid a wreath in Mendel's pea patch. The pictures taken during that visit show grey, balding men with bowed heads.

In the renovated museum I searched for traces of Lysenko, but there were none. At the exit, a guest book lay open on a lectern. Someone had pasted a dried four-leaf clover to the page. 'True science reveals the Lord's greatness', another visitor had opined. Japanese guests had stood here, Australians and Finns, even a biologist from Ecuador. I turned the page and wrote: 'Amazing to see how the dark years of the Lysenko era have been covered up.' Perhaps the airbrushing of Trofim Lysenko out of an exhibition in Mendel's abbey was his just deserts, yet it bothered me. It was as if one were told the story of Galileo without the part about his excommunication by the Vatican.

Martina arrived the next morning on the train from Olomouc, to interpret for me with Dr Orel. I picked her up at the station.

She had her own explanation for why the new exhibition ignored Lysenko: in the Czech Republic, licking one's wounds was reserved for those over fifty. 'Merchandising is what does it these days. And fashion. Things like that.'

Martina had just started work as an assistant lecturer at the literature faculty in Olomouc, a position she had used to good advantage in her correspondence with Orel. Now that she had a genuine university teaching job, she sported not fewer piercings, but more – and also some tattoos she'd had applied at an underground cavern in Prague. I was curious to see what the hermit Orel would make of her.

We arrived at his house too early. The home of Mendel's biographer was on a hillside, beside a lane of maple trees and red and white radio masts. I briefed Martina on what I needed to hear from him. First, whether Lipizzaner herds had been exposed to Lysenko's improvement regimes, and if so, how that had taken place. But I also wanted to hear how Vítězslav Orel himself had survived the Lysenko era. And, if the conversation went smoothly, I hoped to talk about the dystopias, the literary explorations of what could take place in a totalitarian state. I was thinking of Huxley's *Brave New World*, with its happy society of five categories of human clones, generated by egg-cell radiation in accordance with the 'Bokanovsky Process', but also the novel *We* by the Russian Yevgeny Zamyatin, which had cast a pall over the Soviets' utopian ideas when it appeared in 1922. In the society described by Zamyatin, sexual intercourse was arranged by application, regulated by a Sex Bureau which distributed coupons – when I'd read that, it had reminded me of the Soviet marriage manuals that established the optimum coupling time for humans at two minutes. Who knows, maybe Orel could tell me the extent to which those things we in the West had considered fiction were actually put into practice in the communist countries.

Although Martina was of the Yahoo! generation, she still associated the word 'yahoo' with the eighteenth-century *Gulliver's Travels*, in which Jonathan Swift presented his race of Yahoos as a degenerate, depraved strain of humanoids who compared very unfavourably with the refined civilization of the horses, the unpronounceable 'Houyhnhnms'. While we paced back and forth in front of Dr Orel's house, she said she had found a quote from Milan Kundera that might come in handy. It concerned the Creation story, or more precisely God's decision to give man dominion over the animals. 'And then Kundera writes: "Obviously, the Genesis account was written by a man, not by a horse."'

I was flabbergasted and asked where she had found that. All I'd really read of Kundera's was *The Unbearable Lightness of Being*.

'In *The Unbearable Lightness of Being*,' Martina said. She raised her eyebrows in a way that said: bet you never would have guessed!

It was time for Dr Orel. We pushed open the whitewashed gate at number 51 and entered the yard.

'Kundera is from Brno, by the way,' Martina said.

'Milan Kundera? From Brno?!'

Mrs Orel opened the door. 'Please do come in,' she said in a lilting voice. 'My husband is waiting for you.' She took our coats and led us into the hall, in the wake of her perfume. We passed two statues of the Virgin Mary before reaching the living room.

– 248 –

'Welcome to my eagle's nest,' the man of the house called to us. He was sitting by the window in the farthest corner of the room and made no attempt to get up.

'*Orel* means eagle in Czech,' Martina explained. I was still getting my bearings. Turkish rugs on the floor. House plants on the windowsill. A view of Brno in the haze below. Milan Kundera, who came from here.

Only when I was standing in front of him did I see that Dr Orel was in a wheelchair. His legs were covered in a blanket that looked like an ankle-length kilt. A pair of slippers protruded.

His wife had slid up two side tables: one for the reference works, the other for coffee and cakes. Folding her hands like the manager of a rest home, she explained that her husband had been in a road accident in 1989 and was paralysed from the waist down.

Orel cleared his throat and turned to me. Did I – with my background as an agricultural engineer – know in which part of the world animal breeding had first been practised systematically?

I knitted my brow and must have frowned too, but he didn't come to my assistance.

'Do you know who the first person was to describe a cell?'
I admitted that I did not.

'What's your favourite work by Beethoven?'
That provided an opening. 'His ninth symphony,' I said. 'Although I find the claim *Alle Menschen werden Brüdern*, all men will be brothers, a bit too utopian.'

Dr Orel regarded me with piercing blue eyes in an otherwise expressionless face. He spoke German, English and Russian, we had enough languages in common to communicate, but were making no contact.

'Did Darwin ever use the word "evolution"?'

'The term must have been coined later . . .'

'Earlier,' Orel cut me off. He handed me a book about Moravian sheep breeding around the year 1800. In it I would find the answers to all his riddles, helped by the hint that a Moravian sheep breeder featured in each correct answer. 'One of them was so wealthy and well versed in culture that he acted as Beethoven's patron.'

'We simply adore André Rieu, he plays Strauss with such flair,' Mrs Orel interjected. 'He's from Holland, isn't he?'

She had been conversing in Czech with Martina, but apparently following our conversation. 'Our guest', she said slowly and clearly to her husband, 'is less interested in the nineteenth century, and more in the twentieth.'

I saw my angle of approach: 'You studied animal husbandry?'

'After the war, yes,' Dr Orel said. I couldn't tell whether he felt reprimanded, or aggrieved, but he turned away and put another record on the stereo.

'My father raised chickens. He sent me to the agricultural university at Brno because he wanted me to have a better life than he had.' Vítězslav had chosen poultry breeding as his speciality, but before his thesis was accepted the 'February of Triumph' arrived, the 1948 coup, after which the family farm was absorbed by an agricultural collective. 'I was busy at the time with an article about the stupidities of Lysenkoism.'

Had he been expelled from the university?

'No, I was allowed to stay. On condition that I become a faithful follower of Lysenko.'

He had taken the honourable way out and went to work at a poultry farm outside the city. He was not the type who went in for self-pity. His eminent professor, however, now *there* was someone they had put through the wringer. To start with, he was banished to Slovakia. And because he continued in his articles to compare Lysenkoism with denying the force of gravity, he was sentenced to a year and a half in prison. When he was released, in 1959, they withdrew his professorial pension benefits – because the judge ruled that he still 'considered himself superior to the working class'.

Dr Orel rifled among the papers on the table beside his wheelchair. It took him a while to find what he was looking for.

His wife jumped to her feet. 'Do you need your reading glasses?'

'Not necessary,' he said. He held a sheet of paper up close to his face. 'What do think a ram cost in Moravia in 1818?'

Mrs Orel intervened by offering us all a pastry. Martina was sitting there despondently, her shoulders hunched. I noticed that our host had barely acknowledged her presence.

'Dr Orel,' I said as assertively as I could, 'I would like to ask you, as Mendel's biographer, the following question: Do you see Mendel as a tragic figure?'

For the first time, I seemed to get through to him. A silence fell. Orel was thinking. Finally he opened his mouth and began quoting an Augustinian monk. I interrupted him: 'I'm interested in *your* opinion, as his biographer.'

'A tragic figure? Not at all,' the man in the wheelchair said. 'He knew, after all, "My time will come" – and he stuck to that. That's the maxim we hung above the entrance to the Mendelianum.'

'But didn't history deal with his legacy rather cruelly?'

'Not cruelly,' Orel said without batting an eyelid. 'Primitively!' And that was typical of the human condition. The species had not made a great deal of progress; in any case, the development of *Homo sapiens* in no way kept pace with its own, overinflated sense of self-importance. 'The people who maligned Mendel or used him for their own purposes never really made a careful study of the foundations of heredity.'

Those foundations, he went on determinedly, were to be found in the Moravia of two centuries ago, where efforts to improve the Merino breed had been characterized by such expertise and co-operation that it was only a matter of time before a Moravian farmer's son would give birth to the science of genetics.

Part of Orel's mystery was unravelling: he had been confined to his wheelchair in the house on the hill ever since his accident in 1989, at the very point when Eastern Europe had thrown itself into the roiling stream of current events. Removed from that turbulence, he had turned to the past, to the era that had produced his hero Mendel.

I tried once more to turn the conversation to the twentieth century, to the Lipizzaners which had lived within Lysenko's sphere of influence. What had horse breeding been like in Czechoslovakia, Hungary and Romania? Concerning the Ceauşescus, I had read that they wanted to raise as many Lipizzaners as possible, regardless of the quality. The animals were 'produced' in the Carpathians, first for farming purposes, later for export. Black and brown animals were not sold, but went to the Ceauşescus themselves.

Dr Orel appeared to be following me. When it came to horse breeding in Czechoslovakia under Lysenko, he was able to say with certainty that it had happened without the use of statistics – the crux of successfully applying Mendel's insights: you had to count, keep a tally, and then process and calculate the results carefully, so that patterns would emerge and provide concrete points of departure for selection and crossing. But that mathematical approach had been tossed overboard. Between 1948 and 1965, all advances in the field of genetics had completely passed by the Eastern Bloc. What arose instead was a botch-up. He had looked on in dismay at the mess that was made of poultry breeding. A researcher from Prague, operating in the spirit of Lysenko, had applied grafting techniques to animals. He injected blood from one chicken embryo into another, which had produced chicks. Chicks, Orel clarified, that had undergone no genetic change whatsoever. But that didn't matter, the man had received a medal from the government and a long profile in the party newspaper.

'And what about Lipizzaners?'

Orel cocked his head. That depended on how you looked at it. Lysenko's influence had been palpable there, but hadn't led to excesses. It was important to remember that these were not production animals. The 1953 manual *Horse Breeding* explained exactly why Mendel was mistaken and what was wrong with 'bourgeois genetics'. The breeder was taught to 'throw an organism out of balance by means of the powerful effect of environmental influences'. In practical terms, an experiment had been underway to create 'the ideal horse for socialist agriculture': by crossing Lipizzaner stallions with sturdy, coldblood mares.

But in Czechoslovakia, the Lipizzaners had retained their aristocratic status. They were brought together at the Topol'čianky stud farm in the mountains north of Bratislava. There, a new selection criterion was applied, one that had originated in the Soviet Union: the endurance test. Stallions able to cover a demanding, twelve-kilometre course within forty minutes were eligible to serve as sires. This could be seen as part of Lysenko's influence, yet 'stamina' was, of course, hardly a peculiar criterion. The breeders at Topol'čianky had followed the example of the military studs at the foot of the Caucasus, where in 1950 a stallion by the name of Zanos had set a long-distance record of 309 kilometres in twenty-four hours. In the breeding programmes for the Soviet cavalry, pedigrees were largely ignored, and line breeding was declared taboo. In accordance with Lysenko's decrees, the cavalry mounts, young and old, remained outside on the steppes in autumn, preferably without additional food or shelter, until the first snow fell. Only then were they to be brought in – but always with open stable doors and windows, so they could continue to harden.

'So it did happen!' I thought. On the other hand, those were hardly excesses. The methodology really didn't differ much from the regime to which the breed had been subjected for centuries at Lipica. Spartan conditions applied there too, with a minimum of shelter from cold and stormy winds – environmental factors that had helped to shape the Lipizzaner. The Eastern European herds had not been 'distilled' by first causing them to dwindle with the help of hypothermia or starvation; no communist horse breeder had ever gone that far.

The Lysenko era, Dr Orel told us, had come to a definitive end in Czechoslovakia on 16 February 1966. On that day, six months after the opening of the Mendelianum, the government had published Ordinance Number 59, which decreed that all existing biology textbooks be destroyed.

In an attempt to strike a lighter note, I asked whether Czechs had also told Lysenko jokes. The Orels looked at each other. When no reply came, I told one I had heard in Russia. 'Do you know how Mendel proves himself right?' I heard myself say. And then, after a few beats: 'By pointing out the resemblance between you and your son. And do you know how Lysenko does that? By pointing out the resemblance between your neighbour and your son.'

They laughed. Finally, I asked about Lysenko's omission

from the new exhibition at the abbey – what did my host think of that?

'I have nothing to do with that museum, and that suits me down to the ground.' Dr Orel lashed out at the city authorities who had dismantled his Mendelianum. They had confiscated Mendel's spectacles, his microscope and walking stick. Unlawfully. He felt no desire to see what it had been replaced with. 'Apparently, they even use part of the abbey as a guest house these days.'

I kept my mouth shut. What was I supposed to say?

A little later, in the hallway, when we already had our coats on, Mrs Orel said: 'My husband doesn't go outside much any more.'

We walked down the lane of maples to the car. Suddenly Martina remembered what her mother had always said when the collective heating went on the blink again and the snow piled up on the windowsills: 'Oh no, they're subjecting us to *studeny odchov*, cold breeding, again.'

THE COLD WAR CAVALRY

'ATJAN, YOU CALLED . . .'
'Yes, thanks for getting back to me. Listen, where are you at the moment?'

'At home,' I said.

Ever since the Secretary General of the International Lipizzaner Federation had smuggled me into the archives of the Spanish Riding School, we had been on a first-name basis.

'Are you standing close to anything you can hold on to?'

'Why?'

'This Conversano Soja of yours', he started, 'is a horse whose memoirs I wouldn't mind reading. Amazing all the things that stallion must have witnessed.'

I knew next to nothing about Primula's sire. Only that he was born on 22 May 1952 of the mare Soja, who had herself taken part in the exodus from Hostau as a foal.

'He played the lead equine role in *Miracle of the White Stallions*, the Hollywood film about the rescue of the Lipizzaners in 1945.' Atjan Hop claimed that Conversano Soja was the light-grey stallion that performed the school quadrille in the closing scene, the finale which marked the historical 'all's well that ends well' return of the exiled Spanish Riding School to Vienna.

'What makes you think that?' I asked.

He was, as it happened, holding in his hand a description of Conversano Soja, written by Podhajsky himself. Atjan started reading aloud in German. Soja had been a 'stallion among stallions', one who whinnied often and loudly with flared nostrils. Nervous, sensitive. With a heart rate of fifty-two beats a minute and weighing 525 kilos. He was born at Wimsbach, where the breeding mares had been kept until 1952, when they returned to Piber. He had arrived in Vienna in November 1955 as a rough diamond. The 'forces of occupation', for that was how Podhajsky referred to the American, British, French and Soviet troops who had administered former aggressor Austria with a firm military hand since 1945, had left only recently. Amid a raising and a lowering of flags, the final soldiers had marched off home during 1955. At the last moment, the commander of the Russian sector in Vienna had been found willing to clear out the Winter Riding School, which was being used as a scrapyard for wrecked cars. In rapid succession, Austria, a sovereign republic once more, witnessed the ecstatic reopening of the State Opera, the Burgtheater and the Spanish Riding School. ERST HEUTE GEHT FÜR UNS DER KRIEG ZU ENDE (TODAY THE WAR FINALLY ENDS FOR US), the *Neue Kurier*'s headline read on Tuesday, 25 October 1955. Five weeks later, Conversano Soja was among the first batch of new blood that arrived to swell the ranks of high-school horses in Vienna.

'A dapple grey with a thin, black mane,' Atjan read, 'who inherited his looks from his father, Conversano Bonavista, but also his touchiness and rather weak tarsal joints.'

In the Stallburg, Soja had fought with an older stallion in the neighbouring box. Both animals had leapt high against the partitions, Soja had bitten the bars and torn the edge of his tongue. He was sufficiently dazed afterwards to allow a white-coated vet to cut off the chunk of flesh hanging from his mouth ('a strip about five centimetres long') without anaesthetic. He had undergone the whole thing stoically, apparently trusting his medico to do him no harm.

Podhajsky himself had saddle-trained Soja and taught him what he knew and the animal made good progress, but was plagued by injuries. Like a football star, he had to have operations on both hocks. Soja made a complete recovery and since then had shone as the key feature in the quadrille, in which the white horses moved around the ring nose-to-tail, like a string of pearls. You could tell by his grey coat that he was the youngest of the lot, but that didn't stop the director of the Royal Spanish Riding School using him as the lead horse. Soja laid down the tempo and rhythm that the others had to follow. On one occasion, though, disaster struck. With obvious relish, Podhajsky related how, during a visit from the president of a new and otherwise unnamed African country, his horse suddenly froze on entering the ring. At every step, Soja kept his eyes riveted on the 'prominent, dark-skinned guest' in the royal box and, once in the centre of the ring, refused to move 'except under great duress'.

Atjan and I laughed. We could appreciate the absurdity of a 'racist horse', even the least white among them, who apparently struggled coming to grips with a world order marked by changes like decolonization.

In other ways as well, world politics kept pace with the school stallions. After its co-optation by Nazi Germany, the Spanish Riding School was now America's darling. As early as 1950, a grand tour was arranged through the United States that was clearly infused with Cold War sentiment. With their stylized agility, a group of twelve school stallions – shipped across the sea from Bremen – stole the show in the land of the rodeo. Colonel Podhajsky appeared on television wearing the traditional *Zweispitz* riding hat – 'to spread propaganda for our little country, which was once the cultural centre of Europe'. In turn, the Americans never missed a chance to reiterate that they were the ones who had saved that culture from going under, because the Red Army would have been all too pleased to see the horses vanish into their stewpots. Beneath the spotlights of Madison Square Garden, Patton's widow presented a rose to Colonel Podhajsky. The myth-building that began in New York reached a peak twelve years later in the Hollywood rendition of Operation Cowboy, filmed on location in Austria.

During the shooting in 1962, Robert Taylor sat astride Conversano Soja, who was decked out in full regalia for a series of close-ups at a walk and a standstill. But on this occasion too, Soja behaved skittishly and stubbornly, forcing the director to replace him with an older, silvery-white stallion. Podhajsky was dumbstruck; any moviegoer, he felt, would immediately see that the grey horse performing the quadrille (Soja, ridden by Podhajsky himself) was not the same as that receiving a standing ovation at the end.

The exterior scenes were not what they seemed, either. Not a single Austrian Lipizzaner took part in them. The government resisted the idea of having the Piber mares herded by tanks for a second time; the risk of fatal falls or miscarriages was too great, they felt. In order to depict the flight to the free world, the outspokenly anti-communist Walt Disney had therefore been compelled to sign a costly contract with Marshal Tito for the rental of 163 Lipizzaners. Other stand-ins from the Lipizzaner breed were impossible to find, especially in such numbers. Hungary was not far away, but there was no way the Moscow-loyal communists there were going to loan their Lipizzaners for a show of American heroics. It was 1962, and the rivalry between East and West had never been so palpable. The Wall was being raised straight across Berlin, while in the Caribbean the Cuban missile crisis threatened the planet. In the shadow of this political duel, the crew began building replicas of the stables and barracks of Hostau at a military base close to the town of Bruck an der Leitha – still within Austrian territory but close to the Hungarian border. At a sign from the director, more than 150 Lipizzaners from socialist Yugoslavia stormed across the hilly country along the Austro-Hungarian border, moving west, driven and protected by a US Army tank formation, and racing in a cloud of dust in flight from an imaginary Red Army. During their escape the animals were filmed from beneath as they leapt over ditches, from the side by racing command jeeps and even from the air by a low-flying aircraft. Once their escape to freedom had been filmed from all angles and Tito's horses were loaded back into the livestock wagons for the trip home, there turned out not to be 163 of them, but 165. During the orchestrated chaos, two mares had foaled.

'A handsome color film', the *New York Times* ruled. 'In giving a cozy explanation of how Gen. George Patton sent a spearhead of armored forces into Czechoslovakia to grab the herd of Lipizzan mares before the Russians got them, it clearly implies that the peril of a force of American soldiers was as nothing to the future of this great herd of briskly performing horses.'

Besides the show for the silver screen, the Royal Spanish Riding School also gave performances in Helsinki, Stockholm, Copenhagen, Berlin, Aachen, Frankfurt, Rotterdam, Zurich, London, Rome and Seville, where the stallions performed in the huge bullfight arena. Colonel Podhajsky kissed the hand of Pope Pius XII, gave riding lessons to Queen Elizabeth and to Princess Irene of the Netherlands (on Soja!). He had himself awarded – by his rival, Gustav Rau – the highest equestrian medal Germany had to offer and expressed his admiration for Generalissimo Franco, 'who did not at all seem like the iron-fisted dictator he is so often made out to be'.

∪

Atjan Hop had now reached the penultimate paragraph, dedicated in its entirety to Soja. On 3 June 1961, it appeared, he had performed for Jackie Kennedy – at the very moment that her husband was making a timorous impression elsewhere in Vienna during his summit meeting with Nikita Khrushchev. Soja fulfilled his role as captain of the quadrille, without being distracted by the elegant first lady with her beige pillbox hat in the imperial loge.

Barely a year later the stallion was once again in the international limelight. Podhajsky described a special performance he had given with Soja to promote the first communications satellite, Telstar 1, fired into orbit from Cape Canaveral in July 1962, to facilitate direct data communication between the continents. In the race with the Soviet Union – which had achieved a head start with the launch of the first dog (Laika) into space, and the first human (Yuri Gagarin) – the Americans succeeded in broadcasting around the world 'live' TV images of the Statue of Liberty – purportedly to promote 'a better understanding among men'. This latest battle for supremacy in space was only won, however, when images from the Old World were broadcast directly to the New World as well. To that end, Conversano Soja had been curried and saddled and made to perform a real-time piaffe from Vienna for an audience in the western hemisphere.

In 1964, riding the wave of popularity of *Miracle of the White Stallions*, the time was ripe for a new American tour by the Royal Spanish Riding School, a reprise Soja came very close indeed to taking part in. Jackie Kennedy, by then widowed, was the tour's patroness. This time the horses did not have to bob across the Atlantic for days on end – instead, they were flown by KLM air freighter directly to the States, via Amsterdam. Soja, however, whose inflamed joints continued to trouble him from time to time, had been loaned out to Piber to pass down his exceptional genes. During his stay in the Alps he sired forty-two descendants. Among them, in 1967, was his athletically built, smallish son Conversano Primula, who would ultimately grow to adulthood only two kilometres from my family home in the Netherlands.

Alois Podhajsky died in 1973 of a brain haemorrhage, and after his funeral and immediate canonization, the history of the Lipizzaners hit a troubled episode. Austria was briefly startled by the outbreak of a deadly epidemic at the Piber stud, the herpes virus, which raged through the stalls in the spring of 1983, infected forty mares in foal and caused them all to miscarry. Six died of paralysis of the nervous system, and the year 1983 saw the birth of only ten healthy foals. After coping with this setback, which some experts blamed on excessive inbreeding, stud-farm director Dr Lehrner was forced to step down.

The rest of the 1980s, however, were peaceful and calm. The breeding animals were neither endangered nor threatened; the high-school horses ran through their repertoire imperturbably.

But in 1989 this state of routine and stability was rudely interrupted. On 19 August, not far from Bruck an der Leitha, a minor incident took place which was to have major consequences for the Lipizzaners. The reformist government in Budapest announced a daring plan for that day: for a period of three hours, Hungarian border guards would throw open a back road between East and West. An out-and-out provocation, directed at the fraternity of communist countries, and one which received support from an Austrian citizens' platform in the playful form of a 'pan-European picnic'. Hundreds of East German families holidaying at that moment on Lake Balaton were handed invitations to come to the West for a 'picnic'. Weeping in disbelief, 661 East German men, women and children slipped through the hole in the Iron Curtain during that three-hour window. Several dropped to their knees in front of the cameras and kissed the Austrian soil. And so, the ball was set rolling.

I found it remarkable that this half-planned, half-spontaneous human stampede had taken place only a stone's throw from where Walt Disney had shot his Lipizzaner film. What also surprised me was the name of one of the initiators of the picnic: Otto von Habsburg, son of the last Austrian emperor, born in 1912. Though rudely sidelined by the course of twentieth-century events, he had remained politically active. His titles had been removed, his power curtailed, and, as crown prince of the Habsburg dynasty, Otto von Habsburg had been forced to renounce his claim to the throne. But none of this stopped him from knocking a breach, at a crucial moment in the summer of 1989 and a crucial spot between Vienna and Budapest, in the barrier that had divided both his former empire and modern Europe – albeit peacefully and politely, as a member of the European Parliament.

With his protest action, Otto von Habsburg , an amiable old gent with spectacles and a moustache, had also contributed indirectly to the resumed exchange of Lipizzaners between East and West – which was sorely needed for the long-neglected *Blutauffrischung*, the refreshing of blood.

1989 was also the year in which the International Lipizzaner Federation met for the first time in Hungary; that is, in a former Eastern Bloc country. All the stud farms now renewed their contacts – as though no schism had ever taken place.

The euphoria concerning the end of the Cold War was, however, short-lived. After 1989, the Royal Spanish Riding School regained its ceremonious, apolitical character for the first time since that fatal shot was fired in Sarajevo. But with the arrival of the 1990s, shots were once again heard in the capital of Bosnia and Herzegovina.

THE HUMAN ZOO

O N A SATURDAY IN 2008, I found twelve men, women and children of various ethnic backgrounds staring at me from the cover of the weekend science section of my newspaper. Because each portrait photo was circular, it seemed they were peering through the portholes of a ship. Probably some story about multicultural society, I thought. The caption, however, destroyed that illusion: 'They look different, and on the inside the differences are even greater.' I opened the section.

ETHNIC GROUPS SHOWN TO 'CLUSTER' GENETICALLY

As DNA technologies become more advanced, the genetic differences between ethnic groups can be more accurately defined. Scary? 'All research is liable to be abused at some point.'

The article referred to the prominent journal *Science*, which had declared the 'breakthrough of the year 2007' to be the discovery of 'human genetic variation'. Since 2005, a medicine called BiDil – this was not fiction, but fact – had been making waves in the United States as the first 'racist medicine': a vasodilator tailored to 'Afro-American heart patients'. How different this sounded from the mantra I had grown up with, that the difference between black and white is only skin-deep.

'For years, research into racial differences was taboo, but today it is at the centre of attention.' Clearly, I had missed something. Geneticists from the Institut Pasteur had succeeded in identifying the inborn differences between Africans and non-Africans pertaining to digestion, olfactory sensitivity, hair growth and eyesight. 'It is probably only a matter of time before all manner of DNA variations are also found between ethnic groups with relation to intelligence or (aggressive) behaviour.'

Before the law every man was equal, but apparently the same could no longer be said of science.

I read about the 1,000 Genomes Project. This ongoing American–British–Chinese consortium aimed to map all DNA variations between the Japanese, the Maasai, the Chinese, the Tuscans, the Mexicans, the Gujarati Indians and a dozen other groups. With the use of a new generation of DNA-chips – plastic rectangles the size of a credit card – which could compute the entire 'letter combination' of human DNA within twenty-four hours, the catalogue could be ready in just a few years. Thousands of volunteers were taking part in this trans-global project. So what would it finally demonstrate? Differences in aptitude for mathematics? Or leanings towards short-temperedness? How would such revelations be used – and who would be able to control them?

I laid aside the science section. 'Thou shalt not discriminate' was the great pillar beneath the modern constitutional state. *We* do not discriminate – that had been the researchers' way of hedging from the very start. Should one ethnic group turn out to be less intelligent than another, the scientists were merely the bearers of a scientifically verifiable fact. It was a point of view I had always defended: the harm did not lie in the registration of differences. But now I wasn't so sure. People who handled hazardous substances could become contaminated by them; a finding could easily get under one's skin and fester into a prejudice. And were at some point the factual inequality between groups of humans to come into conflict with the principle of equality, which would give way first: the law, or science?

I was reminded of the year I'd graduated from the agricultural university, 1989, and first heard about a DNA automat developed in the United States: a sort of coffee machine with which, by punching the appropriate buttons, gene researchers could order the strand of DNA they desired. Each living organism was reduced to an encrypted roll of film which could be cut and edited at will. If people were able to incorporate a section of human DNA into a cow (like Herman the bull), then why not animal DNA into a human? 'Something' kept us from doing that, but that something was not the practical unfeasibility. Where did the ethical borders of genetic improvement lie, and who actually guarded them these days?

Born in 1990, Herman the bull had been on display – stuffed and mounted and with a steel ring in his nose – in the Naturalis Museum in Leiden since 2006. He had lived to the age of fourteen. His architect, Professor Herman de Boer, was no longer derided as a Dr Frankenstein. Modern geneticists, he told interviewers, are careful about what they do. 'Our conscience has been pricked by Mengele.' And beyond that, he considered himself no more than a farm boy who had followed in his father's footsteps. 'The only difference is that I work the fields of biotechnology.'

In 1997, the first cloned sheep, Dolly, conceived from the mammary gland of a Finn Dorset ewe, had conjured up more glaringly fearful visions than Herman the bull had. But she too had been on display in a museum in Edinburgh for several years already, as a curiosity of scientific history. And horses? The distinction went to Italy, where in 2003 a mare had given birth to her own, genetically identical foal. Not long afterwards, the American gelding Scamper, ten-time national barrel-racing champion, had been duplicated for the sum of $150,000.

That the owner of a Lipizzaner would want to have a genetic copy was something I had never thought possible. But I was wrong. 'Project X' – sponsored by a Florida horsewoman who dearly desired a backup of her stallion Pluto Marcella – resulted on 5 May 2010 in the birth of Pluto II Marcella, while being carried to term in the womb of yet another surrogate dam was a second backup clone, Pluto III Marcella. This presented the stud-book archivists with a dilemma. In the past, they had reluctantly agreed to the introduction of artificial insemination at Piber. Now, suddenly, there was the question of whether clones too could be entered into the book as pure-bred Lipizzaners. And if so, under what heading? There was, after all, already a Pluto Marcella with exactly the same ancestors, born on 24 April 1980 near Chicago.

Curiosity prompted me to examine his pedigree and, lo and behold, the twice-cloned Lipizzaner proved to be a great-grandson of Pluto XX, the horse given to General Patton and shipped to America.

At the age of thirty, his descendant, Pluto Marcella, now had two identical twin brothers, cultivated from his own skin cells. It could have been twenty. Or 200.

∪

Now that the cloning of humans was within sight, most countries had promptly drawn a line in the sand. Cloning people would be taking things too far. Yet the ethicists calling for restraint on the part of the white-coated engineers could, it seemed, barely be heard above the din. Or perhaps they were simply fighting a rearguard action.

Twenty years after the 'dig-ins' organized by The Raging Potatoes, this is how things stand: genetically manipulated crops flourish and grow on seven per cent of the world's farmland. Germany is the only country that does not take part; the sowing of gene crops there – outside a few heavily guarded laboratories – is forbidden. Some corridors in the mansion of heredity research there are still cordoned off with police tape and 'No trespassing' signs – as territory contaminated by the ptomaine of the Holocaust. In 1999, when the philosopher Peter Sloterdijk brought up the 'genetic engineering of human beings' during a lecture entitled 'Rules for the Human Zoo', a wide array of German intellectuals immediately attacked him. Sloterdijk had fretted aloud about the 'general bestialization of humans', as aided and abetted by the media and the entertainment industry, which education and other humanistically inspired attempts at influencing behaviour were unable to counter. 'Nurture' had proved too weak a remedy. Wasn't it time to see what could be done on the 'hardware' side, in the field of 'nature'? Or, in Sloterdijk's own words: 'What can tame man, when the role of human-ism as the school for humanity has collapsed?' Remaining neutral was not advisable, because: 'Those who do not select, will be selected.'

'When I hear this, 'one critic wrote in *Die Zeit*, 'I involuntarily think of the selection on the loading platform at Auschwitz.'

An editor at *Der Spiegel* saw in this a 'summons to purposeful genetic selection under the leadership of a cultural elite' – and said that was 'fascistic'. Sloterdijk was seeking refuge in gene technology. 'The uterus replaces the Utopia.'

Barely ten years later, embryo selection is a fact. At private clinics in countries universally regarded as civilized, parents with hereditary diseases can have several embryos developed simultaneously *in vitro*. In incubators the size of shopping baskets, these prospective babies are allowed to grow to a stage where they can be tested for the presence of the undesirable gene. This is eugenics, plain and simple: only an embryo without the defective gene will be placed in the womb, the rest will be destroyed.

As an article of faith, the preamble to the American Declaration of Independence includes the words: 'We hold these truths to be self-evident, that all men are created equal.' But in the September 2006 issue of the American *Journal of Biosocial Science* one could read that Ashkenazi Jews on the average score strikingly higher on IQ tests than all other ethnic groups. The group also produces proportionally more chess champions. The authors presented this as a solid, proven fact and credited it to the centuries of discrimination against this group in Europe: because its members were not allowed to own land, they often had no choice but to take up professions such as finance and trade, in which great arithmetical skill increased the chances of survival. Over the course of many generations, this societal selection mechanism had genetically embedded in the Ashkenazi Jews the ability to think abstractly. After the article was published, its authors were accused of practising 'institutionalized racism', without any ill effect on their future careers.

Meanwhile, biology forged ahead with the busting of taboos. As late as 1986, the UNESCO 'Seville Statement' censured criminologists who looked for the roots of violent behaviour in neurophysiology. Those who continued to do so would end up making fascism socially acceptable once again – and of course no one was in favour of that. Yet 'evil' also possesses an anatomy, and one which can be manipulated. Using focused electrical impulses, neurologists can now turn off the sources of compulsive behaviour, a technique called deep brain stimulation. With it, the neurosurgeon has a sophisticated instrument for 'resetting' a person's personality – and changing it forever.

Nature and nurture are more complexly interwoven than was supposed in the past, and it is precisely that complexity which is now revealing itself. Mouse mothers submitted to a form of memory training have been shown to pass that acquired trait without fail to their progeny: external stimuli can 'turn on' or 'turn off' certain genes. In other words: Lysenko, Kammerer and Lamarck were – up to a point – right after all. Their central thesis, that acquired traits can be inherited, is now the subject of a new branch of science, epigenetics, which is making progress precisely along the knife-edge dividing the biological views of Hitler and those of Stalin.

The 'eighth day of Creation' dawned some time ago. The human species has not only deduced the workings of evolution, but has succeeded in taking apart its motor, boring out the cylinders and reassembling the whole contraption. On this souped-up moped we then hurtle forwards at breakneck speed – cockily and without a helmet.

U

The letter that came from Atjan Hop, containing a report dating from 1992, brought me back to the raw reality of the not-so-noble human. 'Not exactly fun reading', he had written in the note on top of the pile of photocopies. The title was: *Report on the fate of the Lipizzaner horses killed during the hostilities in and around Lipik, the Croatian Republic, between mid-August and late December 1991.*

The International League for the Protection of Horses, with Britain's Princess Anne as honorary chairperson, had – at the invitation of the Croatian government – performed post-mortems in February 1992 on a dozen carcasses of Lipizzaners found in a hastily covered mass grave. The objective was to establish the cause of death. Could these animals be seen as direct victims of the hostilities? And if so: had they been killed intentionally?

Exhumation at Location 2 in the hamlet of Filipovac produced 13 (thirteen) equine cadavers in various states of decomposition.

The Croatian government had provided hip boots, surgical masks and a mechanical digger. One by one, the limp cadavers of the Lipizzaners were hoisted up by their back legs. They were identified by their brand: an L with a stroke, resembling the sign for the pound sterling. All thirteen horses were found to come from the stud farm at Lipik.

A strong stomach was needed to read on. Even without the sickly smell of decay, the accompanying photos were nauseating. The lungs of nine of the Lipizzaners had been cut open and examined.

The condition of their bronchial tubes shows that they died of smoke inhalation.

This was not the first report I had read about a mass grave in former Yugoslavia, but it was the only one dealing with horses. I felt an impotent rage arise at the thought of the stallion Favory Trompeta, seven years old, dying of suffocation in his burning stall. I would have been hard pressed to say whether the report concerning the execution of 246 Croatians at a pig farm close to Vukovar had, at the time, hit me as hard. That crime, also referred to in Zagreb as 'the second Jasenovac', had been larger in scope and more systematic. Yet I had the uneasy feeling that the death of these horses affected me more deeply. Why was that? Was it the animals' defencelessness? Their innocence, like that of children?

Generally, I mistrusted human tenderness when applied to animals. It was somewhat preposterous. How long ago was it, after all, that it had been normal to go on safari with a rifle, rather than a camera? The love of animals was usually without risk and limited to the fluffier species. The cruellest tyrants, in fact, often showed themselves to be the most soft-hearted animal lovers. Hitler, who pampered his German shepherd. Mussolini, who always carried a few sugar cubes in his pocket. Napoleon, who imposed a ban on the docking of horses' tails. How many mothers' sons had that man put to the sword? He didn't care about them; what he cared about was the inner life of his Arab stallion Vizir. 'How can we be so sure that horses have no language?' he mused in exile on St Helena. 'I believe we only suppose this because we cannot understand them. A horse is filled with memories, knowledge and love.'

Two horses were killed by shrapnel.

One horse died of contusions: the midriff shows signs of dislocation.

In the yard of the stud farm itself ('Location 1'), at least five dead Lipizzaners lay scattered about. The pathologists, who spent two full days poking at the wounds with their latex gloves, could get no closer to the stalls, which still contained unexploded mortar shells.

At university I had learnt that the shift from hunting and gathering to cultivation and husbandry had marked the start of what we call civilization. The cave dweller had crawled out of his cave and built huts and stalls for his animals. He bridled the horse, and when that worked out well, he climbed on its back – an innocuous link in the developmental chain of humanity, or so it seemed. But in so doing, had he not unintentionally knocked the natural scheme of things out of joint? In other words: wasn't the mounting of the horse one of the decisive moves with which man placed himself outside nature – or above it?

Anyone climbing on a horse's back made himself bigger, more important. Galloping through the fields he had the feeling of rising above himself. 'When I bestride him, I soar, I am a hawk: he trots the air; the earth sings when he touches it.' Such is the rider's euphoria, as expressed by Shakespeare.

In equestrian portraits of kings and dukes, the beauty of the horse underscores the power of the man. Employing tricks of perspective, court painters such as Goya and Velázquez were able to emphasize those skewed proportions: the horse's head was made a bit smaller, that of its rider a bit bigger. I was reminded of the paintings of horses *without* a rider, made for the Viennese court. In 1718 the imperial family had brought in an exclusive portraitist of horses, Johann Georg von Hamilton, in whose studio Lipizzaners and Kladrubers posed. And whether those horses were saddled and decked out with braids in their mane or whether they posed completely 'naked', the impression was always one of elegance and refinement, the horse as the epitome of grace. A haughty stallion captured in the midst of a controlled levade was civilization incarnate – the acme of what human culture could produce. So if that was the case, what was one to think of the Lipizzaners in that collective grave at Lipik?

One eight-year-old stallion had been killed at close range by three bullets from an automatic weapon:

On the left side of the chest: three oval wounds. Three ribs are perforated (diameter: 8 mm). Underlying organs destroyed.

As a child I was taught that evil had come into the world

through original sin. Adam and Eve should not have eaten from the tree of knowledge. Once you knew about good and evil, or thought you did, things went downhill fast. Original sin meant that all people knew what it was to act rightly, but were doomed to do the opposite.

A project at secondary school about 'Aggression among humans and animals' had changed my mind about that, though.

That one could always come up with an explanation for aggressive animal behaviour was part of the problem. Whichever way you looked at it, it was invariably in the service of natural selection and therefore neatly in line with the logic of evolution theory. But human aggression assumed forms that didn't make any sense. We mentioned this to our biology teacher and I've never forgotten his answer: patting the chalk dust from his hands, he began to explain the concept of 'enthusiasm' in biological terms. At a first glance, he said, enthusiasm is noble and elevated, a state of mind. We could feel ourselves glowing with it when the Dutch football team reached the World Cup semi-finals, or when our schoolmate Manon Bollegraf became national youth tennis champion – something like that reflected on the whole school. Pure enthusiasm gave you goosebumps, shivers literally ran down your spine.

'Think of a cat arching its back,' our biology teacher said. 'Or a male gorilla standing up and pounding its chest .'

So, our enthusiasm could be traced back to animal behaviour. It flared up in competition with others, or in the face of external threats. Ridiculous as it sounded, goosebumps, by making the hair on your arms stand up, were meant to make the contours of your body seem larger and therefore more threatening. And if at that point a leader appeared who could convince your group that you were threatened, the ranks would close around him. The fury usually attributed to animals jumped the gap to humans like a rabies infection. They let themselves go, uninhibited and unashamed. At worst, this ended in genocide: in the extermination of an entire people. 'Genocide' came from *genos* (sort) and *caedere* (to kill) – and only humans practised it.

Unnatural behaviour, I realized as I laid aside the report, was characteristic of *Homo sapiens*. Creating and destroying he did like no other, that is the Janus face of humanity. In the museum in Vienna you could admire sublime portraits of Lipizzaners, while their descendants, a few hours' drive south, were being dumped in a pit with bullet and shrapnel wounds.

Was there any prospect of change for the better? In technological terms, so much was possible these days – yet the human species seemed immune to all forms of moral improvement. One could wonder whether there was any direction whatsoever in man's development.

Some biologists predicted with great confidence that, within ten to twenty generations, globalization would automatically produce a 'cosmopolitan human'. Due to migration, inexpensive flights and dating services, a human gene pool was being formed in which all variation would gradually be obliterated. You couldn't stop it if you tried, it happened on its own. The melting pot simmered, and the end result was a uniform human, not unlike Colin Powell: coffee-coloured and with slightly frizzy hair.

On the radio I heard an artist describe an experiment he was performing to achieve precisely this with chickens. Under the title 'Cosmopolitan Chicken Project', he had crossed a wide variety of poultry breeds. First the Mechelse koekoek, a breed that was the pride of Belgium, with the French Poulet de Bresse. The mongrels which that produced were then crossed with the English Redcap, and their descendants with the American Jersey Giant, and the following generation in turn with the Dresdner Huhn. Koen Vanmechelen was the artist's name, he was an autodidact. 'As humans,' I heard him say in his velvety Flemish accent, 'this shows us that we need to forget borders and start thinking cosmopolitanly.' Vanmechelen sought to create a super-mongrel as a new starting point for the species *Gallus gallus*. The cosmopolitan chicken, in other words.

Without outside interference, humans would follow the same course. And before long there would be no more grounds for discrimination, persecution, genocide.

I was not convinced. All forms of merger and unification provoked resistance and aversion of their own accord. You could see that in Europe: the bigger the Union became, the more pronounced the nationalism. Before you knew it a leader could make an electorate enthusiastic for an 'own-people-first' platform. Following the eternal to and fro of action and reaction, the pendulum always swung too far: in this case, from the emphasis on *nature* (during the first half of the twentieth century) to *nurture* (during the second) and, at the start of the twenty-first century, powerfully back again to *nature*.

I thought about Tito's goal of creating 'the Yugoslavian', and how that had ended.

Yet, by the same token, once the orgy of ethnic violence had run its course, the survivors had proven themselves capable of resuming with amazing speed the age-old appearance of civilization.

Croatia had simply picked up where it left off as a holiday destination and the motorway between Zagreb and Belgrade was reopened, though there was no longer any mention of brotherhood and unity.

∪

In 2006, close to kilometre marker 100 on the old Highway of Brotherhood and Unity, a new camp museum was opened at Jasenovac. Working on the basis of archive material, the number of the dead was revised by a broad committee of historians. The new balance sheet showed a provisional tally of 69,842 victims – a tenth of Tito's claim, twice that of the president of Croatia. Their names were listed in alphabetical order in a thin-paged volume with the format of a telephone book and the thickness of three paving stones.

Among them were:

39,580	Serbs
14,599	Roma
10,700	Jews
3,462	Croatians
1,501	others

Of whom: 18, 812 children under fourteen years of age

The Tito-era memorial centre now housed the Jasenovac Primary School. The pupils could look out over the meadowlands along the Sava and the ten-metre-high concrete sculpture of the flower. Perhaps they would grow up to become those new world citizens; like everyone else, they had a chance – why not? – even if only a very slim one.

CONVERSANO BATOSTA

I VAN TAKES HIS HANDS off the wheel for a moment, in a how-am-I-supposed-to-explain-this gesture. 'He's a friend of Bono,' he says. 'Of John Malkovich, Bruce Springsteen, Brian Eno.'

At the traffic light, the only one in Lipik, he fishes a CD out of the glovebox. *A Thousand Years of Peace*. On the back is the silhouette of a man wearing a hat.

'He's the biggest pop star in Croatia,' Ivan continues, 'and not because I say so, but because he just is.'

'He' is Nenad. Being short for: Nenad Bach. And he is on his way. Ivan just had him on the phone. Nenad Bach is on the road now and should be here in forty-five minutes.

From the back seat, Jadranka chimes in. 'He performed with Pavarotti too, during a concert for the children of Bosnia.'

It was Jadranka's idea to show me, before Nenad arrives, the classroom where she teaches English and where, one year ago, she and her pupils drew up a petition for the Lipizzaners that had been taken away. In August 2007, as soon as the first grisly photos appeared of the white horses along the Danube, Jadranka went into action. The animals had been located but not yet returned, they were starving and in need, and that was reason enough to post an Internet appeal in Croatian and in English:

> Let's put an end to the suffering of the Croatian Lipizzaners that were taken to Serbia in 1991. Let's bring these final war refugees, along with their children, home to their own stalls in Lipik!

There was a photograph of the mayor of Lipik signing the petition. Even more important was the assistance of Nenad Bach, who awarded the petition a prominent place on his own, highly popular website. Four thousand expressions of sympathy quickly came in, providing enough impetus to get things rolling. And now Nenad Bach was flying in from New York for a hero's welcome in Lipik.

Jadranka and Ivan were the Akelas of the 'Linden Branch' youth organization, which devotes itself to everything concerning the reconstruction of their devastated town. Driving around in Ivan's rattletrap Opel, they give me a quick guided tour of the high points of resurrected Lipik: the new orphanage, the new sanatorium, the new pastel-pink Hotel Lipa – where we will soon be having lunch with the mayor.

Every time we return to the junction of the main street and Empress Maria Theresia Street, the traffic light is red.

'Maria Theresia Street?'

'That's what it's always been called,' Ivan says. 'Except in Tito's day.' Lipik, he tells me, is an old Habsburg spa and was connected by rail with Vienna as early as 1861. 'Did you know that we had electricity here in 1894? That was only twelve years after New York.'

The nineteenth-century spa – a replica, according to Ivan,

of the one at Karlovy Vary – is still surrounded by scaffolding. This art-deco jewel was so badly damaged in 1991, all the way down to the bowling alleys in the cellar, that attempts at restoration seem almost futile.

The Russian bass Fyodor Syalyapin sang here in the period between the world wars, adds Jadranka, who is clearly fonder of opera than of pop music.

At the edge of the park stands a row of stately villas, some of them rebuilt, others still hopeless ruins from which protrude the foliage of tall trees.

'This was the front,' Ivan says, pointing at a turning close to the cemetery. Jadranka's school is in this same district – the only part of town never taken by the Serbs.

The heat – it is a windless Saturday, thirty-five degrees centigrade – hits us full in the face as we climb out of the car. Jadranka takes over, opening the door to the auditorium and leading us, her skirt rustling, to the top floor, where she stops beside a noticeboard. A black hairband keeps her wavy hair pulled back; she radiates a teacher's authority.

The board is hung with poems about Lipizzaners. There is also a photograph of a stallion speaking to the viewer in English in a little cartoon balloon: 'Hello. My name is Conversano Batosta. I was born in 1987.' Beside that, in block letters: UNIVERSAL DECLARATION OF ANIMAL RIGHTS – OCTOBER 1978, PARIS.

Jadranka places her hand on a rubbish bin decorated with horse pictures. 'Our collecting box,' she says. It slowly dawns on me that her pupils toss apples and carrots into it – for the horses that still need to regain their strength.

Also hanging on the board is an eyewitness report, written by Ivan, entitled 'Lipik's soul returns':

13 October 2007

The atmosphere was magical. That evening, Lipik
shook on its foundations. A crowd had gathered at the
stud farm, the mist made people and trees flow together.
Darkness fell, but the glistening of our eyes lit the way
for the horses who were making their journey home.

At 02:21 hrs, the convoy of hope appeared. There was
a honking of horns and cheering, and even though it
was in the middle of the night, the people of Lipik
rushed from their homes. They wept when the horses
appeared out of the darkness which had once, in 1991,
covered them and taken them prisoner.

The drive up to the stud farm was lined on both sides
with 200 inhabitants of Lipik, some of them holding
candles. The trucks drove all the way up to the stables.
As soon as the loading doors opened and the first horses
stepped out hesitantly, a shiver ran through the crowd.
Sixty-six horses from Lipik, Lipizzaners, national
treasure of Croatia, had returned to their own stalls
after sixteen long years.

Everything seems lighter, simpler, now that we know
that our horses sleep under the same sky as we.

Ivan says he didn't go to bed until he had written this down
– spontaneously, straight from the heart – and emailed it to
Nenad Bach. That night he had driven through the town,
honking his horn, as if after a football match. On the final
stretch he had led the convoy, as a sort of one-man escort,
with a Croatian flag out of the open window.

I would get to see the horses soon, I just had to be patient.
A tour of the stud farm was on the programme only after
lunch.

Nenad sends a text message: he has just taken the Lipik/Jasenovac exit.

I ask Jadranka and Ivan whether it was really their petition that had set the horses' return in motion. Jadranka throws me a fatigued glance, and Ivan warns me not to underestimate the power of the Internet. In Germany, a 'fax bombardment' in protest at the horses' treatment had been launched against the Serbian embassy in Berlin, but who cares about faxes? As a matter of principle, Ivan is prepared to share the credit with the Serb group 'Freedom for Animals', who posted photographs of the tracked-down horses on YouTube. Nenad Bach had placed a link to that film clip on his own site, and you could see that it had been viewed thousands of times.

That makes me sit up and take notice: the suffering of the Lipizzaners caused Croatians and Serbs to lend each other a helping hand?

But no, they wouldn't go that far. It's more a generational issue. Anyone, Serb or Croatian, who grew up with the web looks to the future rather than to the past.

Ivan turns the argument around: the older generation couldn't do a thing. 'You can check it out. All their earlier attempts to get the horses back came to nothing.'

He starts working his way down the list of failures. To start with, Croatia had set up a 'Committee for the Return of the Stolen Lipizzaners'. At every peace conference, direct and indirect, the committee members had come up empty-handed. The Serb negotiators acted as though they didn't know what they were talking about. Even Otto von Habsburg hadn't been able to achieve any concrete progress. In 1994, at the age of eighty-two, he had submitted a draft bill in the European Parliament, proposing to place the Lipizzaner on the list of endangered species. It was also a warning to the

Serbs not to harm the Lipik herd, but it turned out to be no more than a paper tiger.

The efforts of the International Lipizzaner Federation had also proven fruitless. All its members were called upon to keep their eyes open for the missing herd. Occasionally, an animal was put up for sale at an auction with the Lipik brand, a sign that the herd, or at least part of it, was still alive and even still being used for breeding (the branding iron had been taken as well). Each and every one of those animals was blacklisted, a boycott which meant that Lipik horses and their offspring became unmarketable. The hope was that this would prompt the horse thief to surrender his spoils of war. The paradox, however, was that horses that had always been placed on the pedestal of nobility were suddenly treated as pariahs – as stateless *sans papiers*.

None of this had helped. When the peace agreements were signed at an airbase in Dayton, Ohio in late 1995, the Lipik horses were not included in the terms. No annexe or separate agreement followed concerning the Lipizzaners and their distribution among the signatories – as was the tradition after the major conflicts of the twentieth century.

The Croatians weren't about to let it go at that. Ten years after the truce, they exerted additional pressure by restoring to its former glory the destroyed nineteenth-century stud farm at Lipik. A new roof was set on the 169-metre-long stable. The yards were raked, the boxwood hedge along the drive trimmed and, on a spring day in 2007, the press was invited in. The sliding stall doors were opened, so that their emptiness could strike the journalists as a powerful indictment. Yet the absence of the white horses produced no stirring media reports.

Those came only that summer, once the all-seeing eye of YouTube zoomed in on the Lipizzaners' suffering.

υ

Nenad Bach is wearing tight white trousers and a collarless white shirt with long, wide sleeves. And, despite the heat, his black hat. We – the mayor of Lipik, a delegation of leading citizens, the young people of Linden Branch and I – stand waiting for him on the steps in front of the Hotel Lipa. After the handshaking and the usual formalities, we are all invited to enter the dining room. The two round tables are set impeccably. The seating arrangement dictates that Ivan and his Linden Branch young people take Table 2. Jadranka has been placed on my right to serve as interpreter. Opposite me at Table 1 are the mayor and the former mayor, Nenad Bach, the city's public works manager, the director of the stud farm and, on my left, Croatia's chief equerry, Mato Čačić, Dipl. Eng. Agr. – according to his business card. He has come by motorcycle from Zagreb. A great hulking fellow with short, bristly hair and carefully cultivated stubble.

'Sorry, mister,' is how he introduces himself , 'I speak English like Tarzan.' He wants me to call him just plain 'Mato'.

In the interests of small talk, I ask Mato whether he, as chief equerry, also owns horses.

'Yes,' he says. 'I own all horses of Croatia.'

Sparkling wine is served, the mayor delivers a toast to the return of the Lipizzaner herd and to Nenad Bach's role in that. A subdued cheer rises from Table 2. The pop star, used to flattery, raises his arms to call for silence – he has no desire for accolades. It is the young people, he says, who he would like to thank today. Nenad Bach has taken off his hat, his thin hair is plastered to his temples. He speaks softly, so that his words are just audible above the monotone purr of the air conditioning.

Rather than launching into a monologue, as men in the Balkans tend to do, he asks questions. Are the horses recovering well? Are they permanently traumatized? And who was it, in the end, who actually brought them back to Lipik?

Although Nenad addresses the mayor, it is the chief equerry who replies. Mato Čačić, it seems, was in contact with the Belgrade authorities for years. On behalf of the Committee for the Return of the Stolen Lipizzaners he had negotiated directly with the Serbs, while remaining in constant consultation with the Croatian Minister of Agriculture via his mobile phone. 'In the end, when things got really exciting, he shouted in my ear: "Mato, I don't care what kind of papers they want you to sign, just sign them, as long as you get those horses back."'

Within a week after the appearance of the photos of the emaciated mares, the Serbs had carried out an inspection of conditions where they were being held, concluding that there were no indications of malnourishment or mistreatment. The Ministry of Agriculture in Belgrade ruled that there was no question here of cruelty to animals. 'And they also said there was nothing to be done legally, because the horses were not state-owned.'

Nenad whistled in consternation.

But that was only the start, Mato says. The man who called himself the owner of the herd turned out to be the boss of a casino in Novi Sad. 'One of those guys who became rich during the war.' Through various channels, Mato and his committee heard that this character was prepared to let the Lipik horses go only if he received 300,000 euros in reparations. Croatia, in other words, could buy back its kidnapped Lipizzaners with a hefty ransom.

Two waiters come in with a huge silver soup tureen. The chicken bouillon has globules of fat floating in it.

'But then,' the chief equerry says, 'your petition and the whole hype got going, and we were invited to perform a reappraisal.'

'And what did your people find?' asks Nenad.

'Complete blackness.'

The waiters ladle the bouillon into our bowls.

'Terminal exhaustion,' Mato goes on. 'And cadavers. The area around that barn on the Danube was an equine grave-yard.' The man who called himself the owner also bred dogs for security firms. He had forty of them, in cages. With his own eyes, Mato Čačić had seen dogs gnawing on the jawbone of a Lipizzaner.

The breeding stallions, each of which had a stall of its own, were in reasonable shape. But the mares that were still alive were covered in wounds, some of them open and untreated. 'The stableman told us that they sometimes attacked each other, on the rare occasions when there was something to eat.'

I asked about that stableman – was that the same one they said had crossed from the Croat side to the Serb, and taken the Lipik herd with him back in 1991?

Mato nods. That's him. Mihajlo Komasović. 'Mile'.

'The horse thief,' Jadranka interprets.

I want to hear more about this Mihajlo, but Mato brushes the subject aside. 'We took blood samples from each horse. For DNA analysis.'

Three weeks later, a deal was reached. The Croatians were allowed to come and fetch them with their own trucks.

'Did money change hands?'

'Not that I know of,' Mato says curtly. 'And to be honest, I don't care.'

On Friday 12 October 2007, they had the horses loaded and ready to go. That sounded simple, but in fact it was like a Wild West round-up. There were mares between the ages of five and seven that had never worn a halter, which Mato and his helpers had to lasso and drag up the ramp. And Serb government officials kept coming by with more and more documents. He had signed them all, sight unseen. Late that evening it looked as though the convoy was actually ready to leave. 'I had our minister on the phone. He said: "Once the lorries are moving, don't stop, don't stop anywhere, just keep driving."'

But at the border crossing at Ilok, they were detained. They remained in custody for two hours, with no reason given. Finally, just after midnight, the barrier was raised and the Lipizzaner convoy was allowed to cross the border.

℧

'I don't want to speak out of hatred,' the mayor remarked, 'but what we can ascertain is this: only a people capable of murdering innocent children is also capable of starving horses to death.'

During the main course – a leg of lamb so tender that the meat falls steaming from the bone – the tone of the conversation changes. The mayor looks at me, the only non-Croatian in the group, and says: 'Back when I travelled through Europe as a student, I felt like a European. But these days I feel like a Croatian.' During the Yugoslavian period, he tells me, he worked as a schoolteacher, with no prospect of ever becoming headmaster. 'The same argument was always used against us – the Jasenovac argument. In other words, Croatians were never to be placed in positions of authority again.' The most recent war had taught him this: 'Anyone who does not love his own people and fatherland is unable to love others.'

'I'm a Croatian too,' the stud-farm director chimes in. 'One hundred per cent, pure to the bone.' When there is a war on, that suddenly becomes important. He knows an excellent example. 'I always got on extremely well with my head stableman. He's a talented breeder who understands his work. Like me, he was born and raised here. But: he is a Serb and I'm a Croatian. He chose to serve his people, I chose mine.'

'That's right!' the mayor says angrily. 'But he did it by taking the herd with him.'

I seize this opportunity to ask about this Serb stableman, who everyone seems certain abducted the horses from Lipik.

Mato Čačić leans over. 'Not for the book, but we brought him back with us. Along with the horses.'

I'm not sure I'm understanding him correctly. Is he saying that they brought Mihajlo 'Mile' Komasović, the Serb who took off with the herd in 1991, back to Croatia?

'We saved his skin,' Mato says. More precisely, they let him travel with the convoy as a stowaway. It was Stableman Komasović, someone explains to me, who had taken the photos of the starving mares and passed them to a newspaper in Novi Sad. He had feared for his life ever since. His boss, the casino owner, had threatened to put a bullet through his head if he ever set foot on his land again. 'I've seen that man, and let me tell you, he's straight out of Las Vegas.' Mato places his index finger against my temple. 'He'd shoot you like that: *boom.*'

But where is Mihajlo Komasović now, I ask: 'Can I meet him?'

'Listen,' Mato says. 'You need to leave Komasović out of this. He's not for the book.'

Other voices are raised in agreement with the chief equerry. Komasović, I should realize, is not really a bad fellow. But to the general public in Croatia he is the kidnapper of the country's living national heritage – an enemy of the state. Nevertheless, Lipik has granted him asylum. He's a Serb in Croatia who has been awarded a flat at the community's expense. But this is not to be bandied about, the wounds of war are still too fresh for such a gesture of reconciliation.

I nod, but what I really want is to hear Komasović's stories and motives in his own words.

'He lives here in Lipik' – that's all the mayor is willing to say.

Mato Čačić proffers: 'In exchange for a place to live, he takes care of the horses. That's what he's done all his life, for ten years here in Lipik, for sixteen years on the other side of the mountains.'

∪

It's time for the high point of the day. We squeeze into a Lipik municipal van. Ivan follows in his Opel, shuttling back and forth to bring the young people to the stud farm, not far outside the town itself.

En route we pass the bottling plant for Lipik mineral water. Towering behind a final row of houses is a grain silo riddled with bullet holes from machine-gun fire, like a giant with acne. The road swings gently to the right and there, alone amid the pastures, lies Ergela Lipik, the Croatian state Lipizzaner stud. A sturdy, elongated building with red roof tiles. Cypress trees line the yard, everything is stately and well ordered.

Mato Čačić, who went ahead on his motorcycle, welcomes Nenad Bach at the open stable doors.

We hear whinnying. Once everyone has arrived we are led

inside, first to the loafing barn for the mares. A group of about thirty white animals looks up from the rustling straw. What first strikes me is that they don't look very emaciated any more. The second thing is that this is June, but they have no foals.

'This last winter they put on weight fairly quickly,' Mato says. 'Next year we'll see whether they can be used for breeding again.'

At the back of the barn, a grey-haired man is pulling apart a bale of hay, like an accordionist working the bellows, and spreading it out in the mangers. Having lost the mares' attention, we move through the farrier's workshop to the separate stalls for the stallions. There are about twelve, and they let us know they are there.

'Gentlemen, it's not feeding time yet!' Mato shouts to them. He unbolts Conversano Batosta's stall and tells us that this stallion had become the primogenitor of the Lipik herd-in-exile. His characteristics – the graceful profile of his back, his friendly character – resulted in him being the one put to stud most often. Mato leads the animal out of his stall, and Batosta gets his picture taken. He has large pink spots on his snout, where there is no pigment. Primula had that too, including the freckles.

I ask about his pedigree. Mato explains that he's currently charting the bloodlines by means of DNA analysis, but that he already knows for certain that, among the sixty-six horses that returned, there are twenty-one half-breds and forty-five pure-bred Lipizzaners. Only eight of those originally came from Lipik – they experienced the war and the abduction first-hand. The rest were born in Serbia. Conversano Batosta is one of the Lipik horses, born on 25 February 1987. He has 'special blood' that runs back to a stallion born during the age of the empire: Conversano Savona.

Suddenly I see him in a different light. The horse thumping his hoof impatiently against the stall door is a second cousin to Conversano Primula.

Mato Čačić continues: 'During the shelling in the autumn of 1991, he was three and a half years old. He had just reached sexual maturity and was still grey.' Now, however, he has become the silvery-white paterfamilias – and, at twenty-one, the oldest horse in the herd.

What age do horses live to, on average? Nenad asks.

Twenty, Mato tells him. But Lipizzaners are a long-lived breed, with a life expectancy of twenty-five.

Nenad Bach puts his hat on. He has to go, he has commitments in Zagreb, but there is one more thing he'd like to know. What is Lipik planning to do with the Lipizzaners?

Arms folded across his chest, the mayor begins sketching a future in which tourists come to Lipik to take the health-giving waters and ride white horses. The only problem is that there are still landmines dotted around.

'Can't you build bridle paths that are guaranteed to be free of mines?' Nenad's suggestion is appreciated, but everyone realizes that, as a selling point, 'guaranteed mine-free' is not a draw to families with children.

The pop star leaves us with the promise that his website is always open for appeals and initiatives on behalf of the Lipizzaners of Lipik.

Everyone gets ready to go, except for me. I ask Jadranka to stay, to interpret.

'For whom?'

Rather than reply, I lead her back to the mares' loafing barn. The old groom who was spreading out hay there before is now at work with a manure fork. He is as thin as a rake and has snowy-white hair.

'You are Mihajlo Komasović,' I say.

The man leans on his fork and looks at me appraisingly. Jadranka stands there, her shoulders drooping, as though she's sorry she let herself be dragged into this.

I ask whether he would like to tell me what happened to him and to the horses.

'Mile' Komasović tugs at his moustache. There are shadows under his deep-set eyes. He sniffs and says: '*Dobro*. All right.'

The stableman, obviously now demoted to stableboy, takes the lead himself. As though his herd had not just returned from the longest exile in the history of the Lipizzaner breed, he begins discussing the quality of their blood. 'All six foundation stallions are represented here,' he says. For the sake of completeness, he wishes they also had a horse from the Tulipan line. On the other hand, though, that's not such a disaster; that line isn't recognized as pure-bred beyond Croatia. And what's more: horses with Tulipan blood are well built but not particularly intelligent.

'Capriola!' Mile Komasović calls over one of the mares, to illustrate an explanation of the classical mare lines and the importance of the mare in general.

I ask about his background: did he study to become a horse breeder?

'We had horses on the farm at home,' Mile says. 'Lipizzaners. My father used them to pull the plough.' He had practised the craft of selection and crossing from an early age.

'He never went to school,' Jadranka interprets as well.

The war broke out in 1991, I say. 'Did you fight too?'

'I was living in Lipik, but I went to the village in the hills where I was born.' He was officially registered as a reservist, but he absconded. He had never worn a uniform. 'My parents taught me that: if a war comes again, run and hide in the hills. There is no such thing as a good war. In a war, the value of a human life sinks to 1 Deutschmark: the price of a bullet.'

Mile was born in 1947. 'I come from Smrtić. In February 1945, there was a raid on the Serb population there. They took away 287 men, large and small, young and old.'

'Took away?' Jadranka asks.

'To Jasenovac, young lady.' Without pausing for breath, he adds: 'My father survived because he had already gone off to fight with the partisans.'

But in 1991, I comment, there was nowhere for the horses to run.

'That's right,' Komasović says. Someone told him that people had tried to have them evacuated before the bombing started – but the army commanders didn't think that was necessary. He had gone to the stud farm twice, under cover of darkness. 'You should have seen them. They were in a terrible way. You couldn't tell a stallion from a mare any more.'

Mile leads us to a window at one side of the building and points to the pastureland between the houses of Lipik and the railway tracks that run along the foot of the hills: that whole open field was no-man's-land, and that was exactly where the mares grazed with their foals. 'At first they would go rushing off whenever a shell exploded. But after a while they grew numb. They would only glance up, or just keep on grazing.'

Jadranka remarks: 'Those mortar shells didn't just drop out of the blue. They were fired from the hills, by Serbs.'

'Young lady,' Mile interrupts her, 'I don't know which side those shells came from.'

Jadranka becomes agitated. Despite the difference in their ages, she comes down on him hard. I recognize a few Croatian swear words, even though there is no English in there at all.

Then suddenly she turns to me. 'Did you hear what he said? He insists he doesn't know which side the shells came from!'

'I heard it,' I say. 'And I'm writing it all down, including your comments.' I have to work hard, but I succeed in stopping her from walking off.

Mile Komasović straightens his T-shirt and slips his fingers into the front pockets of his jeans. At the very end of November 1991, he goes on, he arranged for a truck and had it drive up a back road to behind the stud farm. He and the driver loaded the animals. Mares and stallions together, it didn't matter, they were already so weak from two months in the line of fire.

We hear an anxious whinny. Behind us one of the mares is making to bite a female rival.

'Trompeta!' Mile shouts. 'Calm down!' The mare ceases her hostilities.

'I have three Monteauras,' says the stableman who has now become a stableboy. 'When I call them, they can tell from my voice who I'm talking to.'

I manoeuvre the conversation back to his own wanderings.

The horses were able to move into an *agrokombinat*, a collective farm, just across the Sava in Bosnia, he says. It was a cattle farm, next to a slaughterhouse. But two months later the war broke out there as well. So they'd travelled on to Serbia, to the former stud farm of the Yugoslav People's Army in Karadordevo. Those had been Marshal Tito's elite stables, where his pair of presidential Maestosos spent their twilight years. When Komasović moved in with his Lipik Lipizzaners, the oldest of the two, Maestoso Mara, was still alive – the animal only died in April 1993, blind and worn out, at the record age of forty-one.

'You see?' Jadranka says. 'It *was* a military mission. Not a one-man operation or anything like that.'

'Young lady, I did not steal the horses, I evacuated them. Their lives were in danger and I was their stableman. Besides which, they don't have a nationality, now do they?'

Mile Komasović admits that he let the situation get out of control. Serbia was losing on every front, which brought with it only more and more chaos and poverty. In 1997 the army chiefs decided that from then on the Karadordevo stud should support itself, which the officers in charge there interpreted as permission to set up a back-door trade in horses. Mile saw his herd falling apart, and sought protection ('a roof') from a certain Todor Bukinac, a wealthy man who bred horses and dogs close to Novi Sad.

'Looking back on it, that was my biggest mistake,' Mile says. 'If you ask me whether I regret that decision, I'll tell you: yes, every waking moment.'

The new owner wanted to breed Lipizzaners for the international market. Each horse would make him 8,000–10,000 German marks. The first setback came in the spring of 1999, however, when NATO fighter planes carried out a bombing mission over Serbia in response to the aggression in Kosovo. Hypermodern F-117s homed in on strategic buildings in Belgrade and systematically blew up all the bridges along the Danube. One of those lay only a few hundred metres from Todor Bukinac's yard. The windows of the stable were shattered and chunks of bomb casement landed in the pastures. None of the animals was harmed, but in the weeks that followed most of the mares miscarried. Those that did produce a live foal didn't recognize it as their own and wouldn't allowed it to suckle. 'That sometimes happens when a mare doesn't have any milk,' Mile says. 'But my mares had milk.'

Until the summer of 2003, the casino man believed in his commercial breeding scheme. But when the first animals were brought to auction in Hungary, they proved unmarketable. Despite their lineage and their brand, no one wanted them; their papers were simply ignored.

'Bukinac was furious,' Mile recalls. 'He said he wasn't going to spend another dinar on them.' Mile couldn't forced him to change his mind. His boss felt cheated, and in his frustration he took revenge on a people he hated. How? By harming their animals. The only explanation was that Bukinac had started to see the white mares as Croatian – as Croats. When winter came and the grass was covered in snow, the stableman watched thirty horses die. 'In the end, they were eating their own stalls. They chewed on anything made of wood.'

Bukinac fed the cadavers to his dogs, that gnawed on strips of intestine until their muzzles dripped blood.

Mile told me that he woke every morning wondering, which one is going to die today? When spring came he went begging to the parks service in Novi Sad, asking to take the grass clippings home for his horses. But he was only a refugee on a bicycle, who no one listened to.

The letters he wrote to the Belgrade veterinary inspectorate, warning them about the situation, remained unanswered. In late 2006, the stableman clashed with Bukinac, who banned him from his property. He had gone back once, armed with a camera. He handed the pictures to the editors of the newspaper *Gradanski List* and went into hiding.

Jadranka is twirling a loose strand of hair around her finger. She says she would like to touch one of the mares that survived all the trials of the last sixteen years. Mile wades through the straw and comes back leading a greyish-white animal covered in scars. Neck, chest, stomach, back, shanks – her coat is damaged everywhere. I let the mare lick my hand. Jadranka touches the scars carefully and asks how she got them.

'You can tell by the shape,' Mile says. 'Most of them are sort of sickle-shaped. The ones around the neck are bites, the others are from hooves.' The mares had fought tooth and nail for every clump of hay thrown to them.

I asked whether they had been attacked by dogs as well.

'Not these,' Mile said. 'These were too strong.' The dogs only moved in on animals that were too exhausted to stand upright. They went to work like jackals, circling their prey first and then attacking from behind. 'First they would eat the juiciest parts, the anus and the vagina, where the meat is softest.'

Jadranka looks away. Then she regains her composure and says: ' You've seen the cruellest side of nature.'

'No,' Mile corrects her. 'The cruellest side of human nature.'

ACKNOWLEDGEMENTS

FOR THE LAST TWO and a half years I have worked on this book almost without interruption. That was no solitary labour. An entire range of the initiated, the interested and the expert took part by showing me how to look (at horses, first of all) and helping me to carry on at crucial moments. Piet and Leny Bakker were the first, somewhere in the mid-1970s. When I saw them again, thirty years later, a great deal had changed. But Piet's good-humoured 'Come on, let me show you how to make a horse dance' sounded very familiar. The long-rein exercises with Conversano Nobila that he showed me beside the Zuidlaardermeer often appeared before my mind's eye as I was writing this book.

In April 2009, Piet called me: 'Nobila is dead. He had a tumour in his head. It happened yesterday.'

Conversano Nobila, born in 1986, was twenty-two years old.

The foal Pluto Marcella, the first cloned Lipizzaner, died on 3 August 2010. He was only three months old, while the 'backup clone' – the third Pluto Marcella – was aborted by the surrogate mare two-thirds of the way to term.

Conversano Batosta, on the other hand, is doing well. He has once again been put to stud and, for the first time since

1991, foals have been born in the stable at Lipik. The official reopening of the stud farm took place on 14 May 2009, when a priest sprinkled the young animals with holy water – to protect them against future harm.

While writing this book I consulted a great many sources. A few are noted in the main text, most are not.

The reconstruction of the story of Ehrenfried Brandts' escape, as recounted in the prologue, was based on his own report dealing with December 1945, as found in his book *Pferde zwischen den Fronten* (Munich, 2007). I edited his account here and there, and in other places supplemented it with observations and comments made by Brandts at the age of seventy-two. In addition to the notes taken during our conversation in Munich, our correspondence (by letter and by email) also proved valuable.

The same applies to the information given me by Ulrich Rudofsky, Hans Brabenetz, Ivan Pušćenik, Piet Bakker and Atjan Hop: in addition to our conversations, they sent me a constant flow of emails with explanations, tips, recommendations, commentary and a wealth of documents – all of which were part of the basic material from which I drew.

The passages dealing with the activities of The Raging Potatoes are based in part on two articles that I wrote in 1991 for the magazine *Intermediair*, as well as the raw material on which those articles were based. Statements by and characterizations of Professor Herman de Boer were taken in part from my interview with him ('Regret is an unproductive feeling', *NRC Handelsblad*, 15 June 1995) and from an interview with Jutta Chorus ('Mengele has whetted our conscience', *NRC Handelsblad*, 9 March 2000).

Concerning my sources in book form, I would like to note that I have quoted Xenophon's *Peri Hippikes* in the translation into the Dutch by C. A. van Woelderen, The Hague, 1928.

The quote from Virgil comes from the *Georgics*, based on the translation into Dutch by Ida Gerhardt, The Hague, 1969. Charles Darwin's *On the Origin of Species* from 1859 was a work I studied using the Dutch translation by Ruud Rook, Amsterdam, 2001.

With regard to the spelling of 'Lipica', it should be noted that any number of alternatives are current (Lipitza, Lippiza, Lipizza, Lipica). The spelling often changes in accordance with the proprietor: from Lipiza to Lipizza, for example, during the period of Italian rule from 1919–42. With the exception of a few quotes, I have for the purposes of consistency stuck to the current Slovenian name, Lipica.

A great many particulars concerning the history of the Royal Spanish Riding School and the Lipizzaner breed were taken from the following publications: *Das ehemalige K.u.K. Karster Hofgestüt zu Lippiza 1580–1920* by Emil Finger, Laxenburg, 1930; *Die edlen Lipizzaner und die Spanische Reitschule* by Franz Ackerl and Arthur-Heinz Lehmann, Weimar, 1942; *Spanische Hofreitschule Wien* by Alois Podhajsky, Vienna (photocopy, probably from 1943); *The Spanish Riding School* by Mathilde Windisch-Graetz, London, 1956; *The Spanish Riding School in Vienna* by Ann Tizia Leitich, Munich, 1956; *De Spaanse Rijschool in Wenen* by Hans Handler and Erich Lessing, Bussum, 1972; *Lipica* by Joxe Jurkovid, Koper, 1973; *Piber: Das Gestüt der österreichischen Lipizzaner* by Werner Menzendorf and Heinrich Lehrner, Munich, 1977; *Lipizzaner, the Story of the Horses of Lipica – Commemorating the 400th Anniversary of the Lipizzaner* by Milan Dolenc, Ljubljana, 1981. *Een keizerrijk voor een paard* by Hans-Heinrich Isenbart and Emil Bührer, Haarlem, 1985; *Die Spanische Reitschule zu Wien* by Jaromir Oulehla, Leo Mazakarini and Henri Brabec d'Ipra, Vienna, 1986; *Der Lipizzaner* by Heinz Nürnberg, Magdeburg, 1993, and his *Auf den Spuren der Lipizzaner*, Hildesheim, 1998; *Die Lipizzaner der Spanischen Hofreitschule* by Georg Kugler and Wolfdieter Bihl, Vienna, 2002. I found supplementary information in the undated Italian brochure *L'Allevamento Statale del Cavallo Lipizzano* by Luca Buttazzoni. The fictional *Florian, das Pferd des Kaisers* by Felix Salten, Berlin, 1934, was also useful to me in an indirect fashion.

To get a feeling for the atmosphere in Vienna on the eve of the First World War, I not only relied on Joseph Roth's *Radetzky March*, as noted earlier, but also on his *The Tale of the 1002nd Night* and the autobiographical *The World of Yesterday* by Stefan Zweig. I am also indebted to *Danube* by Claudio Magris.

A number of relevant facts about horses in general were taken from: *La culture équestre de l Occident* by Daniel Roche, Paris, 2008; *100 Jahre Pferdezucht und Pferdesport in Deutschland* by Susanne Hennig, Warendorf, 2005, and *Het paard in de kunst – dertigduizend jaar cultuurgeschiedenis* by Tamsin Pickeral, Baarn, 2007. I found a number of interesting details about Napoleon's horses in *Marengo, The Myth of Napoleon's Horse* by Jill Hamilton, London, 2000.

Specific information about the fate of the Lipizzaners during the Second World War is found in *Gespräche mit einem Pferdemann: Dr Rudolf Lessing*, as told by Dietbert Arnold, Bremen, 1995; in *Pferde zwischen den Fronten* by Ehrenfried Brandts, Munich, 2007 (as noted and quoted from in the main text) and collected magazine articles by Brigitte Peter, published under the title *Hostau 1945: Die Rettung der Lipizzaner – Wagnis oder Wunder?*, Salzburg, 1982. Useful sources on Hostau and surroundings included *Hostau, die Geschichte einer Pfarrei in Böhmen 1836–1938* by Stefan Stippler, Tönning, 2008, and the German–Czech

Wanderungen durch die verschwundenen Ortschaften des Böhmischen Walds, Taus/Domažlice, 2007.

Works of a different nature, which inspired me directly or indirectly while writing this book, included *I Served the King of England* by Bohumil Hrabal, *Kaputt* by Curzio Malaparte and *Red Cavalry* by Isaac Babel.

In addition to his progress reports drawn up during the Second World War (the '*Rau-Berichte*' copied from the archives by Ehrenfried Brandts), I turned as well to Gustav Rau's *Die Reitkunst der Welt an den Olympischen Spielen 1936*, Berlin, 1937. Additional information about him was found in *Gustav Rau, ein Leben für die Pferde* by Karl Schönerstedt, Gießen, 1960. *The Cavalry of World War II* by Janusz Piekalkiewicz, New York, 1980, provided the context in this regard.

Regarding Gregor Mendel, I examined – in addition to the biography *Gregor Mendel, The First Geneticist* by Vítězslav Orel, Oxford, 1996 – the following publications: *Gregor Mendel*, brochure published for the opening of the 'Mendelianum' in Brno, 1965; *Gregor Mendel, der Bahnbrecher der Vererbungslehre* by Alois Fietz, a publication by the NSDAP, *Heft 99* in the series *Heimat und Volk*, Niederdonau, 1944; *Gregor Mendel, de ontdekker der erfelijkheidswetten* by J. G. Meijknecht, Bussum, 1950, and *Gregor Mendel und das Schicksal seiner Vererbungsgesetze* by Ingo Krumbiegel, Stuttgart, 1957.

Concerning the Brothers Heck and their attempts to 'back-breed' primal cattle and horses, I drew from *Aurochs, le retour ... d'une supercherie nazie* by Piotr Daszkiewicz and Jean Aikhenbaum, Paris, 1999. *De oeros, het spoor terug* by Cis van Vuure, Wageningen, 2003 was important in this regard as well. Lutz Heck himself described his experiments with animals, including the tarpan, in *Tiere, mein Abenteuer*,

Vienna, 1954. The book *Op zoek naar volmaaktheid* by Piet de Rooy, Houten, 1991, put me on the trail of numerous publications concerning the life sciences in the early twentieth century. *Biologie en marxisme* by Marcel Prenant (Amsterdam, 1937) sets the tone when it comes to ideologizing biology ('If this book is good, that is *because* it is Marxist and not *although* it is Marxist', the author says in his conclusion. 'If this book is bad, that is not because it is Marxist, but because it is not Marxist enough.') Of a very different nature, but no less curious, is *The Inheritance of Acquired Characteristics* by Paul Kammerer, originally published in 1924, and later in facsimile by High Sierra Books, Gold Beach, 2003. In direct connection with this work, and with Kammerer's suicide, is *The Case of the Midwife Toad* by Arthur Koestler, London, 1971 – in which Koestler goes to great lengths to show that Kammerer did not perpetrate a swindle with his experiments on amphibians, but that he was the victim of a conspiracy.

For reconstructing the ideological–biological clash between Nikolai Vavilov and Trofim Lysenko, the following works were essential: *The Science of Biology Today*, being the transcript of Lysenko's speech to the Lenin Academy for Agricultural Sciences in Moscow, held on 31 July 1948, which appeared unabridged in English in New York, 1948; *Heredity, East and West* by Julian Huxley, New York, 1949; *Lysenko is Right* by James Fyfe, London, 1950; *The Rise and Fall of T. D. Lysenko* by Zhores Medvedev, New York, 1969; *Proletarian Science? The case of Lysenko* by Dominique Lecourt, Oxford, 1970; *New Atlantis Revisited, Akademgorodok, the Siberian City of Science* by Paul Josephson, Princeton, 1997; *A Little Corner of Freedom, Russian Nature Protection from Stalin to Gorbachev* by Douglas Weiner, Berkeley, 1999; 'Freiheit der Wissenschaft versus Primat der Ideologie' by Peter Fäßler:

Zwischen Bodenreform und Kollektivierung, Stuttgart, 2001; *Genetics behind the Iron Curtain* by Anna Matalová and Jirí Sekerák, Brno, 2004, and *The Murder of Nikolai Vavilov* by Peter Pringle, New York, 2008. The Czech handbook on horse breeding mentioned in the main text was published as *Chov Koní* and edited by Frantisek Bílek, Prague, 1953.

The career and insights of Konrad Lorenz are depicted in the biographical *Konrad Lorenz* by Klaus Taschwer and Benedikt Föger, Munich, 2009. I also made use of Lorenz's own *Das sogenannte Böse. Zur Naturgeschichte der Aggression*, translated into Dutch by Dick Hillenius under the title *Over agressie bij dier en mens*, Amsterdam, 1966. A fascinating account of developments in the field of ethology can be found in *Van nature goed, over de oorsprong van goed en kwaad in mensen en andere dieren* by Frans de Waal, Amsterdam, 2005, and *Het geniale dier, een andere antropologie* by René ten Bos, Amsterdam, 2008.

Lorenz's Nazi past has been documented in the wide-ranging *Biologists under Hitler* by Ute Deichmann, London, 1996. Along the same lines, *Nazi Biology and Schools* by Änne Bäumer-Schleinkofer, Frankfurt, 1995, refers among other things to the Nazi textbooks *Vererbung, Rasse, Volk* by Erich Thieme, Leipzig, 1938, and *Familienkunde und Rassenbiologie für Schüler* by Jakob Graf, Munich, 1939. The National Socialist ideas concerning matters biological is dealt with in greater depth in *Das Geschlechtsleben bestimmen wir, Sexualität im Dritten Reich* by Anna Maria Sigmund, Munich, 2008; *Hitler's Vienna, a Dictator's Apprenticeship* by Brigitte Hamann, New York, 1999; *La Société pure de Darwin à Hitler* by André Pichot, Paris, 2001; *Eternal Treblinka, our Treatment of Animals and the Holocaust* by Charles Patterson, New York, 2002; *Heinrich Himmler, de architect van de Holocaust* by Richard Breitman, Oostum, 2005; *De gebroeders Himmler, een Duitse familiegeschiedenis* by Katrin Himmler, Meulenhoff, 2007; *Death Dealer, the memoirs of the SS Kommandant at Auschwitz* by Rudolph Höss, edited by Steven Paskuly, New York, 1992, and *Auschwitz Chronicle 1939–1945* by Danuta Czech, New York, 1990. Background information about the botanical raiding parties carried out by the SS can be found in *Plant Breeding and Agrarian Research in Kaiser Wilhelm Institutes 1933–1945* by Susanne Heim, Boston, 2008.

The chapters dealing with the war in the former Yugoslavia are based on my own experiences as a correspondent, as depicted in part in my book *De brug over de Tara*, Amsterdam, 1999. Also important in this regard was *Croatia, a Nation Forged in War* by Marcus Tanner (New Haven, 1997). The article 'Lipizzaners under Socialism' by Dennison Rusinow in the journal *South-east Europe Series* (volume 12, number 1, New York, 1965) provides insight into the breeding of Lipizzaners under Tito.

Concerning the eugenics movement, Marianne van Herwerden published the book *Erfelijkheid bij de mens en eugenetiek*, Amsterdam, 1926 (an expanded version of which was reissued in 1956). *Out of the Night, a biologist's view of the future* is a plea for racial improvement among humans from a socialist perspective, written by Hermann Joseph Müller, New York, 1935. One of the earliest critiques of eugenics, in novelistic form, is *Darwinia* by Jan Holland (the pseudonym for Annes Johan Vitringa), Deventer, 1876. In assembling my thoughts concerning this theme I was also inspired by *We* by Yevgeny Zamyatin from 1920; *Brave New World* by Aldous Huxley from 1932, and *The Chrysalids* by John Wyndham from 1955. Many of the issues brought up in these dystopian novels are dealt with scientifically in the post-war study by L. C. Dunn, which was eventually published as *Race and Biology, the Race Question in Modern Science*, Paris,

1951. This was one of the documents on which UNESCO's *Statement on Race* was based.

The unravelling of the double helix structure of the DNA molecule has been described first-hand by James Watson in his *The Double Helix: A Personal Account of the Discovery of the Structure of DNA*, New York, 1968. The discussion concerning the use of new gene technologies to breed human beings was stirred up in 1999 by Peter Sloterdijk. The collection *Regels voor het mensenpark*, Amsterdam, 2000, includes his controversial address, along with criticism from the (largely German) press. In *Our Posthuman Future: Consequences of the Biotechnology Revolution*, New York, 2002, Francis Fukuyama takes the debate a step further. Where Fukuyama warns of the dangers in particular, John Harris in *Enhancing Evolution, the Ethical Case for Making Better People*, Princeton, 2007, champions the application of technologies for the improvement of human beings.

U

Finally, I would like to express my deep gratitude to the many people who assisted me with indispensable information and advice: Piet and Leny Bakker, Laurens and Ally Touwen, Frank Verhagen, Hans and Susi Brabenetz, Marko Matz, Ehrenfried Brandts, Ulrich Rudofsky, Atjan and Yolanda Hop, Ines Hubinger, Martina Vitáčková, Vítězslav Orel, Jiří Sekerák, Caitlin Maynard, Ivan Pušćenik, Jadranka Šimunović, Mato Čačić, Milan Božić, Antun Haramija, Stjepan Horvat, Nenad Bach, Brigitte Gawlik, Georg Kugler, Miroslav Rauch, Stefan Stippler, Peter Windrath, Snežana Milovanović and Mihajlo Komasović.

I am particularly grateful to Emile Brugman, Maya Rasker and Anita Roeland for reading critically as the text grew – in a wonderful fashion, all three of you provided me with a solid footing and a sense of direction during the writing of this book.

As with my earlier books, the substantive support bestowed on me by Suzanna Jansen once again exceeded all usual editorial bounds. Without her enthusiasm and that of Vera Adinde Westerman – who encouraged me by taking to horseback herself – I could never have worked on this book with so much pleasure and dedication.

Amsterdam, 18 August 2010